A DIFFERENT JESUS?

The Christ of the Latter-day Saints

Robert L. Millet

William B. Eerdmans Publishing Company
Grand Rapids, Michigan / Cambridge, U.K.

© 2005 Wm. B. Eerdmans Publishing Co.
All rights reserved

Wm. B. Eerdmans Publishing Co.
255 Jefferson Ave. S.E., Grand Rapids, Michigan 49503 /
P.O. Box 163, Cambridge CB3 9PU U.K.

Printed in the United States of America

11 10 09 08 07 06   8 7 6 5 4 3 2

ISBN-10: 0-8028-2876-0
ISBN-13: 978-0-8028-2876-7

www.eerdmans.com

Contents

CONTENTS

Foreword

At a large gathering of scholars of religion several years ago, I ran into a theologian who is well known for his very liberal reinterpretations of traditional Christian ideas. In spite of our rather deep disagreements on matters of faith, we are on friendly terms. On this occasion we agreed to meet later that day for a leisurely dinner together. Our conversation that evening was a stimulating one. We launched quickly into serious theological discussion, and by the end he made it clear that, while he liked and respected me personally, he found my views about Jesus Christ to be deeply offensive. I was insisting that Jesus is the eternal Son of God sent from heaven to do for us what we could never do for ourselves: he offered himself up to the Father as a perfect Sacrifice for our sins. This means, I argued, that no human being can hope to achieve salvation apart from the atoning work of Jesus Christ.

My theological friend was adamant in his endorsement of religious pluralism. As someone reared and educated in the Christian tradition, he testified, he could admit to a special personal "connection" to Jesus of Nazareth. But he was, to use his own word, "outraged" by my insistence that Jesus is a unique Savior. God is larger than any one religion's definitions, he argued, and all of us need to be celebrating the fact that there are many different paths to salvation.

My liberal friend was in a grumpy mood as we left the restaurant to walk back to our hotel, and I was eager to lighten things up. As we walked along a side street, I noticed that someone had scrawled these words on a telephone pole: "Trust Jesus!" I put my arm around my friend's shoulder and directed his attention to the words. "Hey, John," I said in a teasing voice, "I think the Lord is trying to send you a message." He quickly retorted with irritation: "I am not afraid to trust Jesus! But not *your* Jesus! Not *your* Jesus!"

In rather lengthy discussions about Jesus with Mormon scholars over the past several years, I am the one who has been tempted to say accusingly, "Not *your* Jesus! Not *your* Jesus!" I came into those discussions with a firm conception of what the Latter-day Saints (LDS) believe about Jesus, and I was not eager to have them try to convince me that I was operating with preconceived notions that needed correction.

Let me say right up front that I still have some serious misgivings. But I also have to admit that the misgivings do not run quite as deep as they did earlier. Over the past five years I have been a member of a small group of evangelicals who have participated in free-ranging discussions with some Mormon counterparts, all of them scholars from Brigham Young University. Our conversations have often extended over several days, covering key issues that have divided evangelicals and the LDS. In our ongoing conversations we have come to a point where we genuinely listen to each other. Indeed, we have developed enough trust between us that when one of us insists that folks in the other camp have seriously misunderstood us on an important point, we work hard together to clear up the misunderstanding.

Robert Millet, the author of this book, and I have cochaired these discussions, and in the process we have become good friends. Indeed, I encouraged him to write this book, and I urged the Eerdmans folks to publish it. We all agreed that it would be a good idea for me not only to introduce the book but also to offer some afterthoughts for readers who have made their way through his discussion.

In our evangelical-Mormon dialogues, we have talked at length about many important theological topics. But none is more important than the subject of this book. The question of what a person believes about Jesus Christ is not only a central issue for theological discussion; it is one that has eternal significance for all human beings. The jailer in Acts 16 addressed the fundamental question directly to Paul and Silas: "Sirs, what must I do to be saved?" And their answer was equally direct: "Believe on the Lord Jesus, and you will be saved." Our theological discussions about the person and work of Christ are not merely academic excursions. They get at the most basic issue that any human being can confront: How do we get right with God?

In this book Robert Millet addresses the key topics with refreshing candor. Traditional Christians have often seen Mormons as deceptive people who are not being honest with us about what they really believe. It would be wrong to approach this book with such suspicions. Bob Millet is a person of great integrity who wants more than anything else to lay out the issues with clarity. He is not simply telling us what he thinks will please traditional Christians in these pages — he does not shrink from setting forth distinctive LDS beliefs about Jesus and his redemptive mission. But he also explores important commonalities with our convictions about Christ's person and work, and in doing so he demonstrates that he has read our theologians with care.

I hope, then, that traditional Christians will read this book with an open mind. The fact is that many of my Christian friends think they know what the LDS believe, even though they have never seriously attempted to understand those beliefs from the LDS perspective. What they know about Mormonism is what they have learned from books on "the cults" by Christian writers. As an evangelical Christian, I regularly run into people who think they know what I believe because they have heard about people like me from commentators who have warned them about the evils of evangelicalism. Or they have formed their opinions about evangelicalism from a few scattered comments made by various evangelical leaders at some time or another, without bothering to investigate the basic theological understanding that characterizes evangelical life and witness at its best. I know what it is like to want people to set aside what are in fact superficial impressions and give me a fair hearing. That is what Bob Millet is asking in this book. And we owe him that hearing — lest we violate the command from God himself that we not bear false witness against our neighbor.

I will have more to say in an Afterword, after Robert Millet has had the opportunity to make his case. But let me add here that I believe this is an important time for a book like this to come our way. As an evangelical Christian, I am very much aware of the long-standing hostility that has characterized our relations with the LDS. But some interesting changes have taken place on the grassroots level in many communities, where evangelicals and Mormons have worked together in Right-to-Life organizations and in various other causes dealing with issues of public morality. In the light of the friendships that have been formed from these cooperative endeavors, it is especially important to clarify the important points of theology that divide the two sides — as well as exploring the possibilities that we have not adequately understood each other on some key theological matters.

Given the very dangerous trends in our larger culture, this is a crucial time for people of goodwill to be making common cause for social justice — and against the relativism and promiscuity that we confront as citizens together in our "postmodern" world. At the very least, it is necessary for people who share many moral concerns to cultivate a spirit of civility toward each other. Indeed, if evangelicals and Mormons could learn to talk together, about both disagreements and agreements, in calm and mutually respecting tones, this could itself be a wonderful demonstration of civility in our increasingly uncivil world.

The mandate for theological dialogue was brought home to me again recently when an evangelical friend, an influential business leader, asked me whether I had ever studied Mormon thought. When I told him about my participation in a dialogue with Mormon scholars, he was enthusiastic. "I work with Mormons on a regular basis," he reported. "They seem like such fine folks, and often when they speak about spiritual things I sense a rapport with them. But, of course, I have read all the 'anti-cult' stuff, and I have been trained to be suspicious. It bothers me that I don't have a trustworthy account of what they really believe about the basic issues." This is a book for him, and for many others like him.

I am not saying that people like my friend will have all of their theological concerns resolved by reading this book. But they will have some of their misconceptions corrected, so that they can begin to engage their LDS friends on the real issues. That by itself is no small step in the right direction!

RICHARD J. MOUW

Why This Book Was Written

Several years ago two colleagues and I met with three representatives of the Southern Baptist Convention. They were making preparations for a major conference to be held in Salt Lake City and wanted to meet with members of the Religion faculty at Brigham Young University. The meeting, which was held in my office, lasted about two hours. It began quite peacefully, as we exchanged information about where we had lived, gone to school, been employed, etc.

During the second hour our gathering became more animated as we turned our attention to doctrine. Our guests asked questions about our views on such matters as the Fall, the Atonement, grace and works, temples, heaven and hell, and the scriptural canon. Much of our discussion centered on what it means to be saved. One member of their group commented to us that the problem with Latter-day Saints was that we did not really accept the Bible but tended to view things through the lenses of Joseph Smith and what we called the Restoration. We indicated that we respected and revered the Bible, and we did agree that much of what we know about God and his plan for our redemption had come to us through a restoration of gospel truth. We suggested that in many cases present-day Christians tended to view things through the lenses of the early Christian Church councils (beginning in the 4th century) and as formulated in the creedal statements.

At that point, one of our visitors spoke in a rather harsh tone: "Why don't you people just admit it: You worship a different Jesus!" My LDS colleagues and I spent the next half hour or so trying to convince them of our acceptance of Jesus of Nazareth, as set forth in the

New Testament. We left that meeting somewhat frustrated, sensing that we had somehow failed to communicate adequately how deeply the Latter-day Saints feel about Jesus Christ.

I have asked myself many times since that meeting: *Do* we worship the same Jesus worshipped by our friends of other Christian faiths? This question is not answered quickly or easily. It strikes at the heart of *who* the Latter-day Saints are and *what* they really believe. Gordon B. Hinckley, fifteenth president of the Church, asked: "Are we Christians? Of course we are! No one can honestly deny that. We may be somewhat different from the traditional pattern of Christianity. But no one believes more literally in the redemption wrought by the Lord Jesus Christ. No one believes more fundamentally that He was the Son of God, that He died for the sins of mankind, that He rose from the grave, and that He is the living resurrected Son of the living Father."[1]

One might ask: Why does it matter so much to you that some refer to you as a non-Christian sect? For years it didn't; I felt that it really was no big deal that persons of other faiths simply didn't understand who and what we are. That was their problem. In recent years, however, it has become more of a personal preoccupation to assist others to know what we *do* believe and why we claim Christian status. It began to dawn on me when someone commented that "Mormons are not Christians" that major misconceptions were being conveyed. Does it mean we do not believe in the divinity of Jesus Christ or accept the truthfulness or historicity of the New Testament? Do we not believe that our sins can be forgiven and our natures changed through the power of the blood of Christ? Do we not believe we should seek to emulate his matchless life? Do we not believe in the resurrection and the immortality of the soul? Are we like Jews or Muslims or Buddhists or Hindus when it comes to our perception of Jesus?

The chapters that follow focus on what I perceive and believe Latter-day Saint Christianity to be. They explain, to the best of my ability, how the Latter-day Saints view Jesus Christ — his identity, his distinctive mission, his matchless teachings, his sufferings, death and resurrection, and his transforming power. While I owe a deep debt of gratitude to faculty colleagues, ministers and theologians of other faiths, and students who have challenged me to clarify my thinking, I

---

1. *Ensign*, February 1998, 73.

alone am responsible for the conclusions drawn from the evidence cited. This book is a private endeavor and is thus without imprimatur or authorization of The Church of Jesus Christ of Latter-day Saints or Brigham Young University.

Because this is a book about the LDS concept of Christ, I have chosen not to state, again and again, "Latter-day Saints believe" this or that, or "the Mormons teach" such and such. Further, in a topic as controversial as LDS Christology, the fact that persons of differing religious persuasions would challenge or dispute this or that assertion by the Latter-day Saints is obvious; thus I have avoided the constant use of such phrases as "Joseph Smith claimed" or "the alleged manifestation" or "the purported vision" to spare the reader the tedium.

Because the full and proper name of the Church is The Church of Jesus Christ of Latter-day Saints, almost always I have sought to avoid the use of "Mormon Church" or "LDS Church," even though readers may be more familiar with the word Mormon. I have, however, taken occasion to refer to the people as Latter-day Saints, Saints, or to certain beliefs or practices as LDS. LDS folks often refer (as Paul did; see, for example, Romans 1:7; 1 Corinthians 1:2; Ephesians 1:1; 2:19; Philippians 1:1; Colossians 1:2) to first century Christians as the Former-day Saints and to themselves as Latter-day Saints. Saints are members of the body of Christ, believers, church members, those who have taken his name and witness upon themselves. They strive to be worthy of what the word implies, namely, the "sanctified ones," those striving to be holy. Further, except where indicated, all biblical passages are taken from the King James Bible, the authorized and accepted version of the Latter-day Saints in English-speaking countries.

Some readers who are somewhat familiar with the LDS faith may feel frustrated with the fact that I have not covered this or that particular point in the book. First of all, because this is at best an introduction to one dimension of the faith (albeit the central dimension), it is neither possible nor advisable for me to attempt to address every phase of doctrine relative to Jesus Christ. In addition — and this is vital — not everything that was stated or written since 1830, even by prominent Church leaders, is considered to be a part of the doctrine of the Church. Because something is a part of our overall literature does not make it a part of the doctrine that governs the Church today. While Latter-day Saints admire and respect and even revere their Church leaders, we do not believe in prophetic or apostolic infallibility. Latter-day Saints acknowledge that in the past men of God have been moved upon by the Holy Spirit (2 Peter 1:21), but we believe that prophets and apostles are men, "subject to like passions as we are" (James 5:17). They are God's covenant spokesmen, authorized and empowered to declare his word and lead his children, but they are not perfect.

Thus it is not difficult for a critic of the LDS faith to locate some extraneous statement by some leader, spoken some time in the past, a statement that would not be part of the doctrine of the Church today. In the spirit of fairness, it would probably not be difficult for a critic of Evangelicalism to locate a few statements by such beloved spokespersons as Martin Luther, John Calvin, Billy Sunday, D. L. Moody, Billy Graham, or John Stott that would not necessarily represent the majority view on evangelical doctrine. The "doctrine of the Church" today for the Latter-day Saints has a rather narrow focus and direction — it would be found in official Church pronouncements, within current Church manuals and handbooks, and would be a topic discussed regularly in general conferences or other official Church gatherings.

My friend Richard Mouw has written that "The quest for empathy can be helped along by a good dose of *curiosity*. We ought to want to become familiar with the experiences of people who are different from us simply out of a desire to understand the length and breadth of what it means to be human." Further, he added that we need to develop "such a total trust in Christ that we are not afraid to follow the truth wherever it leads us. He is 'the true light, which enlightens everyone' (John 1:9). We do not have to be afraid, then, to enter into dialogue with people from other religious traditions. If we find truth in what they say, we must step out in faith to reach for it — Jesus' arms will be there to catch us!"[2] As one Christian theologian has written: "As the religious pluralization of North America proceeds apace, the task of understanding other religions in theological terms becomes more and more urgent — not merely establishing grounds for apologetic polemics but also clarifying just how these religions figure in the providential plan of God."[3]

---

2. *Uncommon Decency: Christian Civility in an Uncivil World* (Downers Grove, IL: InterVarsity Press, 1992), 63-64, 106.

3. John G. Stackhouse, Jr., *Evangelical Landscapes: Facing Critical Issues of the Day* (Grand Rapids: Baker, 2002), 68; see also 182-83.

This book is not about blending views or jettisoning central verities or blurring important differences between faith groups. It is not, in other words, an effort at ecumenism. It is about understanding, about bridge-building. There are now and will yet be many significant moral and social issues that demand our voice and our vigor, in terms of speaking out and standing up for what is right and denouncing what is wrong. We cannot join hands on moral issues about which we agree wholeheartedly if we permit suspicion and misperception to govern our attitudes and our actions. If we allow unwarranted and unchristian feelings toward those with differing religious views to block our united effort to expose and defeat orchestrated evil, we will have allowed Satan to win a major victory.

Being willing to reach out and understand others is not easy, but it is immensely rewarding. It requires, first of all, what Rich Mouw called "convicted civility," an unquestioned allegiance and devotion to one's own tradition, and at the same time a mind and heart that are open to truth and light, a belief that the God and Father of us all is working in his mysterious ways through good people throughout the earth. It requires us to love people, just as the Master bid us to do (John 13:34-35). In the words of John Stackhouse, "God cares about people more than he cares about 'truth' in the abstract. Jesus didn't die on the cross to make a point. He died on the cross to save people whom he loves. We, too, must represent our Lord with love to God and our neighbor always foremost in our concerns."[4]

---

4. *Humble Apologetics* (New York: Oxford University Press, 2002), 142.

Acknowledgments

Special appreciation is expressed to many people who helped to bring this book to completion. First of all, I am indebted to my friend and colleague Richard Mouw for his recommendation and encouragement to submit the manuscript to Eerdmans. I am also grateful for his desire to provide both a foreword and an afterword to the book.

I appreciate Eerdmans Publishing Company for their openness in publishing a fairly unusual book; this work represents their breadth, their desire to engage hard issues, and their willingness to entertain new perspectives. Jon Pott and Jennifer Hoffman at Eerdmans have been especially helpful, and their keen eyes and recommendations for improvement have sharpened the manuscript considerably.

My longtime assistant, Lori Soza, has, as always, been extremely efficient and helpful in preparing the manuscript for publication. My friends Craig Blomberg, Robert Matthews, David Neff, Craig Hazen, Truman Madsen, Greg Johnson, and David Paulsen have been kind and helpful in reading the manuscript and offering comments about its quality.

The love and encouragement of my wife, Shauna, have proven invaluable in this as in all other endeavors associated with my work.

On Scriptural Citations

Because The Church of Jesus Christ of Latter-day Saints has an expanded canon of scripture, and because many of the distinctive LDS beliefs are set forth in those volumes, it is important at the outset to indicate how scriptural references will be cited. Inasmuch as the King James Version of the Bible is the normative Bible of the Latter-day Saints, I have chosen to quote from it throughout the text of the book. References from the Bible will be kept in the text and placed in parentheses following the passages quoted or cited.

The Book of Mormon is made up of the following fifteen sections, and all but Words of Mormon are called books. These sections will also be cited in parentheses after the quotation or citation.

1 Nephi	Alma
2 Nephi	Helaman
Jacob	3 Nephi
Enos	4 Nephi
Jarom	Mormon
Omni	Ether
Words of Mormon	Moroni
Mosiah	

Thus the citation Alma 12:32 would represent verse 32 of the twelfth chapter of the Book of Alma.

The Doctrine and Covenants is composed of revelations given to or instruction provided by Joseph Smith and five of his successors. Most of the sections came during Joseph's lifetime, dating from 1823 to 1843.

For the most part, the sections are placed in the Doctrine and Covenants in chronological order. The sections quoted or cited will also be found in parentheses. Thus D&C 137:2 would represent the second verse of section 137.

The Pearl of Great Price is a selection from the revelations, translations, and narrations of Joseph Smith. The following are the sections within the Pearl of Great Price:

Selections from the Book of Moses
The Book of Abraham
Joseph Smith-Matthew
Joseph Smith-History
The Articles of Faith

Thus Abraham 5:1 would represent the first verse of the fifth chapter of the Book of Abraham; Joseph Smith-History 1:19 would represent the nineteenth verse of Joseph Smith-History; and Articles of Faith 1:11 would represent the eleventh article of faith.

INTRODUCTION:
How It All Began

One simply cannot understand the Latter-day Saints, and certainly cannot understand their perspective on Jesus Christ, without at least some understanding of their origins. The population of the United States doubled in the first quarter of the nineteenth century. It was a time of revolution, what some historians have called the "Second American Revolution," a time of upheaval, of movement — social, political, economic, and religious. It was the age of Restorationism, an era in America's history when men and women read the Bible, believed its story and message, and sought for a return to "the ancient order of things." Many longed for the reestablishment of primitive Christianity and to enjoy once more the spiritual gifts and divine outpourings that had once graced the ancients.

The Beginnings

Brigham Young expressed the feelings he had had before he encountered Joseph Smith or the Latter-day Saints: "My mind was opened to conviction, and I knew that the Christian world had not the religion that Jesus and the Apostles taught. I knew that there was not a Bible Christian on earth within my knowledge."[1] Wilford Woodruff, fourth president of the Church, said: "I did not join any church, believing that the Church of Christ in its true organization did not exist upon the

---

1. *Journal of Discourses*, 26 vols. (Liverpool: F. D. Richards & Sons, 1851-86), 5:75; cited hereafter as JD.

earth."[2] Willard Richards, later a counselor to Brigham Young, became "convinced that the sects were all wrong, and that God had no church on earth, but that he would soon have a church on earth whose creed would be the truth."[3]

Nothing of consequence emerges in a social or intellectual vacuum, and Joseph Smith and the work he set in motion were no different. What began on the American frontier through the work of an obscure farm boy and would later survive and blossom into a worldwide religious movement would not come into being in "dry ground." Indeed, the ground was prepared through a general dissatisfaction of large groups of people with mainline religious bodies. The roots of a new religion, one representing a restoration, would sink deep into the soil of many souls because individuals were anxious for a "new revelation." People were on the move. Mark Noll has written that "The impetus of creative mobilization rolled on into the 1830s as important new movements continued to take shape, like the Disciples or Christians of Alexander Campbell and Barton Stone, the Adventist followers of William Miller, and the Mormons of Joseph Smith. Well-publicized revival meetings continued to be held by Charles Finney. . . .

"Strains within evangelicalism, which became apparent in the 1830s, also pushed the promise of a thoroughly converted country even further into the future. For some, like veteran Methodist itinerants, consolidations following the explosion of all-out revivalism were taking place too soon; they could be understood only as compromise. By contrast, the followers of Alexander Campbell, Barton Stone, William Miller, and Joseph Smith thought it was far too soon to consolidate. For them, only compellingly fresh reinterpretation of Scripture (Campbell, Stone, Miller) or even new additions to Scripture (Smith) could rescue what was still a spiritually parlous [perilous, dangerous] situation."[4] The Latter-day Saints "managed to give utopianism a good name by refusing to wither away. The group's prophet, Joseph Smith (1805-1844), found no solace in the existing churches, and after

---

2. JD 4:99.

3. *History of The Church of Jesus Christ of Latter-day Saints*, 7 vols., ed. B. H. Roberts (Salt Lake City: Deseret Book, 1957), 2:470.

4. *America's God: From Jonathan Edwards to Abraham Lincoln* (New York: Oxford University Press, 2002), 183, 184.

a vision . . . he embarked on a religious quest to restore the true church."[5]

Joseph Smith, Jr., was born in Sharon, Vermont, on 23 December 1805, the fourth of nine children of Joseph and Lucy Mack Smith. His family moved thereafter to Tunbridge, Vermont; Lebanon, New Hampshire; Norwich, Vermont; and finally in 1814 settled in western New York. After two years of physical labor and financial strain, Joseph Smith, Sr., purchased 100 acres of unimproved land two miles south of Palmyra, New York, on the Palmyra-Manchester town line. In commenting on the religious activity in his own area, young Joseph mentioned that some time in the second year after the family's move to Manchester, "there was in the place where we lived an unusual excitement on the subject of religion." He explained that the excitement "commenced with the Methodists, but soon became general among all the sects in that region of country. Indeed, the whole district of country seemed affected by it, and great multitudes united themselves to the different religious parties" (Pearl of Great Price, Joseph Smith–History 1:5). Between 1816 and 1821 revivals were reported in more towns and more settlers joined churches than at any previous time in New York's history, thus giving rise to the phrase "the burned-over district."[6] "Salvation was what members of the Smith family desperately wanted," Robert Remini has written, "and they responded to these revivals in different ways. After sampling one sect after another, Lucy [young Joseph's mother] finally overcame her prejudice against established churches and joined the Western Presbyterian Church in Palmyra, along with her sons Hyrum and Samuel and her daughter Sophronia. But the two Josephs in the family remained aloof from organized religion, not that they eschewed it totally. Young Joseph leaned toward Methodism, which held one of its greatest revival meetings at that time."[7]

Stephen Prothero has described the religious confusion of the day that young Joseph faced: "Had Smith been raised in colonial New En-

5. Edwin Gaustad and Leigh Schmidt, *The Religious History of America: The Heart of the American Story from Colonial Times to Today* (San Francisco: Harper, 2002), 177.

6. See Milton V. Backman, Jr., "Awakenings in the Burned-Over District: New Light on the Historical Setting of the First Vision," *Brigham Young University Studies* 9, no. 3 (Spring 1969): 302; Whitney R. Cross, *The Burned-Over District* (Ithaca: Cornell, 1950).

7. *Joseph Smith* (New York: Penguin, 2002), 36-37.

gland, where Calvinist theology reigned, predestination theology probably would have brought on his adolescent angst. 'Am I one of the elect, or one of the damned?' he would have wondered, and then he would have gotten about the business of assuring himself of his own election. In upstate New York in the teens and twenties, however, Smith's anxiety took a different shape. It arose not from the rapidly fading theology of predestination but from the reality of religious diversity or, to be more precise, from a combination of religious diversity and Arminian theology. Religious options in the Burned-Over District were as wide as the frontier, and, according to Arminianism, salvation was a matter of individual choice, not divine fiat. But how to choose? Should you cast your lot with the Methodists? The Presbyterians? The Baptists? And if the Baptists, which ones?"[8]

Joseph Jr. attended many of the revivals with his family and became concerned for the salvation of his own soul. In addition, he was particularly troubled about which of all the religious denominations was correct and which he should join. Tradition has it that at one of the revivals a Methodist minister quoted from James 1:5 in the New Testament ("If any of you lack wisdom, let him ask of God") and encouraged the congregation to undertake their religious quest through prayer as well as by study. The fourteen-year-old Joseph then returned to his home and read the same passage from the family Bible. He later wrote of this experience: "Never did any passage of scripture come with more power to the heart of man than this did at this time to mine. It seemed to enter with great force into every feeling of my heart. I reflected on it again and again, knowing that if any person needed wisdom from God, I did; for how to act I did not know" (Joseph Smith-History 1:12). Joseph reported that soon thereafter he walked to a grove of trees not far from his father's farm and knelt to pray. "Information was what I most desired at this time, and with a fixed determination to obtain it I called upon the Lord for the first time."[9] It was the spring of 1820. In describing that occasion almost twenty years later, Joseph stated:

"After I had retired to the place where I had previously designed to

8. *American Jesus: How the Son of God Became a National Icon* (New York: Farrar, Straus and Giroux, 2003), 168.

9. From an 1835 account of the First Vision; in Milton V. Backman, Jr., *Joseph Smith's First Vision,* 2nd ed. (Salt Lake City: Bookcraft, 1980), 159.

go, having looked around me, and finding myself alone, I kneeled down and began to offer up the desires of my heart to God. I had scarcely done so, when immediately I was seized upon by some power which entirely overcame me, and had such an astonishing influence over me as to bind my tongue so that I could not speak. Thick darkness gathered around me, and it seemed to me for a time as if I were doomed to sudden destruction.

"But, exerting all my powers to call upon God to deliver me out of the power of this enemy which had seized upon me, and at the very moment when I was ready to sink into despair and abandon myself to destruction — not to an imaginary ruin, but to the power of some actual being from the unseen world, who had such marvelous power as I had never before felt in any being — just at this moment of great alarm, I saw a pillar of light exactly over my head, above the brightness of the sun, which descended gradually until it fell upon me.

"It no sooner appeared than I found myself delivered from the enemy which held me bound. When the light rested upon me I saw two Personages, whose brightness and glory defy all description, standing above me in the air. One of them spake unto me, calling me by name and said, pointing to the other — This is my Beloved Son. Hear Him!" (Joseph Smith-History 1:15-17).

In an earlier account of the same phenomenon, Joseph explained that "a pillar of light above the brightness of the sun at noon day came down from above and rested upon me and I was filled with the spirit of God. The Lord opened the heavens upon me and I saw the Lord and he spake unto me, saying, Joseph, my son, thy sins are forgiven thee. Go thy way. Walk in my statutes and keep my commandments."[10] In 1842 Joseph Smith prepared a brief history of the Church. That history contains the following description of his experience:

"While fervently engaged in supplication my mind was taken away from the objects with which I was surrounded, and I was enwrapped in a heavenly vision and saw two glorious personages who exactly resembled each other in features and likeness, surrounded with a brilliant light which eclipsed the sun at noon day. They told me that all religious denominations were believing in incorrect doctrines, and that

---

10. From an 1832 account, in Backman, *Joseph Smith's First Vision*, 157, punctuation corrected.

none of them was acknowledged of God as his church and kingdom. And I was expressly commanded to 'go not after them,' at the same time receiving a promise that the fulness of the gospel should at some time be made known unto me."[11]

This experience has come to be known as "Joseph Smith's First Vision" and is fundamental to the faith of the Latter-day Saints. The Saints believe in God, in Jesus Christ, in the Holy Spirit, and in the Holy Bible. They also believe in modern and continuing revelation and latter-day prophets, and the First Vision is foundational to these beliefs. The new prophet-leader and his followers came to extract definite theological principles from the First Vision, such as: (1) a belief in a literal satanic being bent upon the overthrow of all that comes from God; (2) the reality of God the Father as a separate and distinct personage from the resurrected Jesus Christ; (3) the startling realization that no religious denomination on earth had authority to act in the name of God; (4) the need for a restoration — more than a reformation — in order that saving truths and powers could be given anew to persons on earth; and (5) the confidence that it was possible for men and women to pray in faith, to commune with their Maker, and to come to know the things of God.

One historian of religion has written: "Critics of Mormonism have delighted in the discrepancies between the canonical [1838] account and earlier renditions, especially one written in Smith's own hand in 1832. . . . Such complaints, however, are much ado about relatively nothing. Any good lawyer (or historian) would expect to find contradictions in competing narratives written down years apart and decades after the event. And despite the contradictions, key elements abide. In each case, Jesus appears to Smith in a vision. In each case, Smith is blessed with a revelation. In each case, God tells him to remain aloof from all Christian denominations, as something better is in store."[12]

Joseph Smith would later state his position in regard to the actual reality of his experience: "I have thought since, that I felt much like Paul, when he made his defense before King Agrippa, and related the account of the vision he had when he saw a light, and heard a voice; but still there were but few who believed him. . . . Though I was hated and

---

11. From an 1842 account, in Backman, *Joseph Smith's First Vision*, 169.
12. Prothero, *American Jesus*, 171.

persecuted for saying that I had seen a vision, yet it was true; . . . I knew it, and I knew that God knew it, and I could not deny it, neither dared I do it; at least I knew that by so doing I would offend God, and come under condemnation" (Joseph Smith-History 1:24-25).

"My soul was filled with love," Joseph stated, "and for many days I could rejoice with great joy. The Lord was with me but I could find none that would believe the heavenly vision."[13] In speaking more specifically of the opposition he faced, he wrote of an encounter with a Methodist minister some days after the vision: "I took occasion to give him an account of the vision which I had had. I was greatly surprised at his behavior; he treated my communication not only lightly, but with great contempt, saying it was all of the devil, that there were no such things as visions or revelations in these days; that all such things had ceased with the apostles, and that there would never be any more of them" (Joseph Smith-History 1:21).

Modern Revelation and Scripture

Early on, Joseph Smith taught that a vision or revelation from God was not in itself sufficient to enable one to represent Deity. It was while translating the Book of Mormon (to be discussed shortly) that Joseph Smith and his scribe Oliver Cowdery continued to encounter references to baptism and other ordinances (sacraments), as well as the need for proper authority to perform the same. Feeling the need to inquire of God on the matter, they knelt in prayer on 15 May 1829 on the banks of the Susquehanna River near Harmony, Pennsylvania. Joseph and Oliver both reported that an angel appeared and identified himself as John, known in the New Testament as John the Baptist (the one who had prepared the way for and baptized Jesus), laid his hands upon their heads, and ordained them to what John called the Aaronic Priesthood. The Aaronic Priesthood, known also as the Lesser Priesthood or the Preparatory Priesthood, contained the power to teach and preach, to call to repentance, to baptize, and to ordain others to the same authority. John explained that "he acted under the direction of Peter, James,

---

13. From an 1832 account, in Backman, *Joseph Smith's First Vision,* 157, punctuation corrected.

and John, who held the keys of the Priesthood of Melchizedek, which Priesthood, he said, would in due time be conferred on us" (Joseph Smith-History 1:72). Joseph Smith stated that within weeks the three ancient apostles did in fact appear and bestow upon them the higher or Melchizedek Priesthood by the laying on of hands. This authority contained the power to confirm individuals as members of the Church after water baptism and confer the gift of the Holy Ghost. In addition, Joseph taught that the power he received from Peter, James, and John included the holy apostleship, the same authority given by Jesus anciently to bind and seal on earth and in heaven (see Matthew 16:16-19; 18:18).

On 6 April 1830 Joseph Smith met in company with a large group at Fayette, New York, to formally organize what was called on that day the Church of Christ. Later the name was changed to the Church of the Latter Day Saints, and in 1838 to The Church of Jesus Christ of Latter-day Saints. Joseph Smith was then and thereafter acknowledged and sustained by his followers as a prophet, seer, revelator, apostle, and first elder of the Church. Missionaries were sent out from the earliest days, and congregations of Saints were established in New York and Pennsylvania. By 1831 there were two church centers, one in Kirtland, Ohio, and one in Independence, Missouri. Severe persecution in Independence in 1833 and troubles in Ohio in the late 1830s forced the people into other parts of Missouri, and eventually the Saints left the state and settled on the banks of the Mississippi River at Commerce, Illinois. There, from 1839 to 1846, they enjoyed a season of peace and prosperity and built a city that came to be known as Nauvoo, the "city beautiful." Nauvoo grew during the time the Saints were there to become the second largest city in Illinois.

Missionaries were sent abroad, and tens of thousands, especially from Great Britain, converted to The Church of Jesus Christ of Latter-day Saints. Many of these left their homelands as a part of a modern gathering and came to America, the home of their newfound faith. But persecution and contention seemed to be ever a part of the lives of Joseph Smith and the Saints. Fearing his increasing social and political strength and the capacity of the growing Church to wield more and more influence in the state — and being distressed by a number of the beliefs and practices of the Saints, including plural marriage — the enemies (some from among dissident and disaffected members) eventually murdered Joseph Smith and his brother Hyrum in Carthage, Illinois, on 27 June 1844.

Many across the nation felt that the Church would, with the death of its charismatic leader, succumb to this final, stunning blow. But the Latter-day Saints affirmed that their faith was not founded on mortal man; by now the personal conviction of the divine truthfulness of that which Joseph had established was deep, while the vision was broad. There was left to Brigham Young, the senior apostle, the responsibility to regroup the Saints and prepare them for departure from Illinois and then an arduous and now-famous trek across the plains to the Great Basin in what is now Salt Lake City, Utah. The formal date of entry into the Salt Lake Valley was 24 July 1847. Brigham Young served as the Church's second president for thirty years and during that time, although the Saints enjoyed some degree of autonomy in their remote gathering place, there were ongoing struggles with the U.S. government over plural marriage and what was perceived to be the growing theocratic power of Brigham Young himself. Those struggles continued through the nineteenth century until plural marriage was officially discontinued in 1890 and Utah became the forty-fifth state in the union in 1896. Growth and expansion throughout the world have characterized the twentieth-century church, and the work set in motion by Joseph Smith continues to wield an influence in the twenty-first century.

For Joseph Smith and his followers, the traditions of the past regarding scripture, revelation, and canon were altered dramatically by the First Vision. God had spoken again, the heavens were no longer sealed, and a "new dispensation" of truth was under way. The Church's ninth article of faith states: "We believe all that God has revealed, all that He does now reveal, and we believe that He will yet reveal many great and important things pertaining to the Kingdom of God" (Pearl of Great Price, Articles of Faith 1:9). One writer has described this "dynamic scriptural process" as follows:

"Latter-day Saints hold a view of canon that does not restrict itself to God's revelations of the past, whether they be those which they revere in common with their fellow Christians or those believed uniquely by the Saints. Their view is broader: the canon is not closed, nor will it ever be. To them, revelation has not ceased; it continues in the Church. Future revelation is not only viewed as theoretically possible; it is needed and expected, as changing circumstances in the world necessitate new communication from God. This view of canon and scriptural authority is the legacy of Joseph Smith."[14] The LDS canon of scripture, called the "standard works," currently consists of the Bible, Book of Mormon, Doctrine and Covenants, and Pearl of Great Price.

The Book of Mormon

Over three years passed from the time of Joseph Smith's First Vision, and during that period he had refrained from joining any of the existing churches in the area. One evening Joseph knelt in prayer to determine his standing before God, inasmuch as he had enjoyed no further communication with God since 1820. In his own words: "On the evening of the 21st of September, A.D. 1823, while I was praying unto God, and endeavoring to exercise faith in the precious promises of Scripture, on a sudden a light like that of day, only of a far purer and more glorious appearance and brightness, burst into the room, indeed, the first sight was as though the house was filled with consuming fire; the appearance produced a shock that affected the whole body; in a moment a personage stood before me surrounded with a glory yet greater than that with which I was already surrounded."[15] The angel announced himself as Moroni and explained that "God had a work for me to do and that my name should be had for good and evil among all nations, kindreds, and tongues, or that it should be both good and evil spoken of among all people. He said there was a book deposited, written upon gold plates, giving an account of the former inhabitants of this continent, and the source from whence they sprang. He also said that the fulness of the everlasting Gospel was contained in it, as delivered by the Savior to the ancient inhabitants" (Joseph Smith-History 1:34). In describing the plates, as well as the manner in which he translated them, Joseph Smith wrote in 1842:

"These records were engraven on plates which had the appearance

14. Kent P. Jackson, "Latter-day Saints: A Dynamic Scriptural Process," in *The Holy Book in Comparative Perspective,* ed. Frederick M. Denny and Rodney L. Taylor (Columbia, SC: University of South Carolina Press, 1985), 63.

15. *History of the Church* 4:536.

of gold, each plate was six inches wide and eight inches long, and not quite so thick as common tin. They were filled with engravings, in Egyptian characters, and bound together in a volume as the leaves of a book, with three rings running through the whole. The volume was something near six inches in thickness, a part of which was sealed. . . . With the records was found a curious instrument, which the ancients called 'Urim and Thummim,' which consisted of two transparent stones set in the rim of a bow fastened to a breast plate. Through the medium of the Urim and Thummim I translated the record by the gift and power of God."[16]

For the Latter-day Saints, the Book of Mormon is an additional book of scripture, Another Testament of Jesus Christ. The majority of the Book of Mormon deals with a group of Hebrews (descendants of the tribe of Joseph, son of Jacob) who leave Jerusalem in the first year of the reign of King Zedekiah (ca. 600 B.C.), anticipating (being divinely directed concerning) the overthrow of Judah by the Babylonians. The people travel south and eventually set sail for a "promised land," a land "choice above all other lands," the land of America. The early story highlights the dissension between Nephi, a righteous and obedient leader of his people, and his rebellious and murmuring brothers, Laman and Lemuel. Prophet after prophet arises to call the people to repentance and declare the message of salvation. The Nephites are told repeatedly of the coming of Jesus, the Messiah, and the prophet leaders constantly strive to turn the hearts of the people to Christ. (The LDS belief in Christ's "eternal gospel" will be dealt with in chapter 1.) Eventually the internal squabbles result in a total break of the migrants into two separate bodies of people — the followers of Nephi (Nephites) and the followers of Laman (Lamanites). The remainder of the Book of Mormon is essentially a story of the constant rise and fall of the Nephite nation (not unlike the accounts of the children of Israel contained in 2 Kings), as the people either choose to obey God or yield to the enticings of riches and pride.

The book of 3 Nephi, chapters 11–28, contains an account of a visit and brief ministry of Jesus Christ to the Nephites in America, following his death, resurrection, and ascension in the Holy Land. While teaching and comforting these "other sheep" (John 10:14-16; Book of

---

16. *History of the Church* 4:537.

Mormon, 3 Nephi 15:21), Jesus organizes a church and establishes standards for a Christian community. A major feature of his ministry among them was to show them his resurrected glorified body and allow the people to feel and handle and thus experience its tangible nature — to gain an assurance of the resurrection. At one point in the narrative some 2500 men, women, and children become personal witnesses of the Savior's resurrection (3 Nephi 17:25). An era of peace and unity follows for almost two hundred years as the people see to the needs of one another through having "all things in common." The misuse of material blessings eventually leads to pride and class distinctions, resulting in a continuation of the former struggles between good and evil. The story of the Book of Mormon culminates in a final battle between the Nephites and the Lamanites in which the former (who had proven over time to be more wicked than their idolatrous enemies) are exterminated.

The history and divine dealings of the people from the time of Nephi were kept by the prophets and civic leaders, and the final task of completing and then editing and abridging the thousand-year collection of metal plates remained for the prophet-leader Mormon (for whom the book/collection is named) and his son, Moroni, in about A.D. 400. Joseph Smith stated that it was this same Moroni who returned as an angel with the plates in 1823. It is, by the way, because of the Latter-day Saints' acceptance of the Book of Mormon that they have come to be known as "Mormons."

Many persons in the nineteenth century announced revelation from God, claimed visions and oracles. But the Book of Mormon made Joseph's claims somewhat different, inasmuch as it represented to many a tangible evidence of divine intervention in history. People "touched the book," as Richard Bushman has written, "and the realization came over them that God had spoken again. Apart from any specific content, the discovery of additional scripture in itself inspired faith in people who were looking for more certain evidence of God in their lives."[17] In fact, Jan Shipps observed that as important as the First Vision was to the early Saints, "it was this 'gold bible' that first attracted adherents to the movement. As crucial to the success of the

17. *Joseph Smith and the Beginnings of Mormonism* (Urbana: University of Illinois Press, 1984), 142.

whole Latter-day Saint enterprise as is Joseph Smith, it must never be forgotten that in the early years it was not the First Vision but the Book of Mormon that provided the credentials that made the prophet's leadership so effective."[18] "The publication of the Book of Mormon," Peter W. Williams has observed, "signified for Smith's followers a reopening of the canon. . . . Such was an act of religious radicalism only hinted at by the Quakers, who regarded the promptings of the Inner Light as continuing (but not written) revelation. Even the Shakers, who saw Mother Ann Lee as a redemptive figure, did not regard any new body of religious writings as authoritative."[19]

The Doctrine and Covenants

Inasmuch as Joseph Smith claimed divine authority to speak for God, it was but natural that revelations and oracles given to him would be recorded. In 1831 the leaders of the Church began to compile the revelations received by Joseph Smith to date, and by 1833 that collection was known as *A Book of Commandments for the Government of the Church of Christ,* a volume consisting of approximately sixty-four of the present sections of the Doctrine and Covenants. Mob violence in Missouri led to the destruction of the press and the loss of all but a few copies of the Book of Commandments. In August of 1835 Joseph Smith published the first edition of the *Doctrine and Covenants,* an expanded form of the Book of Commandments, a collection that contained an additional forty-five revelations. Today the Doctrine and Covenants (cited hereafter as D&C) consists of 138 divisions called "sections" and two "Official Declarations."

A perusal of the Doctrine and Covenants demonstrates that most of the revelations recorded were received during the Ohio era of the Church's history (1831-37), over twenty were received in Missouri, and fewer than ten were recorded in the Doctrine and Covenants in Illinois. In addition to the revelations through Joseph Smith, there is in the

18. *Mormonism: The Story of a New Religious Tradition* (Urbana: University of Illinois Press, 1985), 33.

19. *America's Religions: From Their Origins to the Twenty-First Century* (Urbana: University of Illinois Press, 2002), 238.

Doctrine and Covenants one revelation received by Brigham Young, one by Joseph F. Smith, sixth president of the Church (served from 1901-1918), and official declarations from Wilford Woodruff (fourth president, served from 1889-1898) and Spencer W. Kimball (twelfth president, served from 1973-1985).

This dynamic scriptural process is illustrated through a brief look at revelations added to the collection in recent years. At the April 1976 general conference of the Church two revelations were added to the canon. One had been received by Joseph Smith in January 1836 but had never been placed in the canon. Another was received by Joseph F. Smith in October 1918. The Saints believe that both of these oracles were inspired of God — that is, they represent the will, mind, voice, and word of the Lord, even from the time they were delivered and recorded. But in 1976 they were added to the standard works, the canon, by a vote of the Church, thus making them canonized scripture. As such they become binding upon the Church, and the members are expected to read and study them and to govern their beliefs and practices according to them.

The Pearl of Great Price

In 1850 Franklin D. Richards, a young apostle, was called to serve as president of the British Mission of the Church. He discovered a paucity of either LDS scripture or Church literature among the Saints in England, this in spite of the fact that a larger number of members resided in the British Isles at that time than in the United States. In 1851 he published a mission tract entitled *Pearl of Great Price,* a collection of translations and narrations from Joseph Smith. Interest in and appreciation for the tract grew over the years, and by 1880 the entire Church voted to accept the Pearl of Great Price as the fourth standard work, the fourth book of scripture in the LDS canon. The Pearl of Great Price contains: (1) doctrinal details concerning Adam (and the Creation and Fall), Enoch, Noah, Moses, and Jesus' Olivet Discourse (Matthew 24) as made known to Joseph Smith as he undertook a serious study of the Bible; (2) more of God's dealings with Abraham; (3) an excerpt from Joseph Smith's 1838 history of the Church; and (4) thirteen statements of religious belief prepared by Joseph Smith, called the Articles of Faith.

The acceptance of modern and continuing revelation, including the addition to the scriptural canon, is one of the distinctives of Mormonism and thus one of the reasons those of other faiths are prone to describe the Latter-day Saints as "non-Christian." And yet, how radical is the idea of modern revelation? Roman Catholics certainly believe that God has directed and will continue to direct the church through the "working out" of church practice and tradition — based upon holy scripture — and that an ongoing form of heavenly guidance comes through such means as papal encyclicals. Pentecostal and Holiness movements within Protestantism believe that spiritual gifts, such as the speaking and interpretation of tongues, is one means by which Deity communicates his will to individuals and groups. And what of evangelicalism? Of my hundreds of evangelical acquaintances, every single one believes that God can and does hear his or her prayers, respond to his or her petitions, and in some cases send an answer through a kind of spiritual illumination that I can only describe as inspiration or revelation.

Further, Roger Olson has pointed out that a too strict adherence to *sola scriptura* and a complete rejection of church tradition (dating, in some cases, to the early church fathers) may lead to problems and challenges for the church. "Evangelicals have lost their memory of the Great Tradition of Christianity before the rise of revivalism and their own free church (less emphasis on creeds and liturgy) movements. We are like people who have forgotten our family tree and our cultural past — rootless wanderers without landmarks from our past to guide us. Is it any wonder, then, that so much of our preaching and teaching is shallow and that we keep repeating the errors of the past? New forms of the heresies that bedeviled the churches in the generations immediately after the apostles' deaths repeatedly appear in evangelical circles. . . . Evangelicalism is in danger of being reduced to a folk religion with little or nothing to say to the world out of its great intellectual heritage. . . .

"What is needed today is a middle way between *sola scriptura* and traditionalism that holds fast to the unique and unsurpassable authority of Scripture even over tradition while requiring respect for the Great Tradition of biblical understanding in the church. . . .

"Evangelicals, with the Reformers, should view the Great Tradition as dynamic and open to correction and revision in the light of Scripture while valuing the achievements of the early church fathers, the medieval theologians, and the Protestant Reformers."[20]

One LDS Church leader remarked that "What makes us different from most other Christians in the way we read and use the Bible and other scriptures is our belief in continuing revelation. *For us, the scriptures are not the ultimate source of knowledge, but what precedes the ultimate source.* The ultimate knowledge comes by revelation . . . through those we sustain as prophets, seers, and revelators."[21]

Conclusion

The Latter-day Saint view of Jesus Christ is thus based upon the teachings and instructions of scripture (the Bible, Book of Mormon, and modern revelations) and pronouncements of latter-day apostles and prophets. "The sacred writings of the Latter-day Saints," observes one writer, "perform a practical function within the faith; they are not used in any kind of ritual situation. They are not used in chanting, reciting, or praying, or in any similar rite . . . , nor is reading them a sacramental act. In Latter-day Saint theology the reading of scripture functions as a means to achieving an important end — education in the principles of the faith so that one can be in harmony with the will of God."[22] Latter-day Saints believe the scriptures are to be read and searched and studied; the reader of scripture is encouraged to open himself or herself to inspiration and to "liken the scriptures" unto their own life situation. In short, though the study of scripture may not be considered a sacramental act, Latter-day Saints believe that one essential key to the receipt of *individual* revelation — to know the mind and will of God in one's life, and to come to know God — is the study of *institutional* revelation.

"Search the scriptures," Joseph Smith counseled the Latter-day Saints, "search the revelations which we publish, and ask your Heavenly Father, in the name of His Son Jesus Christ, to manifest the truth unto

20. Roger E. Olson, "The Tradition Temptation," *Christianity Today,* vol. 47, no. 11 (November 2003), 52, 55.

21. Dallin H. Oaks, "Scripture Reading and Revelation," *Ensign,* January 1995, 7.

22. Jackson, "Latter-day Saints: A Dynamic Scriptural Process," 79.

you, and if you do it with an eye single to His glory nothing doubting, He will answer you by the power of His Holy Spirit. You will then know for yourselves and not for another. You will not then be dependent on man for the knowledge of God; nor will there be any room for speculation. No; for when men receive their instruction from Him that made them, they know how He will save them."[23]

23. *Teachings of the Prophet Joseph Smith,* selected by Joseph Fielding Smith (Salt Lake City: Deseret Book, 1976), 11-12.

1 Jesus Before Bethlehem

From a Latter-day Saint perspective, humankind did not suddenly spring into existence at the time of their mortal birth. We have always lived. Others outside the LDS faith have sensed that there is more to life than living and dying, more to what we do here than meets the physical eye. Many have perceived that this stage of our journey is but a part of a larger drama. William Wordsworth penned the following:

> Our birth is but a sleep and a forgetting:
> The Soul that rises with us, our life's Star,
> Hath had elsewhere its setting,
> And cometh from afar:
> Not in entire forgetfulness,
> And not in utter nakedness,
> But trailing clouds of glory do we come
> From God, who is our home:
> Heaven lies about us in our infancy![1]

Marcel Proust, the influential French novelist, wrote: "Everything in our life happens as though we entered upon it with a load of obligations contracted in a previous existence . . . obligations whose sanction is not of this present life, [that] seem to belong to a different world, founded on kindness, scruples, sacrifice, a world entirely different from

---

1. "Ode: Intimations of Immortality from Recollections of Early Childhood," in *English Romantic Poetry and Prose,* ed. Alfred Noyes (New York: Oxford University Press, 1956), 327-28.

this one, a world whence we emerge to be born on this earth, before returning thither."[2]

The Life Before

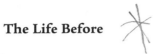

Latter-day Saints believe that men and women are the spirit sons and daughters of God, that we lived in a premortal existence before birth, that we grew and expanded in that "first estate" (Jude 1:6; Pearl of Great Price, Abraham 3:26), all in preparation for this "second estate." In that world men and women were separate and distinct spirit personages, had consciousness, volition, maleness and femaleness, and moral agency. We developed and matured according to our adherence to God's eternal law, and in spite of the fact that we walked and talked with God, it was necessary for us to exercise faith in God's plan for the ultimate salvation of his children. Thus God is literally our spirit Father, and we inherit from him divine qualities and attributes. In the long expanse of time before we were born into mortality, the spirit sons and daughters of God developed talents, strengths, and capacities. In a sense, no two persons remained alike.

Before coming to earth, the sons and daughters of God were told that as mortals they would be required to walk by faith (2 Corinthians 5:7), to operate in this second estate without full knowledge of what they did and who they were in the life before. A veil of forgetfulness would be placed over their minds. One early Church leader suggested what might have been said before we left: "Remember you go [to earth] on this condition, that is, you are to forget all things you ever saw, or knew to be transacted in the spirit world; . . . you must go and become one of the most helpless of all beings that I have created, while in your infancy, subject to sickness, pain, tears, mourning, sorrow and death. But *when truth shall touch the cords of your heart they will vibrate; then intelligence shall illuminate your mind, and shed its lustre in your soul, and you shall begin to understand the things you once knew,* but which had gone from you; you shall then begin to understand and know the object of your creation."[3]

2. In Gabriel Marcel, *Homo Viator* (New York: Harper & Row, 1963), 8.

3. John Taylor, in "The Mormon," 29 August 1857, New York City; in *The Vision,* comp. N. B. Lundwall (Salt Lake City: Bookcraft, n.d.), 146-47, emphasis added.

Jesus the Christ — born in a stable in the humblest of circumstances, reared in Nazareth, trained as a carpenter — is endless and eternal (D&C 19:10). He is God. While he came to earth to obtain a physical body (his condescension or incarnation), yet he was and is the Lord and Master of heaven and earth. "The great Jehovah contemplated the whole of events connected with the earth, pertaining to the plan of salvation, before it rolled into existence. . . . The past, the present, and the future were and are, with Him, one eternal 'now.'[4] The Nativity was in actuality the beginning of Phase II of Christ's eternal ministry. As to what existence was like before our birth as spirits, we really do not know. One Church leader, Bruce R. McConkie, has written that Christ "is described as being 'from everlasting to everlasting' (D&C 61:1), and 'from all eternity to all eternity' (D&C 39:1). . . . He was born, as were all the spirit children of the Father. God was his Father, as he is of all the rest."[5]

Jesus was the firstborn spirit child of God the Father and thus the recipient of the birthright of the royal family. As such, and in that premortal realm, he was the Elder Brother of all of the spirit sons and daughters of the Father. "I was in the beginning with the Father," Christ affirms in a modern revelation, "and am the Firstborn; and all those who are begotten through me are partakers of the glory of the same, and are the church of the Firstborn" (D&C 93:21-22). Over the ages in that premortal world Christ grew in light and truth and knowledge and power until he had become "like unto God" (Abraham 3:24), meaning like unto our Eternal Father. He, above all of his spirit brothers and sisters, exercised "exceeding faith and good works" in our First Estate and thereby was "called with a holy calling," in this case the calling of redemption and salvation (Book of Mormon, Alma 13:3).

As we developed in that pristine existence, we were taught the Great Plan of Happiness, which is the Gospel of God (Romans 1:1; 15:16; 1 Peter 4:17). This was the plan we were to follow in our efforts to become "partakers of the divine nature" (2 Peter 1:4). "After this plan had been taught to all the hosts of heaven; after it was known and understood by all; after all its facets had been debated and evaluated — then the Father asked for a volunteer to put the full terms and all of

---

4. *Teachings of the Prophet Joseph Smith,* selected by Joseph Fielding Smith (Salt Lake City: Deseret Book, 1976), 220.

5. *The Promised Messiah* (Salt Lake City: Deseret Book, 1978), 46.

the conditions of his plan into force."[6] The great question posed to the assembled spirits in the Grand Council was simply "Whom shall I send?" (Abraham 3:27.) Lucifer, a "son of the morning," one who "was in authority in the presence of God" (D&C 76:25), said: "Behold, here am I, send me, I will be thy son, and I will redeem all mankind, that one soul shall not be lost, and surely I will do it; wherefore give my thine honor" (Pearl of Great Price, Moses 4:1). Pride and ambition and self-aggrandizement are everywhere manifest in this response. In contrast, the Firstborn replied: "Father, thy will be done, and the glory be thine forever" (Moses 4:2). These words, though brief, are poignant and all-sufficient: they are the words and wisdom by which Jesus governed his life in both the premortal and mortal realms.

Just how long the discussions and controversy raged in the premortal realm between those who advocated and sustained the plan of the Father and those who accepted Lucifer's amendatory offer is unknown. But surely it must have been the topic of conversation and the object of much teaching over an extended period of time. Joseph Smith explained: "The contention in heaven was — Jesus said there would be certain souls that would not be saved; and the devil said he could save them all, and laid his plans before the grand council, who gave their vote in favor of Jesus Christ. So the devil rose up in rebellion against God, and was cast down, with all who put up their heads for him."[7] "And there was war in heaven; Michael and his angels fought against the dragon; and the dragon fought and his angels, and prevailed not; neither was their place found any more in heaven" (Revelation 12:7-8). Lucifer and one third of the spirit children of God were cast down to the earth. Thereafter the Firstborn was proclaimed as Mediator for man and the Way to the Father; Christ became "the Lamb slain from the foundation of the world" (Revelation 13:8; Moses 7:47).

Under the direction of the Father, who is designated as "God the first, the Creator,"[8] and in company with "the noble and great ones," Christ created this world and all things on the face of it (Abraham 3:22-24; 4:1). In addition, he became the Creator of worlds without

6. McConkie, *The Promised Messiah,* 49.

7. *Teachings of the Prophet Joseph Smith,* selected by Joseph Fielding Smith (Salt Lake City: Deseret Book, 1976), 357; cited hereafter as TPJS.

8. TPJS, 190.

number (D&C 76:24; Moses 1:33). Having been granted a vision of the Lord's majesty and creations, Enoch observed that "were it possible that man could number the particles of the earth, yea, millions of earths like this, it would not be a beginning to the number of thy creations" (Moses 7:30). As "the Lord Omnipotent," He came to be known to the ancients as "the Father of heaven and earth, the Creator of all things from the beginning" (Mosiah 3:5, 8). God the Father "created all things by Jesus Christ" (Ephesians 3:9). He who was "appointed heir of all things" became the one "by whom also [God] made the worlds" (Hebrews 1:2).

The Almighty Jehovah, the premortal God of the ancients, eventually was born on earth as the man Jesus. It was Jehovah who manifested himself to Adam and Eve after the Fall; who revealed himself to Enoch and Noah; who made known the plan of life and salvation to Abraham, Isaac, Jacob and all of the faithful in the Old Testament; and who gave the Law of Moses to ancient Israel (Moses 7:53; 8:19; 1 Nephi 19:10; 3 Nephi 15:5). Further, we believe that the ancients were commanded to offer the firstlings of their flocks as an offering unto the Lord in similitude of the coming sacrifice of Jesus Christ that would bring redemption to all mankind (Moses 5:5-8). Truly, as one Book of Mormon prophet declared, "none of the prophets have written, nor prophesied, save they have spoken concerning this Christ" (Jacob 7:11).

Christ's Eternal Gospel

The Church of Jesus Christ of Latter-day Saints teaches that God our Father has a plan for his children, a program established, from before the foundations of the world, to maximize our growth and insure our happiness. The Book of Mormon prophets speak with grateful hearts for the merciful plan of the great Creator (2 Nephi 9:6), the plan of our God (2 Nephi 9:13), the great plan of mercy (Alma 42:15, 31), the plan of redemption (Jacob 6:8; Alma 12:25-26, 30, 32; 17:16; 18:39; 22:13-14; 29:2; 34:31; 39:18; 42:11, 13), the eternal plan of deliverance (2 Nephi 11:5), the plan of salvation (Jarom 1:2; Alma 24:14; 42:5), and the great plan of happiness (Alma 42:8, 16). Church leaders have explained that the plan of salvation is "always and everlastingly the same; that obedience to the same laws always brings the same reward; that the gospel laws have not changed . . . ; and that always and everlastingly all things pertaining to salvation center in Christ."[9]

The atoning sacrifice is not only timely (for those of us who regularly need its cleansing powers) but *timeless*. Though the act of atonement would not take place until Jesus suffered in the Garden of Gethsemane and on the cross of Calvary, we believe that earth's earliest inhabitants were taught to call upon God in the name of his Beloved Son for deliverance (Moses 5:5-8). In short, the Latter-day Saints believe that God has revealed himself, his plan, including the doctrine of redemption in Christ, from the beginning (Moses 6:59).

Joseph Smith observed that "we cannot believe that the ancients in all ages were so ignorant of the system of heaven as many suppose, since all that were ever saved, were saved through the power of this great plan of redemption, as much before the coming of Christ as since; if not, God has had different plans in operation (if we may so express it), to bring men back to dwell with Himself; and this we cannot believe, since there has been no change in the constitution of man since he fell."[10] This is the context for the apostle Paul's statement that the gospel was preached to Abraham (Galatians 3:8), as well as his observation that the children of Israel "were all baptized unto Moses in the cloud and in the sea; and did all eat the same spiritual meat; and did all drink the same spiritual drink; for they drank of that spiritual Rock that followed them: and that Rock was Christ" (1 Corinthians 10:2-4). Likewise, Moses "refused to be called the son of Pharaoh's daughter; choosing rather to suffer affliction with the people of God, than to enjoy the pleasures of sin for a season; esteeming the reproach of Christ greater riches than the treasures in Egypt" (Hebrews 11:24-26). Truly, as Peter proclaimed, "To [Christ] give all the prophets witness" (Acts 10:43).

Because the Saints believe that the great plan of happiness is eternal and that salvation in any age is accomplished only in and through the mediation of the Redeemer, they also believe that the covenants and ordinances (sacraments) are likewise eternal and unchanging. "Now taking it for granted that the scriptures say what they mean and mean what they say," Joseph Smith noted, "we have sufficient grounds

9. McConkie, *The Promised Messiah*, 4-5.
10. TPJS, 59-60.

to go on and prove from the Bible that the gospel has always been the same; the ordinances to fulfill its requirements, the same, and the officers to officiate, the same; and the signs and fruits resulting from the promises, the same." He continues with an illustration of this principle: "Therefore, as Noah was a preacher of righteousness he must have been baptized and ordained to the priesthood by the laying on of the hands."[11] In short, the Lord "set the ordinances to be the same forever and ever." That is, "Ordinances, instituted in the heavens before the foundation of the world, in the priesthood, for the salvation of men, are not to be altered or changed. All must be saved on the same principles."[12] It is in this light that Latter-day Saints speak of the restored gospel as comprising the new and everlasting covenant. The gospel covenant is new in the sense that it is revealed anew in our day. It is everlasting in the sense that it was had from the beginning.

Remnants of the Faith

It is but reasonable, therefore, that elements of truth, pieces of a much larger mosaic, should be found throughout the world in varying cultures and among diverse religious groups. Further, as the world has passed through phases of apostasy and restoration, relics of revealed doctrine remain, albeit in some cases in altered or even convoluted forms. Joseph F. Smith, sixth president of the Church, had much to say to those who seek to upstage Christianity. Jesus Christ, he taught, "being the fountain of truth, is no imitator. He taught the truth first; it was his before it was given to man." Further, "When I read books scattered . . . through the world, throwing discredit upon words and teachings and doctrines of the Lord Jesus Christ, saying that some of the ideas Jesus uttered, truths that he promulgated, have been enunciated before by the ancient philosophers among the heathen nations of the world, I want to tell you that there is not a heathen philosopher that ever lived in all the world from the beginning, that had a truth or enunciated a principle of God's truth that did not receive it from the fountain head, from God himself. . . .

11. TPJS, 264.
12. TPJS, 168, 308.

"Let it be remembered that Christ was with the Father from the beginning, that the gospel of truth and light existed from the beginning, and is from everlasting to everlasting. The Father, Son, and Holy Ghost, as one God, are the fountain of truth. . . . If we find truth in broken fragments through the ages, it may be set down as an incontrovertible fact that it originated at the fountain, and was given to philosophers, inventors, patriots, reformers, and prophets by the inspiration of God. It came from him through his Son Jesus Christ and the Holy Ghost, in the first place, and from no other source. It is eternal.

". . . Men are mere repeaters of what he has taught them. He has voiced no thought originating with man. The teachings of Jesus did not begin with his incarnation; for, like truth, he is eternal. He not only inspired the ancients, from the beginning, but when he came to earth he reiterated eternal, original truth, and added gloriously to the revelations men had uttered. When he returned to the Father, he still took, and does take, an interest in his children and people, by revealing to them new truths, and by inspiring their actions; and, as men grow in the knowledge of God, they shall become more and more like him unto the perfect day, when his knowledge shall cover the earth as the waters cover the deep."[13]

Being aware that this knowledge was had by many of the ancients, should we be surprised to find legends and myths concerning gods who have divine power but human attributes and passions? Knowing that Adam and Seth and Enos and Cainan and Mahalaleel and others of the antediluvians spoke of the coming of the Messiah, and that the Messiah would come to earth as a man but be possessed of the powers of a God, is it not likely that they also knew that he would be born of a virgin? Should we be surprised to find pagan traditions of virgin births and divine humans?

Men and women in the earliest ages knew of a first estate, a premortal existence. Therefore, is it any wonder that several religious traditions are wedded to an idea of past lives? Inasmuch as the doctrines of rebirth, regeneration, resurrection, and the immortality of the soul were taught from the beginning, why should we flinch when we discover the doctrines of reincarnation, transmigration of souls, and re-

---

13. *Gospel Doctrine* (Salt Lake City: Deseret Book, 1971), 31, 395, 398-400; see also *Journal of Discourses,* 26 vols. (Liverpool: F. D. Richards & Sons, 1851-86), 15:325; cited hereafter as JD.

birth in such traditions as Hinduism, Jainism, and Sikhism, or when we encounter a people like the ancient Egyptians who are obsessed not with death (as some suppose), but with life after death? Elements of enlightenment, remnants of truth, and aspects of the faith of the Former-day Saints may be found in religious traditions throughout the world. The Lord loves his children, all of them, and he delights to "honor those who serve [him] in righteousness and in truth unto the end" (D&C 76:5).

Conclusion

There are good people in the world, men and women who love God, who are earnestly striving to be true to the standards of decency and integrity they have been taught. Indeed, everyone has access to some measure of light and truth from the Almighty. Brigham Young thus declared that there has never been "a man or woman upon the face of the earth, from the days of Adam to this day, who has not been enlightened, instructed, and taught by the revelations of Jesus Christ."[14] C. S. Lewis once stated that there are people "who are slowly becoming Christians though they do not yet call themselves so. There are people who do not accept the full Christian doctrine about Christ but who are so strongly attracted by Him that they are His in a much deeper sense than they themselves understand." Lewis went on to speak of people "who are being led by God's secret influence to concentrate on those parts of their religion which are in agreement with Christianity, and who thus belong to Christ without knowing it."[15]

Latter-day Saints teach that if people will be true to the light within them, they will be led to a higher light found in the covenant gospel, either in this life or in the life to come. "And the Spirit giveth light to every man that cometh into the world; and the Spirit enlighteneth every man through the world, that hearkeneth to the voice of the Spirit" (D&C 84:46-48).[16] In fact, is it not possible that one reason so many parallels

---

14. JD 2:139.

15. *Mere Christianity* (New York: Touchstone, 1996), 178.

16. See Joseph F. Smith, *Gospel Doctrine*, 67-68; Bruce R. McConkie, *A New Witness for the Articles of Faith* (Salt Lake City: Deseret Book, 1985), 260-61.

and resemblances exist between the gospel and the various approxima-tions of the full truth is because men and women are responding to "spirit memories" of the past, those things we once knew but now seem just out of conscious awareness? "All those salient truths," Joseph F. Smith observed, "which come home so forcibly to the head and heart seem but the awakening of the memories of the spirit. Can we know anything here that we did not know before we came?"[17]

17. *Gospel Doctrine,* 13.

2 The Jesus of History,
the Christ of Faith

My memories of the first class I took as a part of a doctoral program in Religious Studies are still very much intact. It was a course entitled "Seminar in Biblical Studies" and dealt with such issues as scripture, canon, interpretation, authorship, eschatology, prophecy, and like subjects. We were but weeks into the seminar when the professor was confronted by a question from an evangelical Christian student on the reality of miracles among ancient Israel. The response was polite but brief: "Well, let me just say that it doesn't really matter whether the Israelites actually crossed the Red Sea on dry ground as a result of some miracle performed by Moses. What matters is that the Israelites then and thereafter saw it as an act of divine intervention, and the event became a foundation for a people's faith for centuries."

About a year later I found myself in a similar setting, this time in a seminar entitled "Critical Studies of the New Testament," the first half of a two-semester encounter with a literary-historical study of the New Testament (NT). The composition of the students in the seminar made for fascinating conversation: a Reform Jew, two Methodists, two Southern Baptists, a Roman Catholic, a Nazarene, and a Latter-day Saint. The professor was a secular Jew. By the time we had begun studying the passion narratives in the Gospels, the question of "historical events" vs. "faith events" had been raised. The professor stressed the importance of "myth" and emphasized that miraculous events in the NT — because in them the narrative detaches itself from the ordinary limitations of time and space such that the supernatural "irrupts" into human history — should be relegated to the category of faith events or sacred story. And then came the punch line, a phrase that had a haunting familiarity: "Now, whether, for example, Jesus of Nazareth came back to life — literally rose from the dead — is not important. What matters is that the Christians thought he did. And the Christian movement is founded on this faith event."

What we are dealing with here is historicity — in simple terms, whether something significant truly took place, whether it was an actual event in actual history. Few normal people doubt that Jesus lived. His appearance on the stage of history is too well attested to doubt. But what is so often doubted is his divinity — his divine Sonship, his miracles, his ability to forgive sins and heal and regenerate human souls, his power over life and death.

In recent years the so-called "Jesus Seminar" has focused our attention on the words of Jesus.[1] These supposed NT scholars have concluded that 82% of the words traditionally attributed to Jesus in the four Gospels were not really spoken by him. In their new translation of the Gospels, the Scholars Version, they employ a system of color coding in which the words formerly attributed to our Lord are classified according to color: (1) words in *red* indicate something definitely spoken by Jesus; (2) words in *pink* are those that the scholars are less certain may be traced back to Jesus or words that have suffered modification in transmission; (3) words in *gray* did not originate with Jesus, though they may well reflect his ideas; and (4) words in *black* are those that were put into the mouth of Jesus in the stories prepared by his followers or admirers (or, in some cases, by his enemies) and are therefore inauthentic. All references in the Scholars Version to Jesus as the Son of God have been declared inauthentic, as have all places that refer to his Messiahship, his preexistence, his resurrection, his forgiveness of sins, and his miraculous healings. For that matter, almost the entire Gospel of John has been printed in black.

My initial reaction to this whole undertaking was a form of quiet rage: How dare they? Who do they think they are? What audacity to suppose that they know enough about our Lord and Savior to set us straight, to tell the world what Jesus said and what he did not say! My next reaction was more somber and poignant: What a pity! How disheartening, how sad that what began as the Quest for the Historical Je-

---

1. See Robert W. Funk, Roy W. Hoover, et al., *The Five Gospels: What Did Jesus Really Say?* (New York: Macmillan, 1993).

sus has brought us to the point where we have sheared the Savior of divinity and reduced to myth and metaphor his capacity to come into the world and transform fallen humanity. How unfortunate it is that basically good men and women, people who have at least an affection or an admiration for holy scripture, should wander so far afield. How did we come to this?

In 1966 Gordon B. Hinckley, at the time a Latter-day Saint apostle and later a president of the Church, said: "*Modern theologians strip [Jesus] of his divinity and then wonder why men do not worship him.* These clever scholars have taken from Jesus the mantle of Godhood and have left only a man. *They have tried to accommodate him to their own narrow thinking. They have robbed him of his divine Sonship and taken from the world its rightful King.*"[2] Some five years later, Church leader Harold B. Lee explained to a group of students at Utah State University: "Fifty years ago or more," he said, "there were the unmistakable evidences that *there was coming into the religious world actually a question about the Bible and about the divine calling of the Master himself.* Now, fifty years later, our greatest responsibility and anxiety is to defend the divine mission of our Lord and Master, Jesus Christ, for all about us, even among those who claim to be professors of the Christian faith, are those not willing to stand squarely in defense of the great truth that our Lord and Master, Jesus Christ, was indeed the Son of God."[3]

Critical of the Criticism

In responding to the issue of the historicity of miracles and divinity in the life and ministry of Jesus the Christ, as a Latter-day Saint Christian I would like to pose a series of questions about much of the Jesus research and then offer a response.

1. To what extent have we accepted "uncritically" the tenets and canons of biblical criticism? Why should we be so willing to "give away the store" and jettison time-honored beliefs and sacred values on the basis of someone else's doubts or a system of scholarship that from the outset precludes the essentials of the Christian message?

2. Conference Report, April 1966, 86, emphasis added.
3. LDS Student Association fireside, Utah State University, 10 October 1971.

Donald Guthrie has noted that "there is a decided difference between a scholar who accepts the divine origin of Scripture and inquires into its historical and literary origins and a scholar who begins his critical inquiries with the assumption that there is nothing unique about the text and who claims the right to examine it as he would any other book. The former is not simply submitting the text to the bar of his own reason to establish its validity, but assumes that the text will authenticate itself when subject to reverent examination. His stance of faith and his critical inquiry in no way invalidate each other."[4]

2. Who was Jesus of Nazareth? To what degree can we trust the canonical Gospels in regard to what Jesus said and did? Has the Christian Church transformed a lowly Nazarene into a God? Is it possible to tear away the faithful film of believing tradition and get back to the way things really were? Can we excise from the biblical text those theological perspectives that preclude an "accurate" view of Jesus? Indeed, the question of the age is, "What think ye of Christ?" (Matthew 22:42).

I add my voice to the growing throng of tens of thousands of irritated Christians and to an increasing number of impatient religious leaders and serious scholars, who certify:

- that Jesus was and is who he and the Gospel writers say he was — the Son of God, the Only Begotten Son in the flesh of the Eternal Father;
- that we have every reason to believe that the four Gospels are true and accurate and that the essential message of historical Christianity — that Christ lived, taught, lifted, strengthened, renewed, healed, prophesied, communed with Deity, suffered, died, rose from the dead, appeared thereafter to hundreds, and will come again in glory — is to be taken seriously;
- that efforts to demythologize or debunk Jesus will in time be shown to be what they in actuality are — shams and charades on the part of people who dare not believe and who work endlessly to proselytize others to share their doubts. Too often the undergird-

---

4. "The Historical and Literary Criticism of the New Testament," in *Biblical Criticism: Historical, Literary and Textual,* ed. R. K. Harrison, B. K. Waltke, D. Guthrie, and G. D. Fee (Grand Rapids: Zondervan, 1978), 87.

ing assumption of those who cast doubt on the historical Jesus as set forth in scripture, in whole or in part, is a denial of the supernatural and a refusal to admit of prophecy, revelation, and divine intervention. J. B. Phillips pointed out that "many otherwise honest intellectual people will construct a neat by-pass around the claim of Jesus to be God. Being people of insight and imagination, they know perfectly well that once to accept such a claim as fact would mean a readjustment of their own purposes and values and affections which they may have no wish to make. To call Jesus the greatest Figure in History or the finest Moral Teacher the world has ever seen commits no one to anything. But once to allow the startled mind to accept as fact that this man is really focused-God may commit anyone to anything! There is every excuse for blundering in the dark, but in the light there is no cover from reality."[5]

3. How have efforts to apply modern scientific principles and methodologies to sacred texts affected our view of Jesus? In what ways do our presuppositions affect our conclusions? If we choose to bracket out divine Sonship, divine intervention, revelation, predictive prophecy, miracles, and physical resurrection, should we be surprised with the product of our investigation?

Perhaps we have been a bit too hasty to apply supposed scientific methodology to sacred texts. A strict application of the scientific method to sacred events, holy words, and miraculous doings is not possible. Some things are not observable or measurable by this world's tools or devices. Some things may only be felt and understood by those possessed of a believing heart. In speaking of applying scientific principles to the study of scriptural texts, my colleague Stephen Robinson pointed out some years ago that "the exclusion of any supernatural agency (including God) from human affairs is fundamental to the methodology of most biblical scholarship." Continuing, "The naturalistic approach gives scholars from different religious backgrounds common controls and perspectives relative to the data and eliminates arguments over subjective beliefs not verifiable by the historical-critical method. However, there is a cost to using the naturalistic approach, for one can never mention God, revelation, priesthood, prophecy, etc., as

5. *Your God Is Too Small* (New York: Touchstone, 1997), 83.

having objective existence or as being part of the evidence or as being possible causes of the observable effect. . . .

"Naturalistic explanations are often useful in evaluating empirical data, but when the question asked involves empirical categories, such as 'Is the Book of Mormon what it purports to be?' it begs the question to adopt a method whose first assumption is that the Book cannot be what it claims to be. This points out a crucial logical difficulty in using this method in either attacking or defending the Church."[6] Simply stated in regard to the NT, why should we be surprised that many biblical scholars conclude that Jesus was not divine, that the miracles did not really occur, that he did not rise from the dead, when the template they place over their reading of the NT is a naturalistic one, a distant objectivity, a feigned detachment that by its very nature precludes such things?

4. To what degree is the effort to demythologize Jesus and Christianity an act of faith? "These men [biblical critics] ask me to believe they can read between the lines of the old texts," C. S. Lewis stated; "the evidence is their obvious inability to read (in any sense worth discussing) the lines themselves. They claim to see fernseed and can't see an elephant ten yards away in broad daylight." Lewis also noted that the typical biblical scholar does not have immediate access to the truth any more than the average man on the street. "Scholars as scholars," he added, "speak on it with no more authority than anyone else. The canon 'If miraculous, unhistorical' is one they bring to their study of the texts, not one they have learned from it. *If one is speaking of authority, the united authority of all the Biblical critics in the world counts here for nothing. On this they speak simply as men;* men obviously influenced by, and perhaps insufficiently critical of, the spirit of the age they grew up in."[7]

5. What of the idea that Christianity is based upon "faith-events" rather than actual historical incidents? Other questions follow: How is my belief in present-day healing, for example, affected by what did or did not take place in the first century? Can I believe that the power to heal is real in our own day if in fact such powers were not operative in

6. From Stephen E. Robinson, "The 'Expanded' Book of Mormon?" in *Second Nephi: The Doctrinal Structure*, ed. Monte S. Nyman and Charles D. Tate, Jr. (Provo: BYU Religious Studies Center, 1989), 393-94.

7. *Christian Reflections* (London: Fount/Harper Collins, 1981), 197, 198, emphasis added.

the first century? Faith is based on evidence, and the stronger the evidence the stronger the faith. To what extent can I trust in a power of redemption if in fact Jesus was not the Savior of humankind? How should I feel about the finality of death if in fact Jesus did not rise from the tomb three days after his crucifixion?

To what degree do my religious beliefs need to be both true and reasonable? One writer affirmed: "There is an excellent objective ground to which to tie the religion that Jesus sets forth. Final validation of this can only come experientially. But it is desperately important not to put ourselves in such a position that the event-nature of the resurrection depends wholly upon 'the faith.' *It's the other way around. The faith has its starting point in the event, the objective event,* and only by the appropriation of this objective event do we discover the final validity of it. . . .

"The Christian faith is built upon Gospel that is 'good news,' and *there is no news, good or bad, of something that didn't happen.* I personally am much disturbed by certain contemporary movements in theology which seem to imply that we can have the faith regardless of whether anything happened or not. I believe absolutely that *the whole Christian faith is premised upon the fact that at a certain point of time under Pontius Pilate a certain man died and was buried and three days later rose from the dead. If in some way you could demonstrate to me that Jesus never lived, died, or rose again, then I would have to say I have no right to my faith.*"[8] Indeed, to what degree can we exercise saving faith and a lively hope in something that did not happen? The Book of Mormon states that "faith is not to have a perfect knowledge of things; therefore if ye have faith ye hope for things which are not seen, *which are true*" (Alma 32:21, emphasis added).

6. Can Jesus be a Galilean guru and not the Son of God? Can he play the role of a Samaritan Socrates and not be divine? In short, what of the idea so prevalent that Jesus was a great moral teacher, a mere man, albeit a brilliant and inspired man, but not the Promised Messiah? In short, is there a difference between the "historical Jesus" and the "Christ of faith"? Do the extant sources allow such a distinction? Did Jesus?

There's a simple syllogism that applies to Jesus. It goes something

8. John Warwick Montgomery, *History and Christianity* (San Bernardino, CA: Here's Life Publishers, 1983), 107, 108, emphasis added.

like this: He was a great moral teacher. He claimed to be the Son of God. He was not the Son of God. Therefore, he could not be a great moral teacher. Robert Stein has written: "On the lips of anyone else the claims of Jesus would appear to be evidence of gross egomania, for Jesus clearly implies that the entire world revolves around himself and that the fate of all men is dependent on their acceptance or rejection of him. . . . There seem to be only two possible ways of interpreting the totalitarian nature of the claims of Jesus. Either we must assume that Jesus was deluded and unstable with unusual delusions of grandeur, or we are faced with the realization that Jesus is truly One who speaks with divine authority, who actually divided all of history into B.C.-A.D., and whose rejection or acceptance determines the fate of men."[9]

One of the most famous statements on this matter, one that forces the issue and exposes the shallowness of many a person's thinking, was made by C. S. Lewis. "I am trying here," he explained, "to prevent anyone saying the really foolish thing that people often say about Him: 'I'm ready to accept Jesus as a great moral teacher, but I don't accept His claim to be God.' That is the one thing we must not say. A man who was merely a man and said the sort of things Jesus said would not be a great moral teacher. He would either be a lunatic — on a level with the man who says he is a poached egg — or else he would be the Devil of Hell. You must make your choice. Either this man was, and is, the Son of God: or else a madman or something worse. You can shut Him up for a fool, you can spit at Him and kill Him as a demon; or you can fall at His feet and call Him Lord and God. But let us not come with any patronizing nonsense about His being a great human teacher. He has not left that open to us. He did not intend to."[10]

7. Stripped of his divinity, his teachings concerning his own Godhood, forgiveness of sins, resurrection, and Second Coming, why would Jesus of Nazareth be so controversial? Why would people dislike such a man? Why on earth would he be crucified?

I have wondered over the years how so many who read the same NT I do could conjure up a Jesus who is basically a simple, nondirective counselor, a sensitive ecologist who came to earth to model quiet pacifism. Given, Jesus of Nazareth was indeed the caring, compassionate,

---

9. *The Method and Message of Jesus' Teachings* (Philadelphia: Westminster, 1978), 118-19.
10. *Mere Christianity* (New York: Touchstone, 1996), 56.

forgiving, serving man described by Matthew, Mark, Luke, and John. He was also, however, God Incarnate, the discerning, fearless, assertive, confrontive, excoriating Being who had little patience with hypocrisy and self-righteousness. John Meir observed: "While I do not agree with those who turn Jesus into a violent revolutionary or political agitator, scholars who favor a revolutionary Jesus do have a point. A tweedy poetaster who spent his time spinning out parables and Japanese koans, a literary aesthete who toyed with 1st-century deconstructionism, or a bland Jesus who simply told people to look at the lilies of the field — such a Jesus would threaten no one, just as the university professors who create him threaten no one. The historical Jesus did threaten, disturb, and infuriate people — from interpreters of the Law through the Jerusalem priestly aristocracy to the Roman prefect who finally tried and crucified him. . . . A Jesus whose words and deeds would not alienate people, especially powerful people, is not the historical Jesus."[11] In addition, as Scot McKnight pointed out, "A social revolutionary would have been crucified (and this partly explains Jesus' death, in my view), but it is doubtful that such a revolutionary would have given birth to a church that was hardly a movement of social revolution."[12]

Conclusion

The Latter-day Saints extend the same invitation that Jesus offered a group of fishermen almost two thousand years ago: "Come and see" (John 1:39). We believe the final great test in determining the living reality of Jesus Christ and the essential truthfulness of the New Testament record is the test of faith, the test of spirit, the test of individual revelation, with the assurance that all can know. For some it is a leap of faith, a faith "that bridges the chasm between what our minds can know and what our souls aspire after."[13]

11. *A Marginal Jew: Rethinking the Historical Jesus,* 3 vols. (New York: Doubleday, 1991), 1:177.

12. "Who Is Jesus? An Introduction to Jesus Studies," in *Jesus Under Fire: Modern Scholarship Reinvents the Historical Jesus,* ed. Michael J. Wilkins and J. P. Moreland (Grand Rapids: Zondervan, 1995), 61-62.

13. Malcolm Muggeridge, *Jesus: The Man Who Lives* (New York: Harper & Row, 1975), 20.

We ask: Must one buy into and imbibe and be held hostage by the traditional mode of thinking or even subscribe to the majority opinion? Jesus stood against the majority opinion in his day; he challenged the religious establishment. While the Latter-day Saints do not subscribe to a position of scriptural inerrancy, they do have a firm conviction that the scriptures mean what they say and say what they mean. They are to be trusted. All Christians would do well to ensure that theirs is a "critical" look at biblical critical presuppositions, methodologies, and conclusions; some things we simply need not swallow. A firm belief in prophecy, revelation, divine intervention, and absolute truths precludes an overwhelming and undiscriminating acceptance of many of the underlying principles of the science of biblical criticism.

A passage from the Book of Mormon has become a kind of caveat with the LDS faith to remind us of the need for a faithful perspective and divine balance when it comes to the academic study of holy things: "O that cunning plan of the evil one! O the vainness, and the frailties, and the foolishness of men! When they are learned they think they are wise, and they hearken not unto the counsel of God, for they set it aside, supposing they know of themselves, wherefore, their wisdom is foolishness and it profiteth them not. And they shall perish. But to be learned is good if they hearken unto the counsels of God" (2 Nephi 9:28-29).

"We have no right to take the theories of men," one Church leader noted in 1915, "however scholarly, however learned, and set them up as a standard, and try to make the Gospel bow down to them, making of them an iron bedstead upon which God's truth, if not long enough, must be stretched out, or if too long, must be chopped off — anything to make it fit into the system of men's thoughts and theories! On the contrary," he said, "we should hold up the Gospel as the standard of truth, and measure thereby the theories and opinions of men."[14]

Howard W. Hunter, fourteenth president of the Church, noted that "There are those who declare it is old-fashioned to believe in the Bible. Is it old-fashioned to believe in Jesus Christ, the Son of the Living God? Is it old-fashioned to believe in his atoning sacrifice and the resurrection? If it is, I declare myself to be old-fashioned and the Church to be old-fashioned. . . .

14. Orson F. Whitney, Conference Report, April 1915, 100.

"In this world of confusing and rushing, temporal progress, we need to return to the simplicity of Christ. We need to love, honor, and worship him. To acquire spirituality and have its influence in our lives, we cannot become confused and misdirected by the twisted teachings of the modernist. We need to study the simple fundamentals of the truths taught by the Master and eliminate the controversial. Our faith in God needs to be real and not speculative. . . . We can be modern without giving way to the influence of the modernist. If it is old-fashioned to believe in the Bible, we should thank God for the privilege of being old-fashioned."[15]

15. *That We Might Have Joy* (Salt Lake City: Deseret Book, 1994), 23, 25-26.

3   Why a Restoration?

Foundational to any understanding of the Latter-day Saint conception of Jesus Christ is the idea of a restoration of divine truth in modern times. Such a concept of a restoration necessarily implies a belief in an apostasy or falling away. Latter-day Saints believe the apostasy of the early Christian church following the death of the apostles was foreseen and foreknown by ancient prophets (see Amos 8:11-12; Isaiah 24:5). Further, warnings of this apostasy can be found in the New Testament (see Acts 20:28-30; 2 Thessalonians 2:1-4; 1 Timothy 4:1-3; 2 Timothy 4:1-4; 1 John 2:18-19). That apostasy entailed the loss or corruption of *divine authority* and true *doctrine*.

Authority and Doctrine

The New Testament clearly teaches the need for divine authority. Jesus ordained the twelve apostles (John 15:16), gave to them the keys of the kingdom of God (Matthew 16:18-19; 18:18), and empowered his servants to perform miracles and take the gospel to all nations (Matthew 10:1, 5-8; 28:19-20). Later, after the Lord's death, the apostles commissioned others to serve in the ministry (Acts 6:1-6; 13:1-3; 14:23; 1 Timothy 4:14; 2 Timothy 1:6; Titus 1:5) and to insure that the saving ordinances (sacraments) were performed only by those properly ordained (Acts 19:1-6, 13-16). This was a power that no man could assume, take upon himself, or even purchase; it came through the laying on of hands by those holding proper authority (Acts 8:18-20; Hebrews 5:4). With the death of the apostles, within approximately one hundred years of the crucifixion of Jesus, this authority, the power to act in the name of God, was lost from the earth.

While Catholics claim apostolic succession (that the bishops of the ancient church have conveyed their priesthood powers down to the pope in our time), and Protestants speak of a "priesthood of all believers," Latter-day Saints teach that God's divine authority was not to be found in the Old World by the middle of the second century A.D. The Roman Church had control of the Christian faith until the sixteenth century, when courageous men objected to, opposed, and broke away from Catholicism. "Finally the heralds of a distant dawn came forth," stated an LDS apostle. "There was a Calvin, a Zwingli, a Luther, a Wesley; there were wise and good men — morning stars who shone more brightly than their fellows — who arose in every nation. There were men of insight and courage who were sickened by the sins and evils of the night. These great souls hacked and sawed at the chains with which the masses were bound. They sought to do good and to help their fellowmen — all according to the best light and knowledge they had.

"In Germany and France and England and Switzerland and elsewhere groups began to break away from the religion of centuries past. A few rays of light were parting the darkness of the eastern sky."[1]

Roger Williams, the man known as the founder of the Baptist faith, later in his life renounced the views of the Baptists and "turned seeker, i.e., to wait for new apostles to restore Christianity." He felt the need "of a special commission, to restore the modes of positive worship, according to the original institution." Williams concluded that the Protestants were "not . . . able to derive the authority . . . from the apostles, . . . [and] conceived God would raise up some apostolic power."[2] In short, Williams held that there was "no regularly constituted church of Christ, on earth, nor any person authorized to administer any church ordinance, nor can there be until new apostles are sent by the great head of the Church, for whose coming I am seeking."[3]

I participated recently in an interfaith dialogue with a wonderful

1. Bruce R. McConkie, Conference Report, April 1978, 16-17.

2. Cited in Milton V. Backman, Jr., *American Religions and the Rise of Mormonism* (Salt Lake City: Deseret Book, 1965), 180-81.

3. Cited in LeGrand Richards, *A Marvelous Work and a Wonder* (Salt Lake City: Deseret Book, 1950), 29.

professor of religion who happens also to be a Protestant minister. We spoke of our respective views of Jesus, focused on where we agreed, emphasized where we disagreed, and then entertained questions from the audience for a half hour or so. Throughout much of the evening my colleague and the members of the audience (most of whom were Protestant or Catholic) used again and again the phrase "traditional Christianity" to refer to what they believed, over against what Latter-day Saints teach. The comments went something like this: "While Latter-day Saints teach that the members of the Godhead are separate and distinct persons and separate Gods, traditional Christianity believes. . . ."

It began to dawn on me how odd the phrase "traditional Christianity" was, as though there were some single, monolithic structure to which everyone else belonged except the Latter-day Saints, some universal church that enjoyed universal agreement on matters doctrinal. Well, I knew enough about present-day Christianity to know there was no such organization. I am fully aware, for example, that there are substantive theological differences between evangelical Christians and Latter-day Saint Christians and have no desire whatsoever to minimize those. I am persuaded, however — and this from very personal experience — that the deeper we look into the central or core doctrines of our respective traditions, the more we will find surprising similarities. But even if there are differences, does this necessitate that insurmountable walls should exist between us? Over the past few years I have read much of evangelical theology. It is clear to me that there are a number of doctrinal and ecclesial matters about which evangelical Christians disagree, including:

1. the inerrancy of scripture;
2. whether God is completely sovereign over all things or whether God limits his control by allowing freedom of the will;
3. whether God possesses a complete knowledge of the future;
4. whether the creation account is literal or figurative, in terms of how long it took to create the earth;
5. the flood in the days of Noah — local or global?
6. whether Christ was both fully God and fully human during his ministry or whether he relinquished his divinity for a season;
7. whether only the predestined are saved or whether all have the potential for full salvation;

8. whether men and women can indeed enjoy eternal security from the moment of their spiritual rebirth or whether they must endure faithfully to the end in order to have the hope of eternal life fully realized;
9. the fate of the unevangelized — the soteriological problem of evil;
10. what happens to babies who die?
11. whether baptism is essential to salvation and to whom it must be administered — infants or mature believers;
12. whether the gifts of the Spirit ceased with the apostles or whether they can and should be enjoyed today;
13. whether women should serve in certain ministerial capacities;
14. the nature of the Rapture, Tribulation, and millennium;
15. whether hell consists of eternal torment and suffering or whether those who reject Christ and his gospel are simply annihilated hereafter;
16. whether man plays a role in his own salvation beyond an initial confession of Christ as Savior — the meaning and place of works;
17. whether one can accept Jesus as Savior but postpone until later a profession of him as Lord and Master — the Lordship controversy;
18. the psychological or social views of the Trinity;
19. whether and how wives should submit to their husbands;
20. life after death.[4]

Some of these are not exactly insignificant issues. In fact, given the divide between persons under the evangelical umbrella on such matters, one wonders why outright rejection or bitter antagonism must or should exist toward any other faith tradition with differing views, including Latter-day Saints.

Because apostolic power was not on the earth, Latter-day Saints believe that alterations in doctrine took place during the Reformation as well, theological shifts away from the teachings of the primitive church in the days of Jesus and the apostles. Such doctrines as predestination, man's inability to come unto Christ on his own, salvation by grace

---

4. See, for example, Gregory A. Boyd and Paul R. Eddy, *Across the Spectrum* (Grand Rapids: Baker, 2002); Roger E. Olson, *The Mosaic of Christian Belief* (Downers Grove, IL: InterVarsity, 2002); John G. Stackhouse, Jr., *Evangelical Landscapes: Facing Critical Issues of the Day* (Grand Rapids: Baker, 2002).

alone (good works not essential to salvation), and *sola scriptura,* the notion of the sufficiency of written scripture — each of which is a vital element within current Christian thinking — do not fully reflect the teachings and doctrine of the first few centuries of the Christian church.[5] So while Latter-day Saints believe that the Protestant Reformation provided a significant measure of correction to the Christian church, it was not sufficient. A complete restoration was needed. In other words, "The Church of Jesus Christ of Latter-day Saints is not a remodeled version of another church. It is not an adjustment or a correction or a protest against any other church."[6] That is, "Whereas Luther had sought to *reform* the existing church-state establishment, others concluded that such an establishment was beyond reforming. So they worked to *restore* primitive Christianity apart from the church-state institution. Since the days of Luther, there have been numerous such movements to restore early Christianity."[7]

The "Only True Church"

Several years ago my colleague Brent Top and I sat with two Protestant ministers for a few hours in what proved to be a delightful and extremely enlightening conversation. Absent was any sense of defensiveness or any effort to argue and debate; we were earnestly trying to understand one another better. Toward the end of the discussion, one of the ministers turned to me and said: "Bob, it bothers you a great deal, doesn't it, when people suggest that Latter-day Saints are not Christian?" I responded: "It doesn't just *bother* me. It *hurts* me, for I know how deeply as a Latter-day Saint I love the Lord and how completely I trust in him."

My Protestant friend then made a rather simple observation, one that should have been obvious to me long before that particular moment. He said: "How do you think it makes us feel when we know of your belief in what you call the great apostasy, of the fact that Christ

5. See David W. Bercot, *Will the Real Heretics Please Stand Up,* 3rd ed. (Tyler, TX: Scroll Publishing, 1999), especially chapters 6-8, 15.

6. Boyd K. Packer, "The Standard of Truth Has Been Erected," *Ensign,* November 2003, 24.

7. Bercot, *Will the Real Heretics Please Stand Up,* 149, emphasis in original.

presumably said to the young Joseph Smith that the churches on earth at that time 'were all wrong,' that 'all their creeds [are] an abomination in my sight,' that 'those professors were all corrupt' (Joseph Smith–History 1:19), and that in your Doctrine and Covenants your church is identified as 'the only true and living church upon the face of the whole earth' (D&C 1:30)?" I can still remember the collage of feelings that washed over me at that moment: it was a quiet epiphany, coupled with feelings of empathy, sudden realization, and a deep sense of love for my friends. For a brief time I found myself, mentally speaking, walking in their moccasins, seeing things through their eyes. It was sobering, and it has affected the way I seek to reach out to men and women of other faiths.

In the first section of the Doctrine and Covenants, a revelation given to Joseph Smith in November 1831, The Church of Jesus Christ of Latter-day Saints is in fact referred to as "the only true and living church upon the face of the whole earth" (D&C 1:30). Admittedly, this is strong language; it is hard doctrine, words that are offensive to persons of other faiths. It may be helpful to consider briefly what the phrase "the only true and living church" means and what it does *not* *mean*. In what follows, I offer my own views, my own perspective. First, let's deal with what the phrase does not mean.

1. It does not mean that men and women of other Christian faiths are not sincere believers in truth and genuine followers of the Christ. Latter-day Saints have no difficulty whatsoever accepting one's personal affirmation that they are Christian, that they acknowledge Jesus Christ as the divine Son of God, their Savior, the Lord and Master of their life. Nor are Latter-day Saints the only ones entitled to personal illumination and divine guidance for their lives.

2. It does not mean that they are worshipping "a different Jesus," as many in the Christian world often say of the Latter-day Saints. Rather, true Christians worship Jesus of Nazareth, the Promised Messiah.

3. It does not mean we believe that most of the doctrines in Catholic or Protestant Christianity are false or that the leaders of the various branches of Christianity have improper motives. Joseph Smith stated: "The inquiry is frequently made of me, 'Wherein do you differ from others in your religious views?' In reality and essence we do not differ so far in our religious views, but that we could all drink into one principle of love. One of the grand fundamental principles of 'Mormonism' is to re-

ceive truth, let it come from whence it may."[8] "Have the Presbyterians any truth?" he asked on another occasion. "Yes. Have the Baptists, Methodists, etc., any truth? Yes. . . . We should gather all the good and true principles in the world and treasure them up, or we shall not come out true 'Mormons.'"[9] In what must have been a tongue-in-cheek effort at toying with various languages to discover meaning, Joseph Smith pointed out that "mormon" means "literally, 'more good.'"[10] President George Albert Smith thus declared to those of other faiths: "We have come not to take away from you the truth and virtue you possess. We have come not to find fault with you nor criticize you. We have not come here to berate you. . . . Keep all the good that you have, and *let us bring to you more good*."[11]

4. It does not mean that the Bible has been so corrupted that it cannot be relied upon to teach us sound doctrine and provide an example of how to live. "When I lived in England a few years ago," said Mark E. Petersen, "I went to the British Museum in London and studied the history of the King James Version of the Bible. I learned that its translators fasted and prayed for inspiration in their work. I am convinced that they received it."[12] Then what of the LDS belief that plain and precious truths and many covenants of the Lord were removed from the Bible before its compilation (1 Nephi 13:20-40; Moses 1:40-41)?[13] While we do not subscribe to a doctrine of scriptural inerrancy, we do believe that the hand of God has been over the preservation of the biblical materials such that what we have now is what the Almighty would have us possess. In the words of Bruce R. McConkie, "we cannot avoid the conclusion that a divine providence is directing all things as they should be. This means that the Bible, as it now is, contains that portion of the Lord's word" that the present world is prepared to receive.[14]

8. *Teachings of the Prophet Joseph Smith* (Salt Lake City: Deseret Book, 1976), 313; cited hereafter as TPJS.

9. TPJS, 316.

10. TPJS, 300.

11. *Sharing the Gospel with Others,* comp. Preston Nibley (Salt Lake City: Deseret News Press, 1948), 12-13, emphasis added.

12. Conference Report, October 1977, 18.

13. See also TPJS, 9-11, 61, 327.

14. "The Bible: A Sealed Book," Eighth Annual Church Educational System Religious Educators' Symposium, August 1984; cited in *Doctrines of the Restoration,* ed. Mark L. McConkie (Salt Lake City: Bookcraft, 1989), 280.

Indeed, although Latter-day Saints do not believe that the Bible now contains all that it once contained, the Bible is a remarkable book of scripture, one that inspires, motivates, reproves, corrects, and instructs (2 Timothy 3:16). It is the word of God. Our task, according to George Q. Cannon, is to engender faith in the Bible. "As our duty is to create faith in the word of God in the mind of the young student, we scarcely think that object is best attained by making the mistakes of translators [or transmitters] the more prominent part of our teachings. Even children have their doubts, but it is not our business to encourage those doubts. Doubts never convert; negations seldom convince. . . . The clause in the Articles of Faith regarding mistakes in the translation of the Bible was never inserted to encourage us to spend our time in searching out and studying those errors, but to emphasize the idea that it is the truth and the truth only that the Church of Jesus Christ of Latter-day Saints accepts, no matter where it is found."[15]

The introductory statement published as a part of the 1981 edition of the Book of Mormon includes these words: "The Book of Mormon is a volume of holy scripture comparable to the Bible. It is a record of God's dealings with the ancient inhabitants of the Americas and *contains, as does the Bible, the fulness of the everlasting gospel*" (emphasis added). In a revelation received in February 1831 that embraces "the law of the Church," the early Saints were instructed: "And again, the elders, priests and teachers of this church shall teach the principles of my gospel, which are *in the Bible and the Book of Mormon, in the which is the fulness of the gospel*" (D&C 42:12, emphasis added). In 1982 Elder Bruce R. McConkie explained to church leaders that "Before we can write the gospel in our own book of life we must learn the gospel as it is written in the books of scripture. The Bible, the Book of Mormon, the Doctrine and Covenants and the Pearl of Great Price — *each of them individually and all of them collectively — contain the fulness of the everlasting gospel*."[16]

While Latter-day Saints do not believe that one can derive divine authority to perform the saving ordinances from the scriptures, we do

---

15. *Gospel Truth: Discourses and Writings of President George Q. Cannon*, 2 vols. in one (Salt Lake City: Deseret Book, 1987), 472.

16. "Holy Writ: Published Anew," Regional Representatives Seminar, 2 April 1982; in *Doctrines of the Restoration*, 237, emphasis added.

say that the Bible contains the fulness of the gospel in the sense that (1) it teaches of groups of people in the past who enjoyed the full blessings of the everlasting gospel; and (2) it teaches (especially the New Testament) the good news or glad tidings of redemption in Christ through the Atonement (3 Nephi 27:13-21; D&C 76:40-42).

5. It does not mean that God disapproves of or rejects all that devoted Christians are teaching or doing, where their heart is, and what they hope to accomplish in the religious world. In April 1843 a Brother Pelatiah Brown sought to silence certain critics of the church by stretching and twisting the meaning of passages from the Book of Revelation to make his point. Brother Brown was disciplined for doing so. Joseph said: "I did not like the old man being called up for erring in doctrine. It looks too much like the Methodists, and not like the Latter-day Saints. Methodists *have creeds which a man must believe or be asked out of their church.* I want the liberty of thinking and believing as I please. It feels so good not to be trammeled. It does not prove that a man is not a good man because he errs in doctrine."[17]

"God, the Father of us all," Ezra Taft Benson said, "uses the men of the earth, especially good men, to accomplish his purposes. It has been true in the past, it is true today, it will be true in the future." Elder Benson then quoted the following from a conference address delivered by Orson F. Whitney in 1928: "Perhaps the Lord needs such men on the outside of His Church to help it along. They are among its auxiliaries, and can do more good for the cause where the Lord has placed them, than anywhere else." Now note this particularly poignant message: "*God is using more than one people for the accomplishment of His great and marvelous work. The Latter-day Saints cannot do it all.* It is too vast, too arduous for any one people." Elder Whitney then pointed out that we have no warfare with other churches. "They are our partners in a certain sense."[18]

In June 1829 Oliver Cowdery and David Whitmer were instructed to "Contend against no church, save it be the church of the devil" (D&C 18:20). B. H. Roberts offered this insightful commentary upon

17. *History of The Church of Jesus Christ of Latter-day Saints,* 7 vols., ed. B. H. Roberts (Salt Lake City: Deseret Book, 1957), 5:340.

18. Conference Report, April 1972, 49; citing Conference Report, April 1928, 59, emphasis added.

this passage: "I understand the injunction to Oliver Cowdery to 'contend against no church, save it be the church of the devil' (D&C 18:20), to mean that he shall contend against evil, against untruth, against all combinations of wicked men. They constitute the church of the devil, the kingdom of evil, a federation of unrighteousness; and the servants of God have a right to contend against that which is evil, let it appear where it will. . . . But, *let it be understood, we are not brought necessarily into antagonism with the various sects of Christianity as such. So far as they have retained fragments of Christian truth — and each of them has some measure of truth — that far they are acceptable unto the Lord; and it would be poor policy for us to contend against them without discrimination. . . . [O]ur relationship to the religious world is not one that calls for the denunciation of sectarian churches as composing the church of the devil.*"

The following remarks by Elder Roberts demonstrate the kind of breadth necessary in reaching out and understanding our brothers and sisters of other faiths: *"All that makes for truth, for righteousness, is of God; it constitutes the kingdom of righteousness — the empire of Jehovah; and, in a certain sense at least, constitutes the Church of Christ.* All that makes for untruth, for unrighteousness constitutes the kingdom of evil — the church of the devil. *With the kingdom of righteousness we have no warfare. On the contrary, both the spirit of the Lord's commandments to his servants and the dictates of right reason would suggest that we seek to enlarge this kingdom of righteousness both by recognizing such truths as it possesses and seeking the friendship and cooperation of the righteous men and women who constitute its membership."*[19]

6. It does not mean that God-fearing Christians who are not Latter-day Saints will not go to heaven. Mormons do not in any way minimize or deny the reality of another person's experience with the Spirit of God, nor should we question the legitimacy of another's commitment to Jesus Christ. To say that another way, we do not doubt that many who claim to have had a mighty change of heart have in fact been "born again."[20] Christians who are somewhat acquainted with LDS beliefs might well respond at this point: "Yes, but do you believe that persons of other faiths will inherit the celestial kingdom?" Latter-day

19. Conference Report, April 1906, 14-15, emphasis added.
20. See Kent P. Jackson, "Am I a Christian?" in *FARMS Review of Books* 14, nos. 1-2 (2002): 131-37.

Saints do believe that baptism by proper authority is necessary for entrance into the highest heaven; the baptismal ordinance is an outward expression of one's personal inward covenant with Christ and acceptance of his gospel. At the same time, LDS doctrine affirms that each man or woman will receive all of the light, knowledge, divine attributes, powers, and heavenly rewards they desire to receive, either in this life or the next. One who seeks with all their soul to come unto Christ will be welcomed eventually into his presence. One who earnestly yearns to qualify for the highest of glories hereafter will have that opportunity. That means that a man or woman who is true to the light they have here will open themselves to greater light.

7. Our belief that we are "the only true and living church" does not mean that Latter-day Saints desire to "do their own thing" or face social challenges on their own. To be sure, we strive earnestly to work together with men and women of other faiths to stand up and speak out against the rising tide of immorality and ethical relativism that are spreading in our world. With most Christian groups, we are persuaded that the changes to be made in our society can only come about "from the inside out" — through the transforming powers of Jesus Christ.[21] Indeed, I am convinced that if we allow doctrinal differences, stereotyping, and demonizing of those who are different to prevent us from joining hands in halting the erosion of time-honored moral and family values, Lucifer will win a major victory.

What, then, does the revelation mean when it states that The Church of Jesus Christ of Latter-day Saints is "the only true and living church upon the face of the whole earth"?

1. "The word *only*," Elder Neal A. Maxwell has written, "asserts a uniqueness and singularity" about the church "as the exclusive ecclesiastical, authority-bearing agent for our Father in heaven in this dispensation."[22]

The word *true* is derived from the Old English word *treowe*, meaning honest, upright, virtuous, straightforward, loyal, faithful, steady and steadfast, constant, fitting, proper, consistent with fact, conforming with reality, conforming to a standard or pattern, accurately positioned, germane, correctly balanced or aligned, precise, and secure. It is

---

21. See Ezra Taft Benson, Conference Report, October 1985, 4-6.
22. *Things As They Really Are* (Salt Lake City: Deseret Book, 1978), 45.

related closely to such words as trust, truce, and betrothed.[23] Thus to refer to the restored church as "the only true church" is to speak of it as being the most steady, sure, and solid institution on earth, the closest to the pattern of the primitive Christian church, in terms of dispensing the mind and will and enjoying the complete approbation of God. It does not suggest that other churches are mostly false or that their teachings are completely corrupt.

"When the Lord used the designation 'true,'" Elder Maxwell pointed out,

> he implied that the doctrines of the Church and its authority are not just partially true, but true as measured by divine standards. The Church is not, therefore, conceptually compromised by having been made up from doctrinal debris left over from another age, nor is it comprised of mere fragments of the true faith. It is based upon the *fulness* of the gospel of him whose *name* it bears, thus passing the two tests for proving his church that were given by Jesus during his visit to the Nephites (3 Nephi 27:8).
>
> When the word *living* is used, it carries a divinely deliberate connotation. The Church is neither dead nor dying. Nor is it even wounded. The Church, like the living God who established it, is alive, aware, and functioning. It is not a museum that houses a fossilized faith; rather, it is a kinetic kingdom characterized by living faith in living disciples.[24]

2. It means that doctrinal finality rests with apostles and prophets, not theologians or scholars. One professor of religion at a Christian institution remarked to me: "You know, Bob, one of the things I love about my way of life as a religious academician is that no one is looking over my shoulder to check my doctrine and analyze the truthfulness of my teachings. Because there is no organizational hierarchy to which I am required to answer, I am free to write and declare whatever I

23. See Joseph Fielding McConkie, *Prophets & Prophecy* (Salt Lake City: Bookcraft, 1988), 174-75; see also *Noah Webster's 1828 First Edition of an American Dictionary of the English Language,* 4th ed. (San Francisco: Foundation for American Christian Education, 1985), s.v. "true"; *The New Shorter Oxford English Dictionary,* 2 vols., ed. Lesley Brown (Oxford: Clarendon, 1993), s.v., "true"; John Ayto, *Dictionary of Word Origins* (New York: Arcade Publishing, 1990), s.v. "true."
24. *Things As They Really Are,* 46, emphasis in original.

choose." I nodded kindly and chose not to respond at the time. I have thought since then, however, that what my friend perceives to be a marvelous academic freedom can become license to interpret, intuit, or exegete a scriptural passage in a myriad of ways, resulting in interpretations as diverse as the backgrounds, training, and proclivities of the persons involved. There are simply too many ambiguous sections of scripture to "let the Bible speak for itself." This was, in fact, young Joseph Smith's dilemma: "The teachers of religion of the different sects understood the same passages of scripture so differently as to destroy all confidence in settling [his religious questions] by an appeal to the Bible" (Joseph Smith-History 1:12). In many cases, neither linguistic training nor historical background will automatically produce the (divinely) intended meaning or clarification of such matters as those mentioned earlier.

"Some things in scripture are not perfectly clear," evangelical pastor and teacher John MacArthur has written. "Sometimes we cannot reconstruct the historical context to understand a given passage. One notable example is the mention of 'baptism for the dead' in 1 Corinthians 15:29. There are at least forty different views about what that verse means. We cannot be dogmatic about such things."[25] Earlier in the same work, MacArthur stated that if you were to attend a typical Bible study you would "probably be invited to share your opinion about 'what this verse means to me,' as if the message of Scripture were unique to every individual. Rare is the teacher who is concerned with what Scripture means to *God*."[26] What is the standard by which we judge and interpret? Who has the right to offer inspired commentary on words delivered by holy men of God who spoke or wrote anciently as they were moved upon by the Holy Spirit (2 Peter 1:21)? While each reader of holy writ should seek to be in tune with the Spirit enough to understand what is intended by the scripture, Latter-day Saints believe the final word on prophetic interpretation rests with prophets. As C. S. Lewis wisely remarked, "Unless the measuring rod is independent of the things measured, we can do no measuring."[27]

25. *Why One Way? Defending an Exclusive Claim in an Inclusive World* (Nashville: W Publishing Group, 2002), 61.

26. *Why One Way?* 24, emphasis in original.

27. From "The Poison of Subjectivism," in *Christian Reflections* (London: Fount/ Harper Collins, 1981), 100.

In writing of *sola scriptura* as a tenet of the Reformation, Randall Balmer observed that "Luther's sentiments created a demand for Scriptures in the vernacular, and Protestants ever since have insisted on interpreting the Bible for themselves, forgetting most of the time that they come to the text with their own set of cultural biases and personal agendas." Balmer continues,

> Underlying this insistence on individual interpretation is the assumption . . . that the plainest, most evident reading of the text is the proper one. Everyone becomes his or her own theologian. There is no longer any need to consult Augustine or Thomas Aquinas or Martin Luther about their understanding of various passages when you yourself are the final arbiter of what is the correct reading. This tendency, together with the absence of any authority structure within Protestantism, has created a kind of theological free-for-all, as various individuals or groups insist that *their* reading of the Bible is the only possible interpretation.[28]

Finally, I have had a number of friends and colleagues from either Protestant or Catholic faiths ask how Latter-day Saints can reconcile the idea of an apostasy of the primitive church with Jesus' commendation of Peter's confession at Caesarea Philippi ("thou art the Christ, the Son of the living God"). We recall that the Savior said: "Blessed art thou, Simon Bar-jona: for *flesh and blood hath not revealed it unto thee, but my Father which is in heaven. And I say unto thee, That thou art Peter, and upon this rock I will build my church; and the gates of hell shall not prevail against it*" (Matthew 16:16-18, emphasis added). Did the Lord not clearly state in this passage that Satan would not prevail over the Christian church?

Well, one thing is sure: the church was not to be built upon Peter or any one individual but rather upon the revealed word, the revelation that came to Peter and affirmed the divine Sonship of the Master.[29] It was as though Christ were saying: "Peter, you have gained the witness of who I am by revelation from God, and it is by revelation, by the immediate direction from heaven to and through my anointed servants, that I will build

---

28. Randall Balmer, *Mine Eyes Have Seen the Glory: A Journey into the Evangelical Subculture in America,* 3rd ed. (New York: Oxford University Press, 2000), 24.

29. Joseph Smith explained: "'Upon this rock I will build my Church, and the gates of hell shall not prevail against it.' What rock? Revelation" (TPJS, 274).

my church. And as long as my people live in such a manner as to enjoy that spirit of revelation — individually and institutionally — the power and dominion of the devil will never be allowed to prevail over my kingdom."

3. It means that while God will bless and strengthen and lead any person who follows the divine light within him or her (John 1:9), each man or woman is responsible to be true to that light which leads unto all truth, to seek and search and weigh and prove all things. A modern revelation attests that "That which is of God is light; and he that receiveth light, and continueth in God, receiveth more light; and that light groweth brighter and brighter until the perfect day" (D&C 50:24), meaning, presumably, the day of resurrection and glorification. A later revelation states that one who is true to the light of conscience, true to what we would know as the Judeo-Christian ethic, will be led to the higher light of the fulness of the gospel, either in this life or the next. "And the Spirit giveth light to every man that cometh into the world; and the Spirit enlighteneth every man through the world, that hearkeneth to the voice of the Spirit. And every one that hearkeneth to the voice of the Spirit cometh unto God, even the Father. And the Father teacheth him of the [gospel] covenant which he has renewed and confirmed upon you" (D&C 84:46-48).

There is a vital balance to be struck here. The Book of Mormon clearly points out that "the Spirit of Christ is given to every man, that he may know good from evil"; "wherefore, I show unto you the way to judge; for every thing which inviteth to do good, and to persuade to believe in Christ, is sent forth by the power and gift of Christ; wherefore ye may know with a perfect knowledge it is of God" (Moroni 7:16). At the same time, the Father of Lights does not desire his children to coast spiritually, to rest content with the light and truth they have, but rather he expects all to grow in perspective and understanding. As C. S. Lewis observed, that God who "will, in the long run, be satisfied with nothing less than absolute perfection, will also be delighted with the first feeble, stumbling effort you make tomorrow to do the simplest duty." Then, quoting his mentor, George MacDonald, Lewis noted that "God is easy to please, but hard to satisfy."[30] Thus the highest *good* that men and women can do is to seek tenaciously for the greatest amount of light and knowledge that God will bestow (see D&C 35:10-12; 84:49-50).

30. *Mere Christianity* (New York: Touchstone, 1996), 174.

Creeds and Christendom

According to one of the accounts of Joseph Smith's First Vision (1838), Joseph learned that "all their creeds were an abomination in his sight; that those professors were all corrupt; that 'they draw near to me with their lips, but their hearts are far from me,' they teach for doctrines the commandments of men, having a form of godliness, but they deny the power thereof" (Joseph Smith-History 1:19). This statement is, of course, considered to be harsh and hurtful to members of other Christian churches. Let's see if we can clarify things somewhat. For example, what were the "creeds" spoken of? Originally the Latin word *credo* meant simply "I believe." In Joseph Smith's day, the word *creed* referred to "a brief summary of the articles of Christian faith" or "that which is believed."[31] A modern dictionary defines a creed as "a system of religious belief" or "a set of opinions or principles on any subject" or "belief or confidence in; an article of faith."[32] As here defined, there is nothing wrong with a creed per se.

Roman Catholic scholar Luke Timothy Johnson has written that "being part of the intelligentsia has meant despising creeds in general and Christianity's creed in particular." Johnson pointed out that "For modernity, belief in a creed is a sign of intellectual failure. Creeds involve faith, and faith makes statements about reality that can't be tested. Everyone knows that statements can be true only when they don't really say anything about the world or when they have been empirically tested. Creeds are therefore structures of fantasy. One cannot be both a believer and a critical thinker." Further: "A significant number of Christians reject any form of the creed. For some, especially in the Anabaptist and Free Church traditions, the creed is too much an instrument of ecclesiastical tradition and power, too much associated with the development of Christianity into Catholicism, too much shaped by philosophy and too little by Scripture."[33]

Alexander Campbell, a contemporary of Joseph Smith and the father of the Disciples of Christ and Church of Christ movements, was

31. *Webster's 1828 American Dictionary of the English Language,* s.v. "creed."
32. *The New Shorter Oxford English Dictionary,* s.v. "creed."
33. *The Creed: What Christians Believe and Why It Matters* (New York: Doubleday, 2003), 1-2, 4.

one who was particularly troubled by creeds. "Following the American Revolution," Milton Backman, Jr. noted, "a number of theologians vehemently condemned all the popular creeds of Christendom. Urging all disciples of Christ to return to the purity of New Testament Christianity, these preachers taught that the Bible should be regarded as the only standard of faith, that every congregation should be autonomous, and that all men are endowed with the capacity to accept or reject God's gift of salvation. Although these resolute leaders were divided concerning the doctrine of the Godhead, they rejected the use of the term 'Trinity,' claiming that such a word was unscriptural."[34]

Joseph Smith was not necessarily opposed to religious creeds in general. In the preface to the first edition of the Doctrine and Covenants (1835) he makes this fascinating remark: "There may be an aversion in the minds of some against receiving any thing purporting to be articles of religious faith, in consequence of there being so many now extant; but if men believe a system, and profess that it was given by inspiration, certainly, the more intelligibly they can present it, the better. It does not make a principle untrue to print it, neither does it make it true not to print it." As an example, Elder McConkie stated that the fifth Lecture on Faith, "in effect, *is a creed announcing who Deity is*. In my judgment, it is the most comprehensive, intelligent, inspired utterance that now exists in the English language — that exists in one place defining, interpreting, expounding, announcing, and testifying what kind of being God is."[35]

Latter-day Saints believe that the creeds spoken of in the First Vision were the post–New Testament creeds that sought to codify beliefs concerning God, Christ, the Holy Spirit, and their relationships, concepts that had evolved during the time following the deaths of the original apostles. Stephen Robinson observed that there is an irony associated with traditional Christians' condemnation of the LDS addition to the canon of scripture. In reality, he suggests, the Protestants do not hold strictly to a belief in *sola scriptura* [the scriptures alone].

34. *Christian Churches in America: Origins and Beliefs*, rev. ed. (New York: Charles Scribner's Sons, 1983), 159.

35. "The Lord God of Joseph Smith," discourse delivered 4 January 1972, *Speeches of the Year* (Provo: Brigham Young University Press, 1972), 4, emphasis added. The Lectures on Faith are a series of seven theological sermons that were prepared by or under the direction of Joseph Smith and delivered during the Winter of 1834-35 in Kirtland, Ohio.

"When they accuse Mormons of not believing the Bible," he wrote, "they usually mean that we do not believe interpretations formulated by postbiblical councils. If evangelicals are going to insist on the doctrine of *sola scriptura* or *ad fontes* ["to the sources"], then they ought to stop ascribing scriptural authority to postbiblical traditions." Robinson elsewhere stated that "Informed Latter-day Saints do not argue that historic Christianity lost *all* truth or became *completely* corrupt. The orthodox churches may have lost the 'fullness' of the gospel, but they did not lose all of it nor even most of it. Many evangelicals caricature or overstate the actual LDS view, which is that the orthodox churches are incomplete rather than corrupt. It is their postbiblical creeds that are identified in Joseph Smith's first vision as an 'abomination,' but certainly not their individual members or their members' *biblical* beliefs."[36]

To the extent that creeds perpetuate falsehood, particularly concerning the nature of the Godhead, then of course our Father in heaven would be displeased with them. Further, to the extent that creeds divide people, categorize people, exclude people, and even lead others to persecute them, one can appreciate why they would be viewed as undesirable. To the extent that they become a badge of belonging, the identifying mark by which a "true Christian" is known, the only way by which one can understand what the scriptures really mean about God and Christ — then to that extent the Christian circle is drawn smaller and smaller and that grace of God that makes salvation available to all humankind (Titus 2:11) is frustrated. The apostle Paul affirmed that our Savior "will have all men to be saved, and to come unto the knowledge of the truth" (1 Timothy 2:4). This is what the Prophet Joseph had in mind when he stated in October 1843: "I cannot believe in any of the creeds of the different denominations, because they all have some things in them I cannot subscribe to, though all of them have some truth. I want to come up into the presence of God, and learn all things; but the creeds set up stakes, and say, 'Hitherto shalt thou come, and no further'; which I cannot subscribe to."[37]

---

36. Craig L. Blomberg and Stephen E. Robinson, *How Wide the Divide? A Mormon and an Evangelical in Conversation* (Downers Grove, IL: InterVarsity Press, 1997), 72, 61, emphasis in original.

37. TPJS, 327. One can gain a deeper insight into the Prophet's frustration and pain

The "professors" mentioned in the First Vision seem to be the antagonistic ministers in Joseph Smith's immediate surroundings. After describing the response of a Methodist minister to his First Vision that "it was all of the devil, that there were no such things as visions or revelations these days; that all such things had ceased with the apostles, and that there would never be any more of them," Joseph reported: "I soon found, however, that *my telling the story had excited a great deal of prejudice against me among professors of religion,* and was the cause of great persecution, which continued to increase . . . and this was common among all the sects" (Joseph Smith-History 1:21-22, emphasis added). In an account of the First Vision found in the Wentworth Letter (1842), Joseph indicates that "They [the Father and Son] told me that *all religious denominations were believing in incorrect doctrines,* and that none of them was acknowledged of God as His Church and kingdom: and I was expressly commanded to 'go not after them,' at the same time receiving a promise that the fulness of the Gospel should at some future time be made known unto me."[38]

Elder William Grant Bangerter once asked students and faculty at BYU: "Do we believe that all ministers of other churches are corrupt? Of course not. Joseph Smith certainly did not intend that. By reading the passage carefully, we find that the Lord Jesus Christ was referring to those ministers who were quarreling and arguing about which church was true — that is, the particular group with which Joseph Smith was involved. . . .

"It is clearly apparent that there have been and now are many choice, honorable, and devoted men and women going in the direction of their eternal salvation who give righteous and conscientious leadership to their congregations in other churches. Joseph Smith evidently had many warm and friendly contacts with ministers of other religions. Quite a few of them joined the Church: Sidney Rigdon, John Taylor, Parley P. Pratt, and others in America and England. Some of

---

concerning the negative impact of religious creeds in his letter to the Saints from Liberty Jail (D&C 123:7).

38. *History of The Church of Jesus Christ of Latter-day Saints,* 4:536, emphasis added. See also similar accounts of the First Vision published by Orson Pratt and Orson Hyde in Milton V. Backman, Jr., *Joseph Smith's First Vision: Confirming Evidences and Contemporary Accounts,* 2nd ed. (Salt Lake City: Bookcraft, 1980), 172, 175.

them who carried the Christian attitude of tolerance did not join the Church. There are many others like them today."[39]

To state that those "professors were all corrupt" is to suggest that they and their teachings had become unsound, spoiled, tainted.[40] Further, as Richard Bushman has pointed out, "At some level, Joseph's revelations indicate a loss of trust in the Christian ministry. For all their learning and their eloquence, the clergy could not be trusted with the Bible. They did not understand what the book meant. It was a record of revelations, and the ministry had turned it into a handbook. The Bible had become a text to be interpreted rather than an experience to be lived. In the process, the power of the book was lost. . . . It was the power thereof that Joseph and the other visionaries of his time sought to recover. Not getting it from the ministry, they looked for it themselves."

"To me," Bushman continues, "that is Joseph Smith's significance for our time. He stood on the contested ground where the Enlightenment and Christianity confronted one another, and his life posed the question, Do you believe God speaks? Joseph was swept aside, of course, in the rush of ensuing intellectual battles and was disregarded by the champions of both great systems, but his mission was to hold out for the reality of divine revelation and establish one small outpost where that principle survived. Joseph's revelatory principle is not a single revelation serving for all time, as the Christians of his day believed regarding the incarnation of Christ, nor a mild sort of inspiration seeping into the minds of all good people, but specific, ongoing directions from God to his people. At a time when the origins of Christianity were under assault by the forces of Enlightenment rationality, Joseph Smith returned modern Christianity to its origins in revelation."[41]

---

39. "It's a Two-Way Street," address delivered on 4 August 1985, in *1984-85 BYU Speeches of the Year* (Provo: Brigham Young University Publications, 1985), 161.

40. *Webster's 1828 Dictionary*, s.v. "corrupt."

41. "A Joseph Smith for the Twenty-First Century," *Brigham Young University Studies* 40, no. 3 (2001): 167-68; see also *Believing History: Latter-day Saint Essays* (New York: Columbia University Press, 2004), 274.

The "More" of Mormonism

Let me state once more that it is a gross exaggeration and misrepresentation to suggest that Latter-day Saints believe all of Christian practice and doctrine since the time of the original apostles has been apostate. Noble and God-fearing men and women who lived through the period that too many have termed the "dark ages" sought to do good and maintain the tenets of Christianity to the best of their ability. John Taylor declared that there were persons during medieval times who "could commune with God, and who, by the power of faith, could draw aside the curtain of eternity and gaze upon the invisible world . . . , have the ministering of angels, and unfold the future destinies of the world. If those were dark ages I pray God to give me a little darkness, and deliver me from the light and intelligence that prevail in our day."[42] Brigham Young explained that many good men before the time of Joseph Smith's call enjoyed "the spirit of revelation" and specifically noted that John Wesley was as good a man as lived on earth.[43]

In speaking of the primitive church, President Boyd K. Packer observed that "the flame flickered and dimmed. . . . But always, as it had from the beginning, the Spirit of God inspired worthy souls. We owe an immense debt to the protesters and the reformers who preserved the scriptures and translated them. They knew something had been lost. They kept the flame alive as best they could. Many of them were martyrs."[44] Similarly, Elder Dallin H. Oaks explained that "We are indebted to the men and women who kept the light of faith and learning alive through the centuries to the present day. We have only to contrast the lesser light that exists among peoples unfamiliar with the names of God and Jesus Christ to realize the great contribution made by Christian teachers through the ages. We honor them as servants of God."[45]

The question that arises from many of other faiths is this: Why should I join your church? What do you have to offer beyond my acceptance of Jesus Christ and the teachings of the Bible? Brigham Young declared that "We, the Latter-day Saints, take the liberty of believing

---

42. *Journal of Discourses* (cited hereafter as JD), 26 vols. (Liverpool: F. D. Richards & Sons, 1851-86), 16:197.

43. JD 6:170; 7:5; 11:126.

44. Conference Report, April 2000, 7.

45. Conference Report, April 1995, 113.

more than our Christian brethren: we not only believe . . . the Bible, but . . . the whole of the plan of salvation that Jesus has given to us. *Do we differ from others who believe in the Lord Jesus Christ? No, only in believing more.*"[46] How so? What is, in fact, the "more" of Mormonism?

1. *Doctrinal Perspective.* Latter-day Saints believe that many of the truths restored through Joseph Smith provide a grander and more elevated perspective on life. For example, to believe that men and women existed before this mortal sphere has immense implications for life here — our joys, our friendships and associations, our likes and dislikes, and our challenges and suffering. Also, consider what difference it makes to believe in "Christ's eternal gospel," the verity that the fulness of the gospel of Jesus Christ has been on earth since the beginning of time.

2. *Doctrinal Consolation.* What difference does it make to know that God has a plan and a timetable by which all of his children will have the opportunity to either accept or reject the message of salvation in Christ? What difference does it make to know that the sweetest associations of this life — marriage and family — can continue uninterrupted beyond the veil of death? What difference does it make to know that those who were unable to be married in this life to one with like passion for the faith, will have that opportunity hereafter?

3. *Doctrinal Clarification and Expansion.* Just as traditional Christians have no hesitation in viewing the events and teachings of the Old Testament through the lenses of the New Testament, so Latter-day Saints do not hesitate to read the Bible through the lenses of the Book of Mormon, modern scripture, and the words of living apostles and prophets. Supplementation is not the same as contradiction. Insights beyond that which is taught in the Bible are available on such topics as the premortal existence of humankind (Alma 13:1-5; Moses 4:1-4; Abraham 3:22-28); the purpose of the Fall and its link to the Atonement (2 Nephi 2; Moses 4-5); the breadth and scope of Christ's infinite atonement (Alma 7:11-13; D&C 76:22-24; Moses 1:32-35); Christ's ministry in the postmortal spirit world (D&C 138); and the "many mansions" (John 14:2) or degrees of glory hereafter (D&C 76, 131).

4. *Doctrinal Confirmation.* One of the major purposes of the Book of Mormon and modern scripture is to convince people "that the records of the prophets and of the twelve apostles of the Lamb are true"

46. JD 13:56, emphasis added.

(1 Nephi 13:39). In the Book of Mormon we find the following: "Therefore repent, and be baptized in the name of Jesus, and lay hold upon the gospel of Christ, which shall be set before you, not only in this record but also in the record which shall come unto the Gentiles from the Jews [the Bible]. . . . For behold, this [the Book of Mormon] is written for the intent that ye may believe that [the Bible]" (Mormon 7:8-9). In the Doctrine and Covenants we read that the Book of Mormon has been delivered in the last days for the purpose of "Proving to the world that the holy scriptures are true, and that God does inspire men and call them to his holy work in this age and generation, as well as in generations of old; thereby showing that he is the same God yesterday, today, and forever" (D&C 20:11-12). In a day when people worldwide have come to doubt the historicity of biblical events, teachings, and values — especially the redemptive role of Jesus the Christ — Latter-day Saint scripture stands as a second witness to their truthfulness and reality.

5. *Doctrinal Consistency.* As indicated earlier, there is a great advantage to a priesthood hierarchy as a means of maintaining doctrinal orthodoxy. While members of The Church of Jesus Christ of Latter-day Saints are perfectly free to think and reflect on whatever they choose and to draw doctrinal conclusions on their own, they are at the same time instructed to "say [to speak in sermons or lessons, or to publish] none other things than that which the prophets and apostles [ancient and modern] have written" (D&C 52:9). The declaration, clarification, and interpretation of doctrine for the church as a whole rest with the presiding councils of the church, the First Presidency and the Quorum of the Twelve Apostles. The pattern is established in the Book of Mormon: "And it came to pass that Alma, having authority from God, ordained priests . . . to preach unto them, and to teach them concerning the things pertaining to the kingdom of God. And he commanded them that they should teach nothing save it were the things which he had taught, and which had been spoken by the mouth of the holy prophets" (Mosiah 18:18-19).

Later the practicality of such a teaching philosophy is given: "Therefore they did assemble themselves together in different bodies, being called churches; every church having their priests and their teachers, and every priest teaching the word according as it was delivered to him by the mouth of Alma." Now note what follows: "And thus, *notwithstanding there being many churches they were all one church, yea, even*

61

the church of God; for there was nothing preached in all the churches except it were repentance and faith in God" (Mosiah 25:21-22, emphasis added).

It was Paul who wrote that the organization of the church — including apostles, prophets, evangelists, pastors, and teachers — had been put in place "For the perfecting of the saints, for the work of the ministry, for the edifying of the body of Christ; *till we all come in the unity of the faith,* and of the knowledge of the Son of God, unto a perfect man, unto the measure of the stature of the fulness of Christ: that we henceforth be no more children, tossed to and fro, and carried about with every wind of doctrine, by the sleight of men, and cunning craftiness, whereby they lie in wait to deceive" (Ephesians 4:11-14, emphasis added).

Conclusion

I have often been challenged in public settings by people who are offended by the LDS notion of being the "only true church" or of our claim to possess the "fulness of the gospel of Jesus Christ." They feel it is unkind, exclusionary, and unchristian. I hasten to add that the complete statement in the Doctrine and Covenants is that Latter-day Saints belong to "the only true and living church upon the face of the whole earth, with which I, the Lord, am well pleased, *speaking unto the church collectively and not individually*" (D&C 1:30, emphasis added). Less than three years later, that same Lord chastened the Saints by observing that "were it not for the transgressions of my people, *speaking concerning the church and not individuals,* they might have been redeemed even now" (D&C 105:2, emphasis added).

On the other hand, doesn't church A believe they have a better insight into this or that doctrine than churches B, C, and D? Doesn't this denomination feel strongly that their beliefs and practices more closely mirror those of the church established by Jesus in the first century? Weren't Hus or Luther or Calvin or Zwingli or Wesley convinced that their efforts to reform the mother church — to cease from the abuses of Roman Catholicism and to return to the scriptures — were inspired and heaven-directed, that their reforms and teachings brought them closer to what the Master had intended from the beginning? Christianity, by its very nature, is exclusive in its perspective on who God is and what it takes to be saved.

J. B. Phillips noted: "The Roman Catholic who asserts positively that ordination in the Anglican Church is 'invalid,' and that no 'grace' is receivable through the Anglican sacraments, is plainly worshipping a God who is a Roman Catholic, and who operates reluctantly, if at all, through non-Roman channels. The ultra-low Churchman on the other hand must admit, if he is honest, that the god whom he worships disapproves most strongly of vestments, incense, and candles on the altar. The tragedy of these examples, which could be reproduced *ad nauseam* any day of the week, is not difference of opinion, which will probably be with us until the Day of Judgment, but the outrageous folly and damnable sin of trying to regard God as the Party Leader of a particular point of view." Phillips went on to state: "*No denomination has a monopoly on God's grace, and none has an exclusive recipe for producing Christian character.*"[47]

If I were asked, "Is God a Mormon? Is the Almighty a Latter-day Saint?" I think I would respond something like this: Our God is the God of all creation, an infinite, eternal, and omni-loving Being who will do all that he can to lead and direct, to bring greater light into the lives of his children, to save as many as will be saved. He is the only true God and thus the only Deity who can hear and respond to the earnest petitions of his children. He is the God of the Catholics, the Protestants, the Buddhists, the Hindus, and all those who seek to know and love and offer praise and adoration to the true and living God. I have been a Latter-day Saint all my life, but I do not in any way believe the Almighty loves Latter-day Saints any more than he loves Anglicans, Jehovah's Witnesses, Unitarians, Jews, or Muslims. He loves us all and is pleased with any and every halting effort on our part to learn of him, serve him, and be true to the light within us.

"If it has been demonstrated that I have been willing to die for a 'Mormon,'" Joseph Smith taught, "I am bold to declare before Heaven that I am just as ready to die in defending the rights of a Presbyterian, a Baptist, or a good man of any other denomination; for the same principle which would trample upon the rights of the Latter-day Saints would trample upon the rights of the Roman Catholics, or of any other

47. *Your God Is Too Small* (New York: Touchstone, 1997), 38-39, emphasis added.

denomination who may be unpopular and too weak to defend themselves."[48] "If I esteem mankind to be in error," Joseph explained, "shall I bear them down? No. I will lift them up, and in their own way too, if I cannot persuade them my way is better; and I will not seek to compel any man to believe as I do, only by the force of reasoning, for truth will cut its own way. Do you believe in Jesus Christ and the Gospel of salvation which he revealed? So do I. Christians should cease wrangling and contending with each other, and cultivate the principles of union and friendship in their midst."[49]

Latter-day Saints cannot jettison what they believe to be the language of the Lord to Joseph Smith in 1820 in order to allay bad feelings or court favor. We hold to the truth that God has spoken anew in our day and restored his everlasting gospel through living prophets.[50] This is our distinctive position, our contribution to a world that desperately needs a belief in God, an understanding of his grand plan of salvation, the promise and hope that come from a Redeemer, and confirming evidence for the historical veracity of the Holy Bible. We can seek to better understand what was meant and intended, but we cannot relinquish the reason we have for being. President Gordon B. Hinckley remarked: "The Lord said that this is the only true and living Church upon the face of the earth with which He is well-pleased. I didn't say that. Those are His words. The Prophet Joseph was told that the other sects were wrong. Those are not my words. Those are the Lord's words. But *they are hard words for those of other faiths. We don't need to exploit them. We just* need to be kind and good and gracious people to others, showing by our example the great truth of that which we believe."[51]

"While one portion of the human race is judging and condemning the other without mercy," Brother Joseph Smith noted solemnly, "the Great Parent of the universe looks upon the whole of the human family with a fatherly care and paternal regard; He views them as His offspring, and without any of those contracted feelings that influence the children of men, causes 'His sun to rise on the evil and the good, and sendeth rain on the just and on the unjust.' He holds the reins of judg-

48. TPJS, 313.

49. TPJS, 314.

50. See Boyd K. Packer, Conference Report, October 1985, 104, 107.

51. Remarks delivered at the North Ogden, Utah Regional Conference, 3 May 1998; as cited in *Church News,* 3 June 2000, emphasis added; see also *Ensign,* June 2004, 3.

ment in His hands; He is a wise Lawgiver, and will judge all men, not according to the narrow, contracted notions of men, but 'according to the deeds done in the body whether they be good or evil.' . . . We need not doubt the wisdom and intelligence of the Great Jehovah."[52]

Latter-day Saints are not naïve enough to believe that early Christianity — with each of the doctrines enunciated perfectly and all of the ecclesiastical structure in place — suddenly fell out of heaven intact; indeed, as is the case with present-day Mormonism, there were questions to resolve, issues to engage, conflicts to handle, and the challenges of growth to face over a period of many years. For the Latter-day Saints, the work of "restoration" is a work in progress, just as it was for those who might be called the Former-day Saints. We are not unmindful that a ferment within the Christian church of the first few centuries is indeed what one might expect.

In 1978 the First Presidency of The Church of Jesus Christ of Latter-day Saints issued the following statement: "Based upon ancient and modern revelation, The Church of Jesus Christ of Latter-day Saints gladly teaches and declares the Christian doctrine that all men and women are brothers and sisters, not only by blood relationship from common mortal progenitors, but also as literal spirit children of an Eternal Father. . . .

"Consistent with these truths, we believe that God has given and will give to all peoples sufficient knowledge to help them on their way to eternal salvation, either in this life or in the life to come.

"We also declare that the gospel of Jesus Christ, restored to his Church in our day, provides the only way to a mortal life of happiness and a fulness of joy forever. For those who have not received this gospel, the opportunity will come to them in the life hereafter if not in this life.

"Our message therefore is one of special love and concern for the eternal welfare of all men and women, regardless of religious belief, race, or nationality, knowing that we are truly brothers and sisters because we are the sons and daughters of the same Eternal Father."[53]

52. TPJS, 218.
53. First Presidency Statement, 15 February 1978.

4 The Christ of the Latter-day Saints

Members of The Church of Jesus Christ of Latter-day Saints claim to be Christians on the basis of their doctrine, their defined relationship to Christ, their patterns of worship, and their way of life. They resonate with C. S. Lewis's words: "It is not for us to say who, in the deepest sense, is or is not close to the spirit of Christ. We do not see into men's hearts. We cannot judge, and are indeed forbidden to judge. It would be wicked arrogance for us to say that any man is, or is not, a Christian in this refined sense. . . . When a man who accepts the Christian doctrine lives unworthily of it, it is much clearer to say he is a bad Christian than to say he is not a Christian."[1]

Beliefs about Christ

The following are fundamental and foundational LDS beliefs about Jesus Christ:

1. Jesus is the Son of God, the Only Begotten Son in the flesh (John 3:16). Latter-day Saints accept the prophetic declarations in the Old Testament that refer directly and powerfully to the coming of the Messiah, the Savior of all humankind. Jesus of Nazareth was and is the fulfillment of those prophecies. He is the Prophet "like unto Moses," the "suffering servant" of Isaiah, the Second David of Jeremiah and Ezekiel.

2. The accounts of Jesus' life and ministry recorded in Matthew, Mark, Luke, and John in the New Testament are historical and thus

---

1. *Mere Christianity* (New York: Touchstone, 1996), 10-11.

truthful. The Jesus of history is indeed the Christ of faith. While Latter-day Saints do not believe the Bible to be inerrant, complete, or the final word of God, they accept the essential details of the Gospels and more particularly the divine witness of those men who walked and talked with Jesus or were mentored by his chosen apostles.

3. Jesus was born of a virgin, Mary, in Bethlehem of Judea in what has come to be known as the meridian of time, the central point in salvation history. From his mother Mary Jesus inherited mortality, the capacity to feel the frustrations and ills of this world, including the capacity to die. Jesus was fully human in that he was subject to sickness, to pain, and to temptation.

4. Jesus is the Son of God the Father and as such inherited powers of Godhood and divinity from his Father, including immortality, the capacity to live forever. Furthermore, Jesus can extend those same attributes and powers to others. While he walked the dusty roads of Palestine as a man, he possessed the powers of a God and ministered as one having authority, including power over the elements and even power over life and death.

5. The Beloved Son was subordinate to his Father in mortality. Jesus came to carry out the will of the Father (John 4:34). He explained: "I seek not mine own will, but the will of the Father which hath sent me" (John 5:30; compare 6:38-40). In addition, the scriptures attest that the Father had power, knowledge, glory, and dominion that Jesus did not have at the time. Truly, "the Son can do nothing of himself, but what he seeth the Father do" (John 5:19). Even what the Son spoke was what the Father desired to be spoken (John 12:49-50). Jesus said: "If ye loved me, ye would rejoice, because I said, I go unto the Father: for my Father is greater than I" (John 14:28).

6. Jesus did not possess a fulness of the glory of the Father at the beginning of his life and ministry, "but received grace for grace; and he received not of the fulness at first, but continued from grace to grace, until he received a fulness." Later, in the resurrection, he "received a fulness of the glory of the Father; and he received all power, both in heaven and on earth, and the glory of the Father was with him, for he dwelt in him" (D&C 93:12-13, 16-17).[2]

2. See Joseph Fielding Smith, *Doctrines of Salvation*, 3 vols., comp. Bruce R. McConkie (Salt Lake City: Bookcraft, 1954-56), 2:269; Bruce R. McConkie, *Mormon Doctrine*, 2nd ed. (Salt Lake City: Bookcraft, 1966), 333.

7. On the other hand, the Father and the Son enjoyed much more than what we would call closeness; theirs was a divine indwelling relationship. Because he kept the law of God, Jesus was in the Father, and the Father was in Jesus (see John 14:10, 20; 17:21; 1 John 3:24). Though they were two separate and distinct persons, they were one — infinitely more one than separate. Their transcendent unity epitomizes what ought to exist between God and all of his children. That is to say, we are under commission to seek the Spirit of God, to strive to be one with the Gods, to have, as Paul wrote, "the mind of Christ" (1 Corinthians 2:16).

8. The Holy Ghost, as the third member of the Godhead, is the minister of the Father and the Son. Christ sends the Comforter (John 15:26; 16:7). That Comforter is not an independent Being in the sense of speaking his own mind and delivering a completely original message. Jesus taught: "When he, the Spirit of truth, is come, he will guide you into all truth: for he shall not speak of himself; but whatsoever he shall hear [presumably, from the Father and/or the Son], that shall he speak: and he will shew you things to come. He shall glorify me: for he shall receive of mine, and shall shew it unto you" (John 16:13-14). The three separate members of the Godhead are one — they bear the same witness and teach the same truths (1 John 5:7).

9. Jesus performed miracles, including granting sight to the blind, hearing to the deaf, life to those who had died, and forgiveness to those steeped in sin and who repented. The New Testament accounts of healings and nature miracles and the cleansing of human souls are authentic and real.

10. Jesus taught his gospel — the glad tidings or good news that salvation had come to earth through him — in order that people might more clearly understand both their relationship to God the Father and their responsibility to each other.

11. Jesus selected leaders, invested them with authority, and organized a church. The Church of Jesus Christ was established, as the apostle Paul later wrote, for the perfection and unity of the saints (Ephesians 4:11-14). "Ye have not chosen me, but I have chosen you, and ordained you" (John 15:16).

12. Jesus' teachings and his own matchless and perfect life provide a pattern for men and women to live by, and we must emulate that pattern as best we can to find true happiness and fulfillment in this life.

He did not just point the way; he *is* the way. He did not just teach the truth; he *is* the truth. He did not just bring resurrection and life to men and women; he *is* the resurrection and the life (John 14:6).

13. Jesus understood clearly who he was and he made it sufficiently clear to others. He knew that he was Jehovah, the God of Abraham, Isaac, and Jacob. He knew that he was God's Only Begotten Son. He knew that people could draw close to God and gain happiness and joy in this life and eternal life in the world to come only through an acceptance of his teachings and his willing sacrifice.

14. Jesus suffered and bled in the Garden of Gethsemane and submitted to a cruel death on the cross of Calvary, all as a willing sacrifice, a substitutionary atonement for our sins. That offering is made efficacious as we exercise faith and trust in him; repent of our sins; are baptized by immersion as a symbol of our acceptance of his death, burial, and rise to newness of life; and receive the gift of the Holy Ghost (Acts 2:37-38; 3 Nephi 27:19-20). While no one of us can comprehend how and in what manner one person can take upon himself the effects of the sins of another — or, even more mysteriously, the sins of all men and women — we accept and glory in the transcendent reality that Christ remits our sins through his suffering. Further, Jesus died, was buried, and rose from the dead, and his resurrection was a physical reality. As the "first fruits" of the resurrection, the effects of his rise from the tomb pass upon all men and women. "As in Adam all die, even so in Christ shall all be made alive" (1 Corinthians 15:22).

15. Men and women cannot overcome the flesh or gain eternal reward through their own unaided efforts. We must work to our limit and then rely upon the merits, mercy, and grace of the Holy One of Israel to see us through the struggles of life and into life eternal (2 Nephi 31:19; Moroni 6:4). While human works are *necessary*, including exercising faith in Christ, repenting of our sins, receiving the sacraments or ordinances of salvation, and rendering Christian service to our neighbors, they are not *sufficient* for salvation (2 Nephi 25:23; Moroni 10:32). Further, one's discipleship ought to be evident in the way they live their lives; those who have come unto Christ by covenant should manifest the "fruit of the Spirit" (Galatians 5:22-25; Alma 7:23-24). As James taught, true faith always manifests itself in faithfulness to the Lord and his word (James 2:17-20). Christian discipleship consists in continuing in his word (John 8:31-32) through obedience to his commandments (Matthew 7:21).

Some Distinctive Contributions

What, then, do the Latter-day Saints feel they can contribute to the world's understanding of Jesus Christ? What can they say that will make a difference in how men and women view and relate to the Savior? Who is the Christ of the Latter-day Saints, the Christ of the Restoration?

The First Vision

Joseph Smith's First Vision represents the beginning of the revelation of God in our day. It is also, therefore, the beginning of the revelation of Jesus Christ. President Gordon B. Hinckley has observed: "To me it is a significant and marvelous thing that in establishing and opening this dispensation our Father did so with a revelation of himself and of his Son Jesus Christ, as if to say to all the world that he was weary of the attempts of men, earnest though these attempts might have been, to define and describe him. . . . The experience of Joseph Smith in a few moments in the grove on a spring day in 1820, brought more light and knowledge and understanding of the personality and reality and substance of God and his Beloved Son than men had arrived at during centuries of speculation."[3] Joseph Smith taught that the Father, Son, and Holy Ghost constitute the Godhead. From the beginning he emphasized that the members of the Godhead are one in purpose, one in mind, one in glory, one in attributes and powers, but separate beings, that they are three distinct Gods.[4] Later in his ministry, he explained: "The Father has a body of flesh and bones as tangible as man's; the Son also; but the Holy Ghost has not a body of flesh and bones, but is a personage of Spirit. Were it not so, the Holy Ghost could not dwell in us" (D&C 130:22).

There was reaffirmed in the First Vision the fundamental Christian teaching — that Jesus of Nazareth lived, died, was buried, and rose from the tomb in glorious immortality. In the midst of the light that shone above the brightness of the sun stood the resurrected Lord Jesus in company with his Father. Joseph Smith knew from the time of the

---

3. *Teachings of Gordon B. Hinckley* (Salt Lake City: Deseret Book, 1997), 236.
4. *Teachings of the Prophet Joseph Smith,* selected by Joseph Fielding Smith (Salt Lake City: Deseret Book, 1976), 370; cited hereafter as TPJS.

First Vision that death was not the end, that life continues after one's physical demise, that another realm of existence — a postmortal sphere — does in fact exist.

The Book of Mormon

Through the Book of Mormon, translated by Joseph Smith, came additional insights concerning the person and powers of Jesus the Christ. Indeed, the Book of Mormon has a high Christology. We learn that our Lord is the Holy One of Israel, the God of Abraham, Isaac, and Jacob (1 Nephi 19:10), and that through an act of infinite condescension he left his throne divine and took a mortal body (1 Nephi 11; Mosiah 3:5). We learn from the teachings of Book of Mormon prophets that he was a man, but much more than man (Mosiah 3:7, 9; Alma 34:11), that he had within him the powers of the Father, the powers of the Spirit (2 Nephi 2:8; Helaman 5:11), the power to lay down his life and the power to take it up again (compare John 10:17-18).

The Book of Mormon provides a balanced perspective on the mercy and grace of an infinite Savior on the one hand, and the labors and works of finite man on the other. One could come away from a careful reading of the second half of the New Testament, for example, somewhat confused on the matter of grace and works, finding those places where the apostles seem almost to defy any notion of works as a means of salvation (Romans 4:1-5; 10:1-4; Ephesians 2:8-10), but also those places where good works are clearly mentioned as imperative (Romans 2:6; James 2:14-20; Revelation 20:12-13). The Book of Mormon is a book about merit, but not about the merits of man. Indeed, as one Book of Mormon teacher noted, "since man had fallen he could not merit anything of himself; but the sufferings and death of Christ atone for their sins, through faith and repentance, and so forth" (Alma 22:14). The doctrinal refrain in the Book of Mormon is that "there is no flesh that can dwell in the presence of God, save it be through the merits, and mercy, and grace of the Holy Messiah" (2 Nephi 2:8). This insight is blended with the realization that the works of men and women, including the receipt of the ordinances of salvation, the performance of duty, and Christian acts of service — in short, being true to our part of the gospel covenant — though insufficient for salvation, are necessary.

While Mormons are criticized occasionally for what some perceive to be a lack of emphasis on Jesus Christ the Son, we feel that too great an emphasis on the second member of the Godhead (almost to the exclusion of the first) can, if we are not careful, tend to shroud in excessive mystery the person and personality of God the Father. Elder Jeffrey R. Holland stated that one of the most uncelebrated aspects of the multi-faceted work of our Divine Redeemer is the fact that Jesus came to earth to reveal the Father, "that in all that Jesus came to say and do, including and especially in His atoning suffering and sacrifice, He was showing us who and what God our Eternal Father is like, . . . trying to reveal and make personal to us the true nature of His Father, our Father in heaven. . . .

"I make my own heartfelt declaration of God our Eternal Father . . . because some in the contemporary world suffer from a distressing misconception of Him. Among those there is a tendency to feel distant from the Father, even estranged from Him, if they believe in Him at all. And if they do believe, many moderns say they might feel comfortable in the arms of Jesus, but they are uneasy contemplating the stern encounter of God. Through a misreading . . . of the Bible, these see God the Father and Jesus Christ His Son as operating very differently. . . .

"In reflecting on these misconceptions we realize that one of the remarkable contributions of the Book of Mormon is its seamless, perfectly consistent view of divinity throughout that majestic book. Here there is no Malachi-to-Matthew gap, no pause while we shift theological gears, no misreading the God who is urgently, lovingly, faithfully at work on every page of that record from its Old Testament beginning to its New Testament end." In short, "what we have in the Book of Mormon is a uniform view of God in all His glory and goodness, all His richness and complexity."[5]

The Cosmic Christ

At the heart of LDS theology is the doctrine of Christ. "The fundamental principles of our religion," Joseph Smith observed, "are the testimony of the Apostles and Prophets, concerning Jesus Christ, that He

5. Holland, "The Grandeur of God," *Ensign,* November 2003, 70-71.

died, was buried, and rose again the third day, and ascended into heaven; and all other things which pertain to our religion are only appendages to it."[6] By means of the Book of Mormon, other scriptural records, and modern prophetic statements, Latter-day Saints testify of the Cosmic Christ, of the Lord and Savior whose name-titles and roles are many. At the risk of being a bit repetitious, we will now set forth some of those divine roles:

1. *The Firstborn.* Modern revelation attests that Jesus was the first-born spirit child of God the Father. "I was in the beginning with the Father," our Lord affirms, "and am the Firstborn; and all those who are begotten through me are partakers of the glory of the same, and are the church of the Firstborn" (D&C 93:21-22).

2. *Jehovah — the Great I AM.* As we have already discussed, the man Jesus was and is the Almighty Jehovah. As Jehovah, he became the chief advocate and proponent of the plan of the Eternal Father, the one who said, "Thy will be done" (Moses 4:2). He was the One who volunteered to put into full effect all of the terms and conditions of that majestic plan. It was Jehovah who manifested himself to Adam and Eve after the Fall, who revealed himself to Enoch (Moses 7:53) and Noah (Moses 8:19), who made known the plan of life and salvation to Abraham, Isaac, Jacob and all of the faithful in the Old Testament (1 Nephi 19:10).

3. *The Creator.* As a premortal spirit, Jehovah grew in knowledge and power to the point where he became "like unto God" (Abraham 3:24), meaning the Father. Under the direction of the Father, he created this world and all things on the face of it. In addition, he became the Creator of worlds without number (D&C 76:24; Moses 1:33; 7:30). As "the Lord Omnipotent," he came to be known to the ancients as "the Father of heaven and earth, the Creator of all things from the beginning" (Mosiah 3:5, 8). To the Book of Mormon people he declared: "Behold, I am Jesus Christ the Son of God. I created the heavens and the earth, and all things that in them are. I was with the Father from the beginning" (3 Nephi 9:15).

4. *The Promised Messiah.* From the dawn of time on this earth men and women looked forward with an eye of faith to that great and last sacrifice (Alma 34:13) that opened the door to redemption. Jehovah

6. TPJS, 121.

would come to earth as the Messiah, the Anointed One, the Christ. From Adam to Zechariah, the prophets of old spoke of the coming of the Holy One of Israel, the Lamb slain from the foundation of the world (Revelation 13:8; Moses 7:47).

5. *The Only Begotten in the Flesh.* Jesus of Nazareth is literally the Son of God, the Only Begotten of the Father in the flesh. He is not the Son of the Holy Ghost, nor is he the Son of the Father in some mystical, metaphorical sense; he is the Son of Almighty God.[7] Truly, "He hath power given unto him from the Father to redeem them from their sins because of repentance" (Helaman 5:10). One prophet "beheld his glory, as the glory of the Only Begotten of the Father, full of grace and truth, even the Spirit of truth, which came and dwelt in the flesh, and dwelt among us" (D&C 93:11).

6. *The Father and the Son.* Though it is true that the word *Father* is generally used in regard to God our Heavenly Father as the Father of our spirits, Jesus is also known as the Father — Father as Creator of the heavens and the earth (Alma 11:39), Father through spiritual renewal and rebirth (Mosiah 5:7; D&C 25:1), and Father by divine investiture of authority.[8] That is, our Savior, as the Word of the Father and the messenger of salvation (D&C 93:8), is authorized and appointed to act and speak on behalf of the Father, in the first person for the Father, as though he were the Father.

7. *The Perfect One.* Jesus of Nazareth was and is the only mortal to traverse earth's paths without committing sin (2 Corinthians 5:21; Hebrews 4:15; 1 Peter 2:22). Joseph Smith taught that Jesus "kept the law of God, and remained without sin, showing thereby that it is in the power of man to keep the law and remain also without sin; and also, that by him a righteous judgment might come upon all flesh, and that all who walk not in the law of God may justly be condemned by the law, and

7. See Ezra Taft Benson, *Come Unto Christ* (Salt Lake City: Deseret Book, 1983), 4. While the Latter-day Saints clearly believe that Jesus is the Son of God the Father, there is no authoritative doctrinal statement within Mormonism that explains how the conception of Jesus was accomplished. One Book of Mormon prophet spoke of Mary as "a virgin, a precious and chosen vessel, who shall be overshadowed and conceive by the power of the Holy Ghost, and bring forth a son, yea, even the Son of God" (Alma 7:10).

8. See "The Father and the Son, A Doctrinal Exposition of the First Presidency and the Twelve Apostles," in James E. Talmage, *The Articles of Faith* (Salt Lake City: Deseret Book, 1975), Appendix 2, note 11, 465-73.

have no excuse for their sins."[9] Jesus never took a backward step and therefore never forfeited the right to the influence of his Father's Spirit. "Where is the man that is free from vanity?" Joseph Smith asked. "None ever were perfect but Jesus; and why was He perfect? Because He was the Son of God, and had the fulness of the Spirit, and greater power than any man."[10] The Savior was and is the Holy One of Israel, the only being in eternity who owed no debt to divine justice and could thereby "claim of the Father his rights of mercy which he hath upon the children of men" (Moroni 7:27).

8. *Gracious Savior.* As early as the spring of 1820 in his First Vision, the boy prophet Joseph Smith was instructed by the Savior: "Joseph, my son, thy sins are forgiven thee. Go thy way, walk in my statutes, and keep my commandments. Behold, I am the Lord of glory. I was crucified for the world that all those who believe on my name may have eternal life."[11] Thus among the first truths imparted to Joseph Smith was the central verity that salvation is in Christ and that redemption and remission of sins come in no other way. All people are thus called upon to "believe the gospel and rely upon the merits of Jesus Christ, and be glorified through faith in his name" (D&C 3:20).

9. *The Deliverer Among the Disembodied.* That the Redeemer's mission spanned the veil of death and continued after his own decease is taught in the Holy Bible, though not with unmistakable clarity (John 5:25-29; 1 Peter 3:18-20; 4:6). Through Isaiah the Lord Jehovah proclaimed: "The Spirit of the Lord God is upon me; because the Lord hath anointed me to preach good tidings unto the meek; he hath sent me to bind up the brokenhearted, to proclaim liberty to the captives, and the opening of the prison to them that are bound" (Isaiah 61:1.) That Jesus was indeed the realization of this prophecy is clear from his own self-testimony (Luke 4:18-19).

Joseph F. Smith, sixth president of The Church of Jesus Christ of Latter-day Saints and nephew of Joseph Smith, recorded a vision in October 1918 in which the postmortal spirit world ministry of Christ was made known. The account of that vision constitutes section 138 of the

9. *Lectures on Faith* (Salt Lake City: Deseret Book, 1985), 5:2.

10. TPJS, 187-88.

11. From an 1832 account, in Milton V. Backman, Jr., *Joseph Smith's First Vision,* 2nd ed. (Salt Lake City: Bookcraft, 1980), 157, spelling and punctuation corrected.

Doctrine and Covenants. In short, Latter-day Saints believe that all men and women will be granted the opportunity to receive the gospel of Jesus Christ, either in this life or in the life that continues after one's mortal death before the resurrection. This doctrine addresses the age-old query in the Christian world: What about those who never heard of Jesus Christ? We will speak in more detail of Christ's postmortal ministry in chapter 6.

10. *The King of kings and Lord of lords.* Most Christians believe that Jesus of Nazareth was and is the Christ, the Holy One of Israel. We know that he came to earth to teach, to cleanse and sanctify human hearts, and to die and rise from the tomb. In addition, Latter-day Saints teach that he came to earth as a legal administrator, empowered to empower others. He ordained and set apart and bestowed priesthoods and authorities, and he thereby established his church and kingdom on earth. As mentioned earlier, the Saints feel that the Church of Jesus Christ fell away after the death of the apostles and the keys of authority were lost to the world for almost two millennia. Thus the call of Joseph Smith signaled not only a restoration of divine truths, but also a restoration of the powers necessary to reestablish the kingdom of God on earth, this time to remain forever. The restoration of divine truth, begun in the spring of 1820, will continue into and through the Millennium. Jesus the Christ will then, in that magnificent day of peace and glory, reign as the Second David, the King of Israel and of all the earth, the King of kings. And this earth will be his.

Extra-Biblical Witnesses

One of the main reasons Latter-day Saints are often relegated to the category of cult or non-Christian is because they accept scripture beyond the Bible. To be sure, they love the Bible. They cherish its sacred teachings and delight in reading and teaching it. They seek to conform their lives to its marvelous precepts. But they do not believe that the Bible contains all that God has spoken or will yet speak in the future. John Stackhouse warned of being so wedded to the Bible that one cannot recognize truth elsewhere. "Bible texts in some evangelical traditions," he wrote, "replace even the cross as the symbol emblazoned on the front wall of the sanctuary. . . . Indeed, among the criticisms most frequently leveled against evangelicals is that we are *too* focused on the Bible at the expense of not taking other God-given theological resources as seriously as we should, whether tradition, reason, or experience. . . . These attitudes combine to form a syndrome that places the text of the Bible at the center of evangelical life and in fact displaces the Holy Spirit's role as primary teacher, thus amounting to a bibliolatry."[12]

Occasionally we hear that certain Latter-day Saint teachings — like some of those concerning the Savior that I have detailed earlier — are *unbiblical* or of a particular doctrine being *contradictory* to the Bible. Let's be clear on this matter. The Bible is one of the books within the LDS standard works, the scriptural canon. There are times, of course, when latter-day revelation provides clarification or additional information to the Bible. But *addition* to the canon is hardly the same as *rejection* of the canon. Supplementation is not the same as contradiction. All of the prophets, including the Savior himself, brought new light and knowledge to the world; in many cases, new scripture came as a result of their ministry. That new scripture did not invalidate what went before, nor did it close the door to subsequent revelation.

Let me reason now from a Latter-day Saint perspective on the matter of an "open canon." Most New Testament scholars believe that Mark was the first Gospel written and that Matthew and Luke drew upon Mark in the preparation of their Gospels. One tradition is that John the Beloved, aware of the teachings of the Synoptic Gospels, prepared his Gospel in an effort to "fill in the gaps" and thus deal more with the great spiritual verities that his evangelistic colleagues chose not to include (see John 20:30-31). How many people in the Christian tradition today would suggest that what Matthew or Luke did in adding to what Mark had written was illegal or inappropriate or irreverent? Do we suppose that anyone in the first century would have so felt?

Would John's effort, presumably written many years after the synoptics, have been viewed with disdain or suspicion by the Saints of the first or second century? I would not think so. Would anyone accuse Matthew or Luke or John of writing about or even worshipping a "different Jesus" because they were bold enough to add to what had been

---

12. *Evangelical Landscapes: Facing Critical Issues of the Day* (Grand Rapids: Baker, 2002), 54, 169-70.

incompletely recorded already? Surely not. Why? Because Matthew and Luke and John were inspired of God, perhaps even divinely commissioned by the church to pen their testimonies.

If Luke (in his Gospel, as well as in Acts) or John chose to write of subsequent appearances of the Lord Jesus after his initial ascension into heaven, appearances not found in Mark or Matthew, are we prone to criticize, to cry foul? No, because these accounts are contained in the Christian canon, that collection of books that serves as the rule of faith and practice in the Christian world. And here we come face to face with an age-old question: Is a writing authoritative because it is in the canon, or is it in the canon because it is authoritative?

F. F. Bruce observed that "there is a distinction between the canonicity of a book of the Bible and its authority. Its canonicity is dependent upon its authority. For when we ascribe canonicity to a book we simply mean that it belongs to the canon or list. But why does it so belong? Because it was recognized as possessing special authority. People frequently speak and write as if the authority with which the books of the Bible are invested in the minds of Christians is the result of their having been included in the sacred list. But the historical fact is the other way about; they were and are included in the list because they were acknowledged as authoritative." Bruce concludes: "Both logically and historically, authority precedes canonicity."[13]

The authority of scripture is tied to its source. The living, breathing, ever-relevant nature of the word of God is linked not to written words, not even to the writings of Moses or Isaiah or Malachi, not to the four Gospels or the epistles of Paul, but rather to the spirit of prophecy and revelation that illuminated and empowered those who recorded them in the first place. The Bible does in fact contain much that can and should guide our walk and talk; it contains the word and will of the Lord to men and women in earlier ages, and its timeless truths have tremendous normative value for our day. But we do not derive authority to speak or act in the name of Deity on the basis of what God gave to his people in an earlier day.

Just how bold is the Latter-day Saint claim? How strange is it to

---

13. *The Books and the Parchments* (Westwood, NJ: Fleming H. Revell Co., 1963), 95-96; see also Bruce, *The New Testament Documents: Are They Reliable?* (Grand Rapids: Eerdmans, 1974), 27.

propose that we require a living tree of life in our day? In a letter to his Uncle Silas in 1833, Joseph Smith wrote the following:

"Seeing that the Lord has never given the world to understand by anything heretofore revealed that he had ceased forever to speak to his creatures when sought unto in a proper manner, why should it be thought a thing incredible that he should be pleased to speak again in these last days for their salvation? Perhaps you may be surprised at this assertion that I should say 'for the salvation of his creatures in these last days' since we have already in our possession a vast volume of his word [the Bible] which he has previously given. But you will admit that the word spoken to Noah was not sufficient for Abraham. . . . Isaac, the promised seed, was not required to rest his hope upon the promises made to his father Abraham, but was privileged with the assurance of [God's] approbation in the sight of heaven by the direct voice of the Lord to him. . . . I have no doubt but that the holy prophets and apostles and saints in the ancient days were saved in the kingdom of God. . . . I may believe that Enoch walked with God. I may believe that Abraham communed with God and conversed with angels. . . . And have I not an equal privilege with the ancient saints? And will not the Lord hear my prayers, and listen to my cries as soon [as] he ever did to theirs, if I come to him in the manner they did? Or is he a respecter of persons?"[14]

Latter-day Saints feel a deep allegiance to the Bible. It seems odd to us, however, to be accused of being irreverent or disloyal to the Bible when we suggest to the religious world that the God of heaven has chosen to speak again. We feel our challenge is hauntingly reminiscent of that faced by Peter, James, John, or Paul when they declared to the religious establishment of their day that God had sent new truths and new revelations into the world, truths that supplemented and even clarified the Hebrew scripture. Any effort to add to or take away from that collection of sacred writings was suspect and subject to scorn and ridicule.

Latter-day Saints declare, as did the apostle Paul to Felix: "But this I confess unto thee, that after the way which they call heresy, so worship I the God of my fathers, believing all things which are written in the law and in the prophets" (Acts 24:14; compare 26:22). The LDS wit-

---

14. *Personal Writings of Joseph Smith*, rev. ed., ed. Dean C. Jessee (Salt Lake City: Deseret Book, 2002), 321-24, spelling and punctuation corrected.

ness is that the Lord Jehovah, who revealed himself to Adam and Abraham and Micah; the God of our fathers who spoke through the mouths of Jacob and Joseph and Jeremiah; the same being who came to dwell in the flesh and who taught Andrew and Nathaniel and Matthew — this same being, Jesus the Christ, has revealed himself and his everlasting gospel in these last days. The Latter-day Saints have received a commission to make these things known to the world. It would be unchristian *not* to share what has been communicated to them.

Conclusion

Jesus Christ is the central figure in the doctrine and practice of The Church of Jesus Christ of Latter-day Saints. He is God the Second, the Redeemer.[15] He is the Prototype of all saved beings, the standard of salvation.[16] Jesus explained that "no man cometh unto the Father, but by me" (John 14:6). Latter-day Saints acknowledge Jesus Christ as the source of truth and redemption, as the light and life of the world, as the way to the Father (John 14:6; 2 Nephi 25:29; 3 Nephi 11:11). They worship him in that they look to him for deliverance and redemption and seek to emulate his matchless life (D&C 93:12-20). Truly, as one Book of Mormon prophet proclaimed, "We talk of Christ, we rejoice in Christ, we preach of Christ, . . . that our children may know to what source they may look for a remission of their sins" (2 Nephi 25:26). We have been invited to come unto Christ — to learn of him, to listen to his words, to walk in the meekness of his Spirit (D&C 19:23) — and thereby grow into a meaningful spiritual relationship with him.

15. TPJS, 190.
16. *Lectures on Faith* 7:9.

5 Salvation in Christ

It is not uncommon for a member of The Church of Jesus Christ of Latter-day Saints to be asked the following questions by a caring or curious Christian: "Are you a saved Christian?" or "Have you been saved?" Almost without exception, Latter-day Saints will stumble over their words and wrestle with how to respond, for to us salvation is generally associated with the life to come, and being saved has to do with gaining eternal life following death and eventual resurrection.

Here, as in other theological matters, we use the same or similar words as our Christian neighbors to describe a Christian concept but discover upon more serious investigation that what we mean is at least slightly different. In that vein, I would suggest that for Latter-day Saints being saved is a *process,* one that has something to do with what has been accomplished in the past, what is going on now, and what will yet take place in the future. Thus our hesitation to respond to a rather straightforward question about being saved derives, not from any effort to avoid the issue or to suggest that we do not believe in the saving role of Jesus Christ, but rather from the fact that the question is not easily answered.

In this chapter I will attempt to provide a Latter-day Saint perspective on the matter of salvation in Christ and will suggest where our beliefs parallel but also differ from those of other Christian traditions.

The Greatest Gift

Salvation or eternal life (for in most all of our scriptural sources, these two terms are synonymous) is "the greatest of all the gifts of God"

(D&C 14:7; see also 6:13). It is not something for which we can barter, nor something that may be purchased with money. Nor in the strictest sense is it something that may be *earned*.[1] More correctly, salvation is a gift, a gift most precious, something gloriously transcendent that may only be inherited and bestowed.

A Book of Mormon prophet explained that "the Spirit is the same, yesterday, today, and forever. And the way is prepared from the fall of man, and salvation is free" (2 Nephi 2:4). One Latter-day Saint leader, Bruce R. McConkie, has written: "Salvation is free. Justification is free. Neither of them can be purchased; neither can be earned; neither comes by the Law of Moses, or by good works, or by any power or ability that man has. . . . Salvation is free, freely available, freely to be found. It comes because of his goodness and grace, because of his love, mercy, and condescension toward the children of men. . . . The questions then are: What salvation is free? What salvation comes by the grace of God? With all the emphasis of the rolling thunders of Sinai, we answer: All salvation is free; all comes by the merits and mercy and grace of the Holy Messiah; there is no salvation of any kind, nature, or degree that is not bound to Christ and his atonement."[2]

Our Plight

Cornelius Plantinga has written: "In the film *Grand Canyon,* an immigration attorney breaks out of a traffic jam and attempts to bypass it. His route takes him along streets that seem progressively darker and more deserted. Then the predictable . . . nightmare: his expensive car stalls on one of those alarming streets whose teenage guardians favor expensive guns and sneakers. The attorney does manage to phone for a tow truck, but before it arrives, five young street toughs surround his disabled car and threaten him with considerable bodily harm. Then, just in time, the tow truck shows up and its driver — an earnest, genial man — begins to hook up the disabled car. The toughs protest: the truck driver is interrupting their meal. So the driver takes the leader of

1. See Dallin H. Oaks, *With Full Purpose of Heart* (Salt Lake City: Deseret Book, 2002), 75.

2. *The Promised Messiah* (Salt Lake City: Deseret Book, 1978), 346-47.

the group aside and attempts a five-sentence introduction to meta-physics: 'Man,' he says, 'the world ain't supposed to work like this. Maybe you don't know that, but this ain't the way it's supposed to be. I'm supposed to be able to do my job without askin' you if I can. And that dude is supposed to be able to wait with his car without you rippin' him off. Everything's supposed to be different than what it is here.'"[3]

No, things aren't the way they ought to be. And they haven't been since Adam and Eve left the Garden of Eden. This is a fallen world, and we are brought face to face on a regular basis with the fact that for this temporal time and season not all well-laid plans will come to fruition. Times change. Things break down. Youth fades. Bodies grow old and decay. I look at the date and recall that in June 2001 I was rushed to the hospital because of a serious heart attack. I'm grateful to be alive, but I walk a little slower now, don't have the stamina I once had, and in general feel like the old tabernacle is losing the battle against mortality.

What, then, is the nature of man? Is he prone to choose the right, serve others, and make noble contributions to society? Or, on the other hand, is man a depraved creature, a sinful infidel who seeks only the gratification of the flesh? Which is it? How should we feel about our-selves — elated or depressed? John Stott pointed out that "human be-ings are the product of both the creation and the Fall. So, then, every-thing in us that is attributable to our creation in the image of God we gratefully affirm, while everything in us that is attributable to the Fall we must resolutely repudiate or deny. Thus we are called both to self-affirmation and to self denial."[4] To resolve this dilemma, we must first recognize that some statements from LDS literature speak of man's eternal nature, while others speak of his mortal or fallen nature.

To be sure, Joseph Smith taught that man is an eternal being. He declared that the intelligence of man "is not a created being; it existed from eternity, and will exist to eternity. Anything created cannot be eternal."[5] Subsequent Church leaders have explained that the attri-butes, powers, and capacities possessed by our Father in heaven reside

3. *Not the Way It's Supposed to Be: A Breviary of Sin* (Grand Rapids: Eerdmans, 1995), 7.

4. *Why I Am a Christian* (Downers Grove, IL: InterVarsity, 2003), 78.

5. *Teachings of the Prophet Joseph Smith*, selected by Joseph Fielding Smith (Salt Lake City: Deseret Book, 1976), 158; see also 181, 352-54; cited hereafter as TPJS.

83

in men and women in rudimentary and thus potential form. There is a sense, then, in which we might say that men and women, being spiritual heirs to godliness, are good by nature; that is, they are good because they are related to and are products of the Highest Good, a spark of divinity from the Father of lights (James 1:17). As the scriptures declare, men and women are created in the image of God (Genesis 1:26). God is good, even the embodiment and personification of all that is noble, upright, and edifying, and we are from him. It is vital that the religious world grasp the concept that "the Creator endowed us with a cluster of rational, moral, social, and spiritual faculties that make us like God and unlike the animals. Human beings are Godlike beings, and the divine image in us, although it has been marred, has not been destroyed."

Christ "not only taught it; he exhibited it. His whole mission demonstrated the value he placed on people. He treated everybody with respect — women and men, children and adults, the sinner and the righteous. . . .

"Christian teaching on the dignity and worth of human beings is of the utmost importance today, not only for our own self-image and self-respect but also for the welfare of society. When human beings are devalued, everything in society tends to turn sour. . . . But when human beings are valued as persons, because of their intrinsic worth, everything changes. Why? Because people matter. Because every man, woman and child has worth and significance as a human being made in God's image and likeness."[6]

Because Latter-day Saints believe in a "fortunate fall," that the fall of our first parents was as much a part of the plan of God as the Atonement — indeed, the Atonement derives from the Fall — they do not believe in the doctrine of human depravity. "When our spirits took possession of these tabernacles," Brigham Young observed, "they were as pure as the angels of God, wherefore total depravity cannot be a true doctrine."[7] On another occasion, he taught: "The spirits that live in these tabernacles were as pure as the heavens, when they entered them. They came to tabernacles that are contaminated, pertaining to the

---

6. John Stott, *Why I Am a Christian,* 106-107.

7. *Journal of Discourses,* 26 vols. (Liverpool: F. D. Richards & Sons, 1851-86), 10:192; cited hereafter as JD.

flesh, by the Fall of man. The Psalmist says, 'Behold, I was shapened in iniquity, and in sin did my mother conceive me.' (Psalms 51:5.) This scripture," Brother Brigham continues, "has established in the minds of some the doctrine of total depravity, that it is impossible for them to have one good thought, that they are altogether sinful, that there is no good, no soundness, and no spiritual health in them. This is not correct, yet we have a warfare within us. We have to contend against evil passions, or the seeds of iniquity that are sown in the flesh through the Fall. The pure spirits that occupy these tabernacles are operated upon [by God's Spirit], and it is the right of Him that sent them into these tabernacles to hold the preeminence, and to give them the spirit of Truth to influence the spirits of men, that [the Spirit of God] may triumph and reign predominantly in our tabernacles."[8]

C. S. Lewis did not hold to a traditional Christian view of human depravity. For one thing, Lewis concluded that if people are depraved they cannot even decide between what is good and what is evil. "If God is wiser than we," he stated, "His judgement must differ from ours on many things, and not least on good and evil. What seems to us good may therefore not be good in His eyes, and what seems to us evil may not be evil. On the other hand, if God's moral judgement differs from ours so that our 'black' may be His 'white,' we can mean nothing by calling Him good." This particular problem would affect our relationship to God, including our obedience to him. "If He is not (in our sense) 'good' we shall obey, if at all, only through fear — and should be equally ready to obey an omnipotent Fiend. The doctrine of Total Depravity — when the consequence is drawn that, since we are totally depraved, our idea of good is worth simply nothing, may thus turn Christianity into a form of devil-worship." Lewis also observed: "I disbelieve that doctrine [total depravity], partly on the logical ground that if our depravity were total we should not know ourselves to be depraved, and partly because experience shows us much goodness in human nature."[9]

Thus Brigham Young explained that the spirit, the eternal part of us, can be and is influenced by our fallen nature, our flesh. "Now I want to tell you," he pointed out, "that [Satan] does not hold any power over

8. JD 10:105.

9. *The Problem of Pain* (New York: Touchstone, 1996), 32, 59; see also *Christian Reunion and Other Essays* (London: William Collins Sons & Co., 1990), 60.

man, only so far as the body overcomes the spirit that is in a man, through yielding to the spirit of evil. The spirit that the Lord puts into a tabernacle of flesh is under the dictation of the Lord Almighty; but the spirit and body are united in order that the spirit may have a tabernacle, and be exalted; and the spirit is influenced by the body, and the body by the spirit. In the first place the spirit is pure, and under the special control and influence of the Lord, but the body is . . . under the mighty influence of that fallen nature that is of the earth."[10] Hence the debate between those who argue for man's nobility and those who argue for man's ignobility is resolved by asking the question: which nature are we speaking of? Man is basically good, at least his eternal nature is. Man is basically fallen, at least his mortal nature is.

Because Adam and Eve transgressed by partaking of the forbidden fruit they were cast from the Garden of Eden and from the presence of the Lord; they experienced spiritual death. As a result came blood, sweat, toil, opposition, bodily decay, and, finally, physical death. Even though the Fall was a vital part of the great plan of the Eternal God, our state, including our relationship to and contact with God, changed dramatically. While Latter-day Saints do not subscribe to a belief in an "original sin," the scriptural word does not permit them to minimize the effects of the Fall. To say that we are not accountable for or condemned by the fall of Adam is not to say that we are unaffected by it. The world is filled with people — Christian and non-Christian alike — who believe that "good people go to heaven." They simply want to receive from God hereafter, or at least they say they do, what they *deserve*. The scriptural view is actually quite different. "Jesus taught that good people *don't* go to heaven. Furthermore, he taught that God was intent on not giving people what they deserved. Jesus claimed that God desires to give men and women exactly what they do *not* deserve." The sobering fact is that Jesus "declared that even the best among them was not good enough to reach God on his own merit." Further, "the reason good people don't go to heaven is that there aren't any good people. There are only sinners. . . . Good people don't go to heaven. *Forgiven* people go to heaven."[11]

---

10. JD 2:255-56.

11. Andy Stanley, *How Good Is Good Enough?* (Sisters, OR: Multnomah, 2003), 49-50, 90, emphasis in original.

Joseph Smith did not believe that human beings, because of intrinsic carnality and depravity, are incapable of choosing good over evil. And he did not believe that children are born in sin, that they inherit the so-called sin of Adam, either by sexual union or by birth. But he did believe in the powerful pull of the Fall. "There is one thing under the sun which I have learned," Joseph stated in 1843, "and that is that *the righteousness of man is sin* because it exacteth over much; nevertheless, the righteousness of God is just, because it exacteth nothing at all, but sendeth the rain on the just and the unjust, seed time and harvest, for all of which man is ungrateful."[12]

The propensity for and susceptibility to sin are implanted in our nature at conception, just as death is (Psalm 51:5; Moses 6:55). Both death and sin are present only as potentialities at conception, and therefore neither is fully evident at birth. Death and sin do, however, become actual parts of our nature as we grow up. Sin comes spontaneously, just as death does. In the case of little children, we believe that responsibility for the results of this fallen nature (sinful actions and dispositions) are held in abeyance by virtue of the Atonement until they reach the age of eight, the time of accountability (D&C 29:46; 68:25-27; 74:7; Moses 6:53-54). When children reach the time of accountability, however, they become subject to spiritual death and must thereafter repent and come unto Christ by covenant and through the sacraments or ordinances of the gospel.

The glad tidings, the good news is that redemption from the Fall and reconciliation with the Father are possible. That redemption and reconciliation come through the finished work of Jesus the Christ. In short, salvation is in Christ. Redeemed man is man who has partaken of the powers of Christ through the Atonement, repented of his sins, and been renewed through the sanctifier, who is the Holy Ghost. The Holy Ghost is the midwife of salvation. He is the agent of the new birth, the sacred channel and power by which men and women are changed and renewed, made into new creatures. This new birth brings membership in the family of God: such persons are redeemed from the Fall, reconciled to the Father through the Son, made worthy of the designation of sons and daughters of God. They come to see and feel and understand things that the spiritually inert can never know. They be-

---

12. TPJS, 317, emphasis added.

come participants in the realm of divine experience. Brigham Young summed up our position on the Fall this way: "It requires all the atonement of Christ, the mercy of the Father, the pity of angels and the grace of the Lord Jesus Christ to be with us always, and then to do the very best we possibly can, to get rid of this sin within us, so that we may escape from this world into the celestial kingdom."[13]

A Plan of Salvation

Fundamental to the plan of God is moral agency, the divine right and capacity to choose. Agency is a gift of God, one that comes through the blessings of the Atonement of Jesus Christ. A Book of Mormon prophet explained that "the Messiah cometh in the fulness of time, that he may redeem the children of men from the fall. And because that they are redeemed from the fall, they have become free forever, knowing good from evil; to act for themselves and not to be acted upon. . . . Wherefore, men are free according to the flesh; . . . And they are free to choose liberty and eternal life, through the great Mediator of all men, or to choose captivity and death, according to the captivity and power of the devil" (2 Nephi 2:26-27). Some six hundred years later another spiritual leader declared that "whosoever perisheth, perisheth unto himself: and whosoever doeth iniquity, doeth it unto himself: for behold, ye are free; ye are permitted to act for yourselves; for behold, God hath given unto you a knowledge and he hath made you free" (Helaman 14:30; compare D&C 58:27-28; Moses 7:32).

As pointed out in chapter 1, Latter-day Saints believe that Christian doctrines have been taught and Christian sacraments administered by Christian prophets since the beginning of time. In this sense, the Saints do not accept a type of developmental or evolutionary approach to the Old and New Testaments. They do not accept the view that the antediluvians, for example, were primitives or that the so-called Christian era we generally associate with the birth or ministry of Jesus is in some way superior, on a higher plane, or more spiritually progressive than those of the Old Testament patriarchs or the prophets. It is true that we speak of the Christian era as "the meridian of time," but this

13. JD 11:301.

has reference to the centrality of Christ's ministry, teachings, and atoning sacrifice more than to the uniqueness of the message delivered in the first century.

God has revealed himself and his plan of salvation during different periods of the earth's history called *dispensations*. The Adamic dispensation was the first. LDS scripture declares that Adam and Eve, after their expulsion from the Garden of Eden, called upon God in prayer and came to know the course in life they should pursue through God's voice, by the ministry of angels, and by revelation through the power of the Holy Ghost. This gospel was then taught to their children and their grandchildren, and thus the knowledge of God, of a coming Savior, and of a plan for the redemption and reclamation of wandering souls was in effect early on (see Moses 5:1-8, 58).

Other dispensations followed, periods of time wherein the heavens were opened, prophets were called and empowered, and new truths and new authorities restored to the earth, usually following a time of falling away or apostasy. Thus the ministries and teachings of Enoch, Noah, Abraham, Moses, Jesus, and Joseph Smith introduced major dispensations, periods wherein God — his person and plan — was revealed anew. Lest there be misunderstanding at this point, I hasten to add that Jesus Christ is chief, preeminent, and supreme over all the prophets. Jesus was a prophet, a restorer, a revealer of God, but he was also the divine Son of God. While the prophets were called of God, he is God. Under the Father, his is the power by which men and women are forgiven, redeemed, and born again unto a new spiritual life. All the prophets from the beginning testified of Christ; all of those called as spokesmen or mouthpieces for God were, first and foremost, witnesses of the Redeemer, inasmuch as "the testimony of Jesus is the spirit of prophecy" (Revelation 19:10).

The Atonement

Gospel means "good news" or "glad tidings." The bad news is that because of the fall of our first parents we are subject to the effects and pull of sin and death. The bad news is that because of the fall men and women experience spiritual death — separation and alienation from the presence and influence of God and of things of righteousness. The

89

bad news is that every man, woman, and child will one day face the grim reaper, the universal horror we know as physical death. The good news is that there is help, relief, extrication from the pain and penalty of our sins. The good news is that there is reconciliation with God the Father through the mediation of his Son, Jesus Christ. The good news is that there is an atonement, literally an at-one-ment with the Father. The good news is that the victory of the grave and the sting of death is swallowed up in the power of One greater than death (1 Corinthians 15:54-55; see also Isaiah 25:8). The good news is the promise of eventual life after death through the resurrection. That victory and divine help begin in this life; we do not need to wait until after death. In short, the gospel is the good news that Christ came to earth, lived and taught and suffered and died and rose again, all to the end that those who believe and obey might be delivered from death and sin unto eternal life (D&C 76:40-42). This good news we share with Christians throughout the world.

Jesus did what no other man or woman has ever done, could do, or will do — he lived a perfect life. He was tempted in all points just as we are, but did not yield (Hebrews 4:15; 1 Peter 2:22). Jesus was the Truth and he taught the truth, and his teachings stand as the formula for happiness, the guide for personal, interpersonal, and world peace. His messages, as contained in the New Testament, are timely and timeless; they are a treasure house of wisdom and divine direction for our lives. But other men and women have spoken the truth, have offered wise counsel for our lives, and even provided profound insight as to who we are and what life is all about. Jesus did what no other person could do — he atoned for our sins and rose from the dead. Only a god, only a person with powers over death, could do such things.

While everything Jesus did from the time of his baptism until his final ascent into heaven was in some way contributive to his mission of atonement, Latter-day Saints believe that the final phase of the atonement of Christ began in the Garden of Gethsemane and was consummated on the cross of Calvary. Professor Douglas Davies has written: "Christians have paid relatively little attention to what befell Jesus in the Garden of Gethsemane compared to what happened to him at the Last Supper and on Calvary. This is as true for artists as it is for theologians. There are innumerable paintings of the Crucifixion but relatively few dealing with Christ's Passion in the garden. So, too, with theology: there is much written about the Eucharist and Christ's death but much less on his personal trial in the garden." Davies goes on to describe the master's anguish in Gethsemane as a betrayal of sorts, one instance among many during the long hours of atonement, in which Jesus was left alone, this time by the Father himself.[14]

Pastor/teacher John MacArthur, in writing of the "bitter cup" Jesus was called upon to imbibe, observed: "Never was so much sorrow emanating from the soul of one individual. We could never comprehend the depth of Christ's agony because, frankly, we cannot perceive the wickedness of sin as He could. Nor can we appreciate the terrors of divine wrath the way He did." Further, he asked: "What is the cup? It is not merely death. It is not the physical pain of the cross. It was not the scourging or the humiliation. It was not the horrible thirst, the torture of having nails driven through His body, or the disgrace of being spat upon or beaten. It was not even all of those things combined." Rather, MacArthur adds, "what Christ dreaded most about the cross — the cup from which He asked to be delivered if possible — was the outpouring of divine wrath He would have to endure from His holy Father. . . . In some mysterious way that our human minds could never fathom, God the Father would turn His face from Christ the Son, and Christ would bear the full brunt of the divine fury against sin. . . . In other words, on the cross, God imputed our sin to Christ and then punished Him for it."[15]

One of the direct consequences of sin is the withdrawal of the Father's Spirit, resulting in feelings of loss, anxiety, disappointment, fear, alienation, and guilt. Latter-day Saint scripture and prophet leaders affirm that Jesus experienced the withdrawal of the Father's Spirit and thus suffered in both body and spirit, both in the Garden of Gethsemane and on the cross of Calvary (D&C 19:15-20.) The withdrawal of the Spirit lasted for a period of hours in Gethsemane and reoccurred on the cross the next day. It was for this reason that Jesus cried out from the cross: "My God, my God, why hast thou forsaken me?" (Matthew 27:46). A Book of Mormon prophet thus described our Lord's sufferings as follows: "And he cometh into the world that he may save all men

14. *Private Passions: Betraying Discipleship on the Journey to Jerusalem* (Norwich: Canterbury Press, 2000), 77-87.
15. *The Murder of Jesus* (Nashville: Word, 2000), 63-71.

if they will hearken to his voice; for behold, he suffereth the pains of all men, yea, the pains of every living creature, both men, women, and children, who belong to the family of Adam" (2 Nephi 9:21). The difference for Latter-day Saints is their belief that the Savior's suffering in Gethsemane was not just prelude to the Atonement but a vital and important part of it. In the Book of Mormon, a prophet-king, speaking of the coming of the Messiah, said: "And lo, he shall suffer temptations, and pain of body, hunger, thirst, and fatigue, even more than man can suffer, except it be unto death; for behold, *blood cometh from every pore, so great shall be his anguish for the wickedness and the abominations of his people*" (Mosiah 3:7, emphasis added).

In a revelation given through Joseph Smith in March 1830 to Martin Harris, the resurrected Lord declared: "Therefore I command you to repent — repent, lest I smite you by the rod of my mouth, and by my wrath, and by my anger, and your sufferings be sore — how sore you know not, how exquisite you know not, yea, how hard to bear you know not. For behold, I, God, have suffered these things for all, that they might not suffer if they would repent; . . . *which suffering caused myself, even God, the greatest of all, to tremble because of pain, and to bleed at every pore*, and to suffer both body and spirit — and would that I might not drink the bitter cup and shrink — Nevertheless, glory be to the Father, and I partook and finished my preparations unto the children of men" (D&C 19:15-16, 18-20, emphasis added).

It was Brigham Young who spoke specifically on the subject of what made Jesus sweat blood in the garden. "God never bestows upon this people," President Young pointed out, "or upon an individual, superior blessings without a severe trial to prove them, to prove that individual, or that people. . . . For this express purpose *the Father withdrew His Spirit from His Son, at the time He was to be crucified.* Jesus had been with His Father, talked with Him, dwelt in His bosom, and knew all about heaven, about making the earth, and about the transgression of man, and what would redeem the people, and that he was the character who was to redeem the sons of earth, and the earth itself from all sin that had come upon it . . . , consequently at the very moment, at the hour when the crisis came for him to offer up his life, *the Father withdrew Himself, withdrew His Spirit, and cast a vail [sic] over him. That is what made him sweat blood. If he had had the power of God upon him, he would not have sweat blood;* but all was withdrawn from him, and a vail was cast over him, and he then pled with the Father not to forsake him."[16]

How this took place is unknown. We believe in Christ and trust in his redeeming mercy and grace. We accept the word of scripture, both ancient and modern, in regard to the ransoming mission of Jesus the Christ. We know from personal experience — having been transformed from pain to peace, from darkness to light — of the power in Christ to renew the human soul. But, like the rest of the Christian world, we cannot rationally comprehend the work of a God. We cannot grasp how one man can assume the effect of another man's error, and, more especially, how one man, even a man possessed of the power of God, can suffer for another's sins. The Atonement, the greatest act of mercy and love in all eternity, though real, is, for now, incomprehensible and unfathomable.

Very often I am asked why the Latter-day Saints do not believe in the saving efficacy of the cross. In point of fact, we do. As I previously mentioned, what began in Gethsemane was completed, brought to its conclusion, on the cross. President Ezra Taft Benson explained: "In Gethsemane and on Calvary, He [Christ] worked out the infinite and eternal atonement. It was the greatest single act of love in recorded history. Thus He became our Redeemer."[17] In short, it was necessary that Jesus (1) forgive our sins and thereby deliver us from spiritual death; and (2) die and then rise from the dead, to offer the hope of resurrection, thereby overcoming physical death. One Book of Mormon prophet foresaw the time, some six hundred years ahead, when Jesus would be *"lifted up upon the cross and slain for the sins of the world"* (1 Nephi 11:33, emphasis added). Notice the language of the risen Lord to the people of the Book of Mormon: "Behold, I have given unto you my gospel, and this is the gospel which I have given unto you — that I came into the world to do the will of my Father, because my Father sent me. And *my Father sent me that I might be lifted up upon the cross;* and after that I had been lifted up upon the cross, that I might draw all men unto me, that as I have been lifted up by men even so should men be lifted up by the Father, to stand before me, to be judged of their works, whether they be good or whether they be evil" (3 Nephi 27:13-14, emphasis

16. JD 3:205-206, emphasis added.
17. *Teachings of Ezra Taft Benson* (Salt Lake City: Bookcraft, 1988), 14.

added). In that spirit, Joseph F. Smith, sixth president of the Church, reminded us that "having been born anew, which is the putting away of the old man sin, and putting on of the man Christ Jesus, we have become soldiers of the Cross, having enlisted under the banner of Jehovah for time and for eternity."[18] Although Jesus was "Crushed by the ruthless power of Rome, he was himself crushing the serpent's head (as was predicted in Genesis 3:15). The victim was the victor, and the cross is still the throne from which he rules the world."[19]

Physical death is the separation of the spirit from the body. Following death, that spirit goes into a postmortal spirit world to await the time when spirit and body are reunited, the time we know as the resurrection. Latter-day Saints accept the account in the New Testament that Jesus of Nazareth died on the cross, and that his body was taken down by his disciples and placed in a tomb. On the third day he rose from the dead. His physical body was joined again with his spirit. With that physical body he walked and talked and taught and ate and ministered. The resurrection of Jesus is of monumental importance; it was the first occurrence of a resurrection on this earth and stands as a physical proof of his divine Sonship (1 Corinthians 15:12-17; 2 Nephi 9:8-9; 3 Nephi 11). Again, in a way that is incomprehensible to finite minds, Christ's rise from the tomb opened the door for all men and women to rise one day from death to life. In short, because he rose, we shall also, in the proper time.

In the Pearl of Great Price are recorded the following words of God to Moses the Lawgiver: "For behold, this is my work and my glory — to bring to pass the immortality and eternal life of man" (Moses 1:39). This is a capsule statement, a succinct summary of the work of redemption in Christ. From an LDS perspective, there are two types of salvation made available through the atonement of Jesus Christ — universal and individual. All who take a physical body — good or bad, evil or righteous — will be resurrected. That is, all men and women will one day rise from death to life, their spirits reuniting with their bodies, never again to be divided. "For as in Adam all die, even so in Christ shall all be made alive" (1 Corinthians 15:22). This is universal salvation. It is salvation from physical death, a salvation available to all. *Im-*

---

18. *Gospel Doctrine* (Salt Lake City: Deseret Book, 1971), 91.
19. John Stott, *Why I Am a Christian*, 61.

mortality is salvation from the grave. It is endless life. It is a universal gift.

Individual salvation is another matter. Though all salvation is available through the goodness and grace of Christ, there are certain things that must be done in order for divine grace and mercy to be activated in the lives of individual followers of the Christ. Persons must come unto him, accept him as Lord and Savior, and have faith on his name. The products of that faith include repentance, baptism, the reception of the Holy Spirit, and dedicated discipleship until the end of one's life. Eternal Life comes to those who believe and obey. Christ is "the author of eternal salvation unto all them that obey him" (Hebrews 5:9). One Book of Mormon prophet thus observed: "And he [Christ] shall come into the world to redeem his people; and he shall take upon him the transgressions of those who believe on his name; and these are they that shall have eternal life, and salvation cometh to none else. Therefore the wicked remain as though there had been no redemption made, except it be the loosing of the bands of death; for behold, the day cometh that all shall rise from the dead and stand before God, and be judged according to their works" (Alma 11:40-41).

Latter-day Saints believe that all men and women have the capacity to be saved. "We believe," Joseph Smith wrote in 1842, "that through the Atonement of Christ, all mankind may be saved, by obedience to the laws and ordinances of the Gospel" (Articles of Faith 1:3). Stated another way, there is no person who comes to earth who is outside the reach of Christ's power to save, no soul beyond the pale of mercy and grace. God is no respecter of persons, as Peter pointed out, "but in every nation he that feareth him, and worketh righteousness, is accepted with him" (Acts 10:34-35). Thus Latter-day Saints do not believe in predestination, that men and women are chosen or elected unconditionally to salvation or damnation. Joseph Smith taught that "unconditional election of individuals to eternal life was not taught by the Apostles. God did elect or predestinate, that all those who would be saved, should be saved in Christ Jesus, and through obedience to the Gospel; but He passes over no man's sins, but visits them with correction, and if His children will not repent of their sins He will discard them."[20]

20. TPJS, 189.

The highest rewards hereafter and the greatest happiness here are reserved for those who come unto Christ and accept his gospel. Though we acknowledge the decency of men and women of good will everywhere — the effort of many outside the Christian faith to make a positive difference in the world, and the nobility and refined character of so many who adopt other religious views — still we hold to the position that Jesus is the Christ, the Messiah, the Savior of all men and women. His message and redemptive labors are infinite in scope and meant to be accepted by all. He will one day return in glory to the earth, assume responsibility for the purification of this planet, and reign as King of kings and Lord of lords.

And so while the "wages of sin is death," the gift of God "is eternal life through Jesus Christ our Lord" (Romans 6:23). As indicated, a gift must be received. Although there is no question that salvation is in Christ and that the renovation of men and women's souls is the work of a God, persons who choose to come unto Christ are expected to be more than grateful and passive observers of the changes taking place within them. Men and women have a role to play. "We can't know Jesus as the Messiah," John MacArthur pointed out, "until we surrender to Him. . . . You will never know whether Jesus can save your soul from hell, give you new life, re-create your soul, plant His Holy Spirit there, forgive your sin, and send you to heaven until you give your life totally to Him. That is self-denial, cross bearing, and following Him in obedience. . . . I don't believe anyone ever slipped and fell into the kingdom of God. That's cheap grace, easy-believism, Christianity Lite, a shallow, emotional revivalist approach."[21] "We profanely assume," C. S. Lewis noted, "that divine and human action exclude one another like the actions of two fellow-creatures so that 'God did this' and 'I did this' cannot both be true of the same act except in the sense that each contributed a share." He continued: "In the end we must admit a two-way traffic at the junction. . . . We have nothing that we have not received; but part of what we have received is the power of being something more than receptacles."[22] As Lewis stated elsewhere, "Christians have

---

21. *Hard to Believe: The High Cost and Infinite Value of Following Jesus* (Nashville: Thomas Nelson Publishers, 2003), 67, 84.

22. *Letters to Malcolm: Chiefly on Prayer* (San Diego: Harcourt, Brace, & Co., 1964), 49-50.

often disputed as to whether what leads the Christian home is good actions, or faith in Christ. I have no right really to speak on such a difficult question, but it does seem to me like asking which blade in a pair of scissors is most necessary. . . . You see, we are now trying to understand, and to separate into water-tight compartments, what exactly God does and what man does when God and man are working together."[23]

Latter-day Saints have often been critical of those who stress salvation by grace alone, while we have often been criticized for a type of works-righteousness. We believe that the gospel is, in fact, a gospel *covenant*. The Lord agrees to do for us what we could never do for ourselves — to forgive our sins, to lift our burdens, to renew our souls and re-create our nature, to raise us from the dead and qualify us for glory hereafter. Whereupon, we strive to do what we *can* do: have faith in Christ, repent of our sins, be baptized, love and serve one another, and do all in our power to put off the natural man and deny ourselves of ungodliness. In short, we believe that more is required of men and women than a verbal expression of faith in the Lord, more than a confession with the lips that we have received Christ into our hearts. Without question, the power to save us, to change us, to renew our souls, is in Christ. True faith, however, always manifests itself in *faithfulness*. Thus, the real question is not whether one is saved by grace or by works but rather, In whom do we trust? On whom do we rely?

Few things would be more sinister than encouraging lip service to God while discouraging obedience and faithful discipleship. On the other hand, surely nothing could be more offensive to God than a smug self-assurance that comes from trusting in one's own works or relying upon one's own strength. What is perhaps the most well known passage in LDS literature on this delicate matter is found in the Book of Mormon: "For we labor diligently to write, to persuade our children, and also our brethren, to believe in Christ, and to be reconciled to God; *for we know that it is by grace that we are saved, after all we can do*" (2 Nephi 25:23, emphasis added; see also 10:24; Alma 24:10-11). That is, above and beyond all we can do, in spite of all we can do, notwithstanding all we can do, we are saved by the grace of Christ. Further, the more we learn

---

23. *Mere Christianity* (New York: Touchstone, 1996), 131-32; see also *Christian Reunion*, 18.

to trust the Lord and rely upon his merits and mercy, the less anxious we become about life here and hereafter. "Thus, if you have really handed yourself over to Him, it must follow that you are trying to obey Him. But trying in a new way, a less worried way."[24]

Justification and Sanctification

At the time of the organization of The Church of Jesus Christ of Latter-day Saints in April of 1830, Joseph Smith recorded the following revelation: "And we know that all men must repent and believe on the name of Jesus Christ, and worship the Father in his name, and endure in faith on his name to the end, or they cannot be saved in the kingdom of God." Now note these words: "And we know that justification through the grace of our Lord and Savior Jesus Christ is just and true; and we know also that sanctification through the grace of our Lord and Savior Jesus Christ is just and true, to all those who love and serve God with all their mights, minds, and strength" (D&C 20:29-31).

One Church leader, Elder D. Todd Christofferson, pointed out that "Justification and sanctification are at the center of God's gracious plan of salvation." In speaking of justification, he wrote that "Pardon comes by the grace of Him who has satisfied the demands of justice by His own suffering, 'the just for the unjust, that he might bring us to God' (1 Peter 3:18). He removes our condemnation without removing the law. We are pardoned and placed in a condition of righteousness with Him. We become, like Him, without sin. We are sustained and protected by the law, by justice. We are, in a word, *justified*. Thus, we may appropriately speak of one who is justified as pardoned, without sin, or guiltless."[25]

Sidney B. Sperry wrote that "justification seems to anticipate for a Christian a decision of 'acquittal' or of being regarded as 'righteous' in a future divine judgment. Can a member of the Church of Christ be regarded in the present time as being justified by faith? If he has truly been 'born again' of the Spirit and continues in a newness of life, we may answer 'yes.' In anticipation of his continued observance of the re-

---

24. C. S. Lewis, *Mere Christianity*, 131.
25. "Justification and Sanctification," *Ensign*, June 2001, 18, 20.

quirements of God, he may be regarded as 'acquitted' or as 'righteous,' and so is in divine favor. A comparison may be made by reference to a man on an escalator. We anticipate that he will reach a given floor if he stays on the escalator. So a person will eventually be justified, but may be regarded as being so now, if he retains a remission of sins (Mosiah 4:26) and continually shows his faith in God."[26]

Elder Christofferson added that "to be sanctified through the blood of Christ is to become clean, pure, and holy. If justification removes the punishment for past sin, then sanctification removes the stain or effects of sin. . . . This marvelous pardon that relieves us of the punishment that justice would otherwise exact for disobedience and the purifying sanctification that follows are best described as gifts. . . . *Given the magnitude of the gift of grace, we would never suppose, even with all the good we could possibly do in this life, that we had earned it. It is just too great.*"[27]

To say this another way, justification is a legal term; being justified establishes my righteous *standing* before God. On the other hand, sanctification is an ongoing work of the Holy Spirit, one that deals with the gradual purification of my *state*. One early twentieth-century leader, B. H. Roberts, insightfully taught that the forgiven soul may still continue to "feel the force of sinful habits bearing heavily upon him. He who has been guilty of habitual untruthfulness, will at times find himself inclined, perhaps, to yield to that habit. He who has stolen may be sorely tempted, when opportunity arises, to steal again. While he who has indulged in licentious practices may again find himself disposed to give way to the seductive influence of the siren. So with drunkenness, malice, envy, covetousness, hatred, anger, and in short all the evil dispositions that flesh is heir to.

"*There is an absolute necessity for some additional sanctifying grace that will strengthen the poor human nature, not only to enable it to resist temptation, but also to root out from the heart concupiscence — the blind tendency or inclination to evil.* The heart must be purified, every passion, every propensity made submissive to the will, and the will of man brought into subjection to the will of God.

"*Man's natural powers are unequal to this task;* so, I believe, all will tes-

---

26. *Paul's Life and Letters* (Salt Lake City: Bookcraft, 1955), 176.
27. "Justification and Sanctification," 22, emphasis added.

tify who have made the experiment. *Mankind stand in some need of a strength superior to any they possess of themselves, to accomplish this work of rendering pure our fallen nature. Such strength, such power, such a sanctifying grace is conferred on man in being born of the Spirit — in receiving the Holy Ghost.* Such, in the main, is its office, its work."[28]

The Doctrine and Covenants poses this question: "For what doth it profit a man if a gift is bestowed upon him, and he receive not the gift? Behold, he rejoices not in that which is given unto him, neither rejoices in him who is the giver of the gift" (D&C 88:33). Thus while we are justified and sanctified through the mercy of God, yet such gifts must be received, must be accessed. This comes through what are known as the first principles and ordinances of the gospel — namely, faith in Jesus Christ, repentance, baptism, and the receipt of the Holy Ghost by the laying on of hands. Joseph Smith also called these the "articles of adoption," the means by which men and women are adopted into the family of the Lord Jesus Christ.[29] Again, in a very real sense, repentance, baptism, and confirmation are the *effects* that flow from saving faith.

Orson Pratt, an early LDS apostle and contemporary of Joseph Smith and Brigham Young, wrote that "Faith alone will not save men: neither will faith and works save them, unless they are of the right kind. . . . The first effect of a true faith is a sincere, true, and thorough repentance of all sins; the second effect is an immersion in water, for the remission of sins; the third is the reception of the ordinance of the laying on of the hands for the baptism of the Holy Ghost: these are the first commandments in the Gospel. No man has a saving faith without attending to these three requirements. . . . Indeed these are the introductory principles, and the only principles by which men and women can be born into the kingdom of Christ, and become his sons and daughters. . . .

"A faith, then, that brings remission of sins or justification to the sinner, is that which is connected with repentance and baptism. Faith alone will not justify; faith and repentance alone will not justify; faith and baptism alone will not justify; but faith, repentance, and baptism will justify and bring remission of sins through the blood of Christ.

---

28. *The Gospel and Man's Relationship to Deity* (Salt Lake City: Deseret Book, 1966), 169-70, emphasis added.

29. TPJS, 328; see also *Orson Pratt's Works* (Salt Lake City: Deseret News Press, 1945), 48.

What does Paul mean when he says, 'Therefore being justified by faith, we have peace with God, through our Lord Jesus Christ?' He means that *faith is the starting point — the foundation and cause of our repentance and baptism which bring remission or justification;* and being the cause which leads to those results, it is not improper to impute justification to faith."

And then, in commenting on the apostle Paul's teaching that "by grace are [we] saved" in Ephesians 2, Brother Pratt explained: "We are to understand from these passages, that the grace and faith by which man is saved, are the gifts of God, having been purchased by him not by his own works, but by the blood of Christ. Had not these gifts been purchased for man, all exertions on his part would have been entirely unavailing and fruitless. Whatever course man might have pursued, he could not have atoned for one sin; it required the sacrifice of a sinless and pure Being in order to purchase the gifts of faith, repentance, and salvation for fallen man. *Grace, Faith, Repentance, and Salvation, when considered in their origin, are not of man, neither by his works; man did not devise, originate, nor adopt them; superior Beings in Celestial abodes, provided these gifts, and revealed the conditions to man by which he might become a partaker of them.* Therefore all boasting on the part of man is excluded. He is saved by a plan which his works did not originate, a plan of heaven, and not of earth."[30]

In short, as one has faith, repents, and is baptized, he or she is justified before God. Thereafter, by virtue of the Atonement, as well as the baptism which has taken place, a person may plead for forgiveness and receive from God a remission of sins. "None of us, of course, is perfectly obedient, and thus we rely on our baptismal covenant to bring a remission of sins after baptism just as it has done for our lives before baptism. We rely on repentance to reinvigorate that covenant [or to "renew" one's covenant], to bring the Holy Spirit and, with it, atoning grace. The process of cleansing and sanctifying through the baptisms of water and of the Holy Ghost can be continued weekly as we worthily partake of the sacrament of the Lord's Supper."[31] To be sure, the sacrament or ordinance of baptism does not save, nor does partaking of the

---

30. "The True Faith," in *A Series of Pamphlets* (Liverpool: Franklin D. Richards, 1852), 3-9, emphasis added; see also *Orson Pratt's Works,* 51.

31. Christofferson, "Justification and Sanctification," 24.

emblems of the Savior's broken body and spilt blood, for salvation is in Christ the Person; rather, baptism and the sacrament of the Lord's Supper are channels of divine grace that help to activate the power of God in a person's life.

In one sense, a person is sanctified at the time he or she enters the kingdom of God following baptism. The initiate is cleansed of sin and accounted a Saint, a sanctified one, a member of Christ's Church (1 Corinthians 1:2). At the same time, the process of sanctification goes forward for the rest of one's life. Brigham Young explained that sanctification "consists in overcoming every sin and bringing all in subjection to the law of Christ. God has placed in us a pure spirit; when this reigns predominant, without let or hindrance, and triumphs over the flesh and rules and governs and controls as the Lord controls the heavens and the earth, this I call the blessing of sanctification. Will sin be perfectly destroyed?" Brigham Young inquired. "No, it will not, for it is not so designed in the economy of heaven. . . . Do not suppose that we shall ever in the flesh be free from temptations to sin. Some suppose that they can in the flesh be sanctified body and spirit and become so pure that they will never again feel the effects of the power of the adversary of truth. Were it possible for a person to attain to this degree of perfection in the flesh, he could not die neither remain in a world where sin predominates. Sin has entered into the world, and death by sin. I think we shall more or less feel the effects of sin so long as we live, and finally have to pass the ordeals of death. . . . If we live our religion it will enable us to overcome sin that it will not reign in our mortal bodies but will become subject to us, and the world and its fulness will become our servant instead of our master."[32]

Prevenient Grace

One group of scholars have defined prevenient grace as follows: "A designation of the priority of God's gracious initiative on behalf of humans." This prevenient grace "precedes all human response to God's initiative." For Calvinists, it "is bestowed only on those God elects to eternal life through faith in Jesus Christ." For Arminians, it "is the

---

32. JD 10:173.

Holy Spirit's work in the hearts of all people, which gives them the freedom to say yes to the gospel."[33]

Although Latter-day Saints believe that salvation is available to all men and women (Articles of Faith 1:3), they acknowledge at the same time that the effects of the Fall tend to entice humankind away from God, from godliness, and from an acceptance of the gospel of Jesus Christ. To counteract this influence, there are unconditional blessings and benefits — graces that flow from the Almighty. For one thing, Latter-day Saints believe that every man and woman born into mortality possesses the Light of Christ or the Spirit of Jesus Christ. This inner light is given to each of us to lead us to God, to Christ, and to the gospel. One important manifestation of the Light of Christ is what we call conscience, a kind of moral monitor by which people know right from wrong, good from evil, important from insignificant. If persons are true to this light within them, they will in time be led to higher light and deeper understanding (Moroni 7:12-19; D&C 84:44-48).

Note this language from an early Book of Mormon prophet: "Adam fell that men might be; and men are, that they might have joy. And the Messiah cometh in the fulness of time, that he may redeem the children of men from the fall." Now pay particular attention to the following: "And *because that they are redeemed from the fall they have become free forever, knowing good from evil; to act for themselves and not to be acted upon*. . . . Wherefore, men are free according to the flesh. . . . And they are free to choose liberty and eternal life, through the great Mediator of all men, or to choose captivity and death, according to the captivity and power of the devil; for he seeketh that all men might be miserable like unto himself" (2 Nephi 2.25-27, emphasis added; compare 2 Nephi 10:23).

Some six hundred years later, a prophet pleaded with a wayward people: "And now remember, remember, my brethren, that whosoever perisheth, perisheth unto himself; and whosoever doeth iniquity, doeth it unto himself; for behold, ye are free; ye are permitted to act for yourselves; for behold, God hath given unto you a knowledge and he hath made you free. He hath given unto you that you might know good

---

33. Stanley J. Grenz, David Guretzki, and Cherith Fee Nordling, *Pocket Dictionary of Theological Terms* (Downers Grove, IL: InterVarsity, 1999), 95.

from evil, and he hath given unto you that you might choose life or death" (Helaman 14:30-31). In the Doctrine and Covenants the early Latter-day Saints were instructed that "men should be anxiously engaged in a good cause, and *do many things of their own free will, and bring to pass much righteousness; for the power is in them, wherein they are agents unto themselves*" (D&C 58:27-28, emphasis added).

Saved: Today and Tomorrow

Do Latter-day Saints, then, consider themselves to be "saved Christians"? In April of 1998 LDS Apostle Dallin H. Oaks addressed this question in a general conference of the Church. He pointed out that the Latter-day Saints use the words *saved* or *salvation* in several ways: saved from the permanence of physical death through the resurrection of Christ; saved in the sense of having been born again, having died to sin and come alive to things of righteousness; saved in the sense of having escaped ignorance concerning God, Jesus Christ, and the plan of salvation; saved from the second death or final spiritual death; saved from sin on conditions of repentance; and saved in the sense of being exalted through the receipt of temple ordinances, a matter which will be discussed shortly.[34]

Latter-day Saints identify, to some extent, with the following from evangelical theologian John Stott: "Salvation is a big and comprehensive word. It embraces the totality of God's saving work, from beginning to end. In fact, salvation has three tenses, past, present, and future. . . . I have been saved (in the past) from the penalty of sin by a crucified Saviour. I am being saved (in the present) from the power of sin by a living Saviour. And I shall be saved (in the future) from the very presence of sin by a coming Saviour. . . .

"If therefore you were to ask me. 'Are you saved?' there is only one correct biblical answer which I could give you: 'yes and no.' Yes, in the sense that by the sheer grace and mercy of God through the death of Jesus Christ my Saviour he has forgiven my sins, justified me and reconciled me to himself. But no, in the sense that I still have a fallen nature and live in a fallen world and have a corruptible body, and I am

34. See Conference Report, April 1998, 75-79.

longing for my salvation to be brought to its triumphant comple-tion."[35]

Well then, do the Latter-day Saints believe they are saved? What about "eternal security"? Or do they, as some have suggested to me, live in constant anxiety and morbid fear because they sense they must "save themselves"? Whereas the ultimate blessings of salvation do not come until the next life, there is a sense in which people in this life may enjoy the assurance of salvation and the peace that accompanies that knowl-edge (D&C 59:23). True faith in Christ produces *hope in Christ* — not worldly wishing but *expectation, anticipation, assurance.* As the apostle Paul wrote, the Holy Spirit provides the "earnest of our inheritance," the promise or evidence that we are on course, in covenant, and thus in line for full salvation in the world to come (2 Corinthians 1:21-22; 5:5; Ephesians 1:13-14). That is, the Spirit of God operating in our lives is like the Lord's "earnest money" on us — his sweet certification that he seriously intends to save us with an everlasting salvation. Thus if we are striving to cultivate the gift of the Holy Spirit, we are living in what might be called a "saved" condition.

David O. McKay, ninth president of the Church, taught that "The gospel of Jesus Christ, as revealed to the Prophet Joseph Smith, is in very deed, in every way, the power of God unto salvation. It is salvation here and now. It gives to every man the perfect life, here and now, as well as hereafter."[36] On another occasion, President McKay taught: "Sometimes we think of salvation as a state of bliss after we die. *I should like to think of salvation as a condition here in life today.* I like to think that my Church makes me a better man, my wife a better woman, a sweeter wife, my children nobler sons and daughters, here and now. I look upon the gospel as a power contributing to those conditions."[37] Brigham Young stated: "*It is present salvation and the present influence of the Holy Ghost that we need every day to keep us on saving ground. . . . I want present salvation. . . . Life is for us, and it for us to receive it today, and not wait for the Millennium. Let us take a course to be saved today,* and, when evening comes, review the acts of the day, repent of our sins, if we have any to re-

35. *Authentic Christianity from the Writings of John Stott,* ed. Timothy Dudley-Smith (Downers Grove, IL: InterVarsity, 1995), 168; see also *Why I Am a Christian,* 83.

36. *Gospel Ideals* (Salt Lake City: The Improvement Era, 1953), 6.

37. Remarks at the dedication of the San Mateo, California, meetinghouse on 22 February 1953; reported in *Church News,* 28 February 1953, emphasis added.

pent of, and say our prayers; then we can lie down and sleep in peace until the morning, arise with gratitude to God, commence the labors of another day, and strive to live the whole day to God and nobody else."[38]

"I am in the hands of the Lord," President Young pointed out, "and never trouble myself" about my salvation, or what the Lord will do with me hereafter."[39] As he said on another occasion, our work "is a work of the present. *The salvation we are seeking is for the present, and sought correctly, it can be obtained, and be continually enjoyed.* If it continues today, it is upon the same principle that it will continue tomorrow, the next day, the next week, or the next year, and, we might say, the next eternity."[40]

I like the thought that has been expressed that heaven "is not, so to speak, the reward for 'being a good boy' (though many people seem to think so), but is the continuation and expansion of a quality of life which begins when a man's central confidence is transferred from himself to God-become-man [Jesus Christ]." It is fascinating "that Jesus Christ on more than one occasion is reported to have spoken of 'eternal life' as being entered into *now*, though plainly to extend without limitation after the present incident we call life. The man who believes in the authenticity of His message and puts his confidence in it already possesses the quality of 'eternal life' (John 3:36; 5:24; 6:47). He comes to bring men not merely 'life,' but life of a deeper and more enduring quality (John 10:10; 10:28; 17:3)."[41]

Salvation is a process, one that begins with hearing the word, being transformed by the power of that word, coming into the kingdom of God by covenant and ordinance, and then remaining in the gospel harness. One's spiritual growth and maturity take place line upon line, precept upon precept, here a little and there a little (Isaiah 28:10; 2 Nephi 28:30). Truly, as Paul wrote, "now is our salvation nearer than when we believed" (Romans 13:11). The Saints can thus be possessed of that confidence that "he which hath begun a good work in you will perform it until the day of Jesus Christ" (Philippians 1:6). Our task is

---

38. JD 8:124-25, emphasis added.
39. Ibid., 6:276.
40. Ibid., 1:131, emphasis added.
41. J. B. Phillips, *Your God Is Too Small* (New York: Touchstone, 1997), 115.

thus to "stand still, with the utmost assurance, to see the salvation of God" (D&C 123:17; compare Exodus 14:13).

While a man or woman may receive the conditional assurance of salvation in this life through the influence of the Spirit — the quiet but compelling realization that one is on course and thus in line for full salvation hereafter — the Latter-day Saints also speak a great deal about "enduring to the end," that is, remaining constant, steadfast and immovable in the faith (Mosiah 5:15) until he or she is called upon to pass through death. Thus the promise is that "whosoever repenteth shall find mercy; and he that findeth mercy and endureth to the end the same shall be saved" (Alma 32:13). Also: "And, if you keep my commandments and endure to the end you shall have eternal life, which gift is the greatest of all the gifts of God" (D&C 14:7). Finally, "blessed are they who are faithful and endure, whether in life or in death, for they shall inherit eternal life" (D&C 50:5). Endurance to the end entails walking in the light as Christ is in the light (1 John 1:7), striving to manifest our faith through our faithfulness. Truly, "The only visible evidence you will ever have of your salvation is a life lived in the direction of obedience; it is the proof that you genuinely have bowed to the lordship of Jesus Christ and been transformed by His grace into a servant of His righteousness."[42]

A Broad Concept of Salvation

As early as February 1832 Joseph Smith declared that the life beyond consists of more than heaven and hell. He recorded a revelation known as "The Vision of the Glories" or simply "The Vision" (D&C 76). This vision serves as a type of commentary on the Master's words that "in my Father's house are many mansions" (John 14:2) and on the apostle Paul's passing comment to the Corinthians about types of bodies in the resurrection (1 Corinthians 15:40-42). Joseph stated that God revealed to him the concept of three main divisions in the afterlife — in descending order (in terms of the greatest eternal reward), the celestial kingdom, terrestrial kingdom, and telestial kingdom, each of which is a kingdom of glory.

42. MacArthur, *Hard to Believe*, 112-13.

The Latter-day Saints believe that hell has two meanings: (1) that division of the postmortal spirit world where those who have lived wickedly and have spurned morality and decency reside following their death and until the time of their resurrection; and, ultimately, (2) the final abode of those called the "sons of perdition," persons who deny and defy the truth, who come to know God and then fight against him and his plan of salvation (D&C 76:31-35). The sons of perdition are the only ones who face the second death, meaning the second or final spiritual death. They inherit a kingdom of no glory. Everyone else will come forth from the grave to inherit a kingdom of glory.

In that sense, Latter-day Saints believe in a type of universal salvation, not in the sense that everyone will one day dwell with God and be like God, but rather that all (who do not defect to perdition) will enjoy a measure of God's goodness and grace through inheriting a heaven of some type.[43] For one thing, all persons who have had a physical body will be resurrected, "for as in Adam all die, even so in Christ shall all be made alive" (1 Corinthians 15:21-22). Or, as a Book of Mormon prophet put it, "the day cometh that all shall rise from the dead and stand before God, and be judged according to their works" (Alma 11:41). As stated in the Vision, "And this is the gospel, the glad tidings, . . . that he came into the world, even Jesus, to be crucified for the world, and to bear the sins of the world, and to sanctify the world, and to cleanse it from all unrighteousness; that through him all might be saved whom the Father had put into his power and made by him; who glorifies the Father, and saves all the works of his hands, except those sons of perdition who deny the Son after the Father has revealed him" (D&C 76:40-43).

This idea is not totally foreign to other Christians. In the words of popular writer Bruce Wilkinson, "Although your eternal destination is based on your belief [in Jesus Christ as Lord and Savior], how you spend eternity is based on your behavior while on earth." Thus "The Unbreakable Link" is stated as follows: "Your choices on earth have direct consequences on your life in eternity." Discipleship flows from true conversion. That is, "Doing is a servant's language of devotion." In

---

43. See John A. Widtsoe, *Evidences and Reconciliations* (Salt Lake City: Bookcraft, 1960), 198-201.

short, "there will be degrees of reward in heaven."[44] Jonathan Edwards stated that "There are many mansions in God's house because heaven is intended for various degrees of honor and blessedness. Some are designed to sit in higher places there than others; some are designed to be advanced to higher degrees of honor and glory than others are."[45] Similarly, John Wesley spoke of some persons enjoying "higher degrees of glory" hereafter. "There is an inconceivable variety in the degrees of reward in the other world. . . . In worldly things men are ambitious to get as high as they can. Christians have a far more noble ambition. The difference between the very highest and the lowest state in the world is nothing to the smallest difference between the degrees of glory."[46]

While I was sitting with a group of religious scholars once, they commented to me that the problem with the LDS conception of heaven is that *everyone* is saved. I thought of that conversation as I later read the following from a Roman Catholic scholar, Richard John Neuhaus: "The hope that all may be saved . . . offends some Christians. It is as though salvation were a zero-sum proposition, as though there is only so much to go around, as though God's grace to others will somehow diminish our portion of grace. . . . If we love others, it seems that we must hope that, in the end, they will be saved. We must hope that all will one day hear the words of Christ, 'Today you will be with me in paradise.' Given the evidence of Scripture and tradition, we cannot deny that hell exists. We can, however, hope that hell is empty. We cannot know that, but we can hope it is the case."[47]

While our faith and conduct in this mortal experience are vital, learning and growth and redemption continue well beyond the grave. "When you climb up a ladder," Joseph Smith explained only two months before his death, "you must begin at the bottom, and ascend step by step, until you arrive at the top; and so it is with the principles of the gospel — you must begin with the first, and go on until you learn all the principles of exaltation. But it will be a great while after you have passed through the veil [of death] before you will have learned them. It is not all to be comprehended in this world; it will be a great

---

44. *A Life God Rewards: Why Everything You Do Today Matters Forever* (Sisters, OR: Multnomah Publishers, 2002), 23, 25, 73, 98.

45. Jonathan Edwards, cited in Wilkinson, *A Life God Rewards*, 119.

46. John Wesley, cited in Wilkinson, *A Life God Rewards*, 120-21.

47. *Death on a Friday Afternoon* (New York: Basic Books, 2000), 57, 61.

work to learn our salvation and exaltation even beyond the grave."[48] As Charles W. Penrose once stated, "While there is one soul of this race, willing and able to accept and obey the laws of redemption, no matter where or in what condition it may be found, Christ's work will be incomplete until that being is brought up from death and hell, and placed in a position of progress, upward and onward, in such glory as is possible for its enjoyment and the service of the great God."[49]

Temples and Salvation

It is not uncommon to have one of my Christian friends, particularly one who knows me well and senses my commitment to Jesus Christ, ask me: "Bob, if you sincerely believe in the ransoming power and completed work of Jesus Christ, why do you as a people build and attend temples? Is salvation really in Christ, or must you enter the temple to be saved?" This is an excellent question, one that has forced me to ponder carefully upon the place and meaning of temples in LDS theology. President Gordon B. Hinckley taught that "Each temple built by The Church of Jesus Christ of Latter-day Saints stands as an expression of the testimony of this people that God our Eternal Father lives, that He has a plan for the blessing of His sons and daughters of all generations, that His Beloved Son, Jesus the Christ, who was born in Bethlehem of Judea and was crucified on the cross of Golgotha, is the Savior and Redeemer of the world, whose atoning sacrifice makes possible the fulfillment of that plan in the eternal life of each who accepts and lives the gospel." "These unique and wonderful buildings," he stated on another occasion, "and the ordinances administered therein, represent the ultimate in our worship. These ordinances become the most profound expressions of our theology." Thus the temple is "a statement that we as a people believe in the immortality of the human soul. . . . It speaks of life here and life beyond the grave."[50]

Like most Christians, we believe that the ancient tabernacle and temples were types of the Savior. That is, the "placement, the furniture,

---

48. TPJS, 348.
49. "Mormon Doctrine" (Salt Lake City: George Q. Cannon & Sons, 1897), 72.
50. *Teachings of Gordon B. Hinckley* (Salt Lake City: Deseret Book, 1997), 623, 636, 638.

the clothing — each item was specified by the Lord to bear witness, in typology, symbolism and similitude of Jesus Christ and his atoning sacrifice."[51] This appears to be the message of Hebrews, chapters 9-10. "Accordingly," one LDS writer has observed, "it should not seem surprising that the Atonement is a focal point of modern temple worship, just as it was in ancient times."[52] The temple and its ordinances are the highest channel of grace, indeed, the culminating channel, the means by which men and women are endowed with power from on high (see Luke 24:49). These ordinances serve as extensions and reminders of the Lord's infinite and eternal Atonement. In that sense, "The rebirth that climaxes all rebirths is in the House of the Lord."[53]

The covenants and ordinances of the temple "embody certain obligations on the part of the individual," such that he or she promises "to observe the law of strict virtue and chastity, to be charitable, benevolent, tolerant and pure; to devote both talent and material means to the spread of truth and the uplifting of the race; to maintain devotion to the cause of truth; and to seek in every way to contribute to the great preparation that the earth may be made ready to receive her King — the Lord Jesus Christ."[54] As Tad Callister has written, "An integral part of the temple experience is the making of covenants. Why? Because faithful observance of these covenants can help to bring about the broken heart and contrite spirit that allow us to more fully enjoy the infinite blessings of the Atonement." Further, "It is our privilege, in the sanctuary of these holy places, to commune and reflect more meaningfully upon the Savior and his vicarious act of love for each of us, and then to receive of that endowing power that lifts us heavenward." In short, "The Atonement is the focal point of each saving ordinance."[55]

Because the ordinances or sacraments are essential — inasmuch as they represent, symbolize, and consummate our covenants with Christ — each son or daughter of God must receive the sacraments in order to gain the highest of eternal rewards. If the opportunity to receive such rites is not possible in mortality, it will be made available in the world

51. Tad R. Callister, *The Infinite Atonement* (Salt Lake City: Deseret Book, 2000), 294.
52. Ibid., 295.
53. Truman G. Madsen, "The Temple and the Atonement," in *Temples of the Ancient World*, ed. Donald W. Parry (Salt Lake City: Deseret Book and FARMS, 1994), 72.
54. James E. Talmage, *The House of the Lord* (Salt Lake City: Deseret Book, 1969), 84.
55. *The Infinite Atonement*, 296.

to come. Thus temples become the place of covenant, the place of ordinance, for both the living and the dead. A living person may thus enter the temple and be baptized, for example, in behalf of one who has died. "This is a sanctuary of service," President Hinckley pointed out. "Most of the work done in this sacred house is performed vicariously in behalf of those who have passed beyond the veil of death. I know of no other work to compare with it. It more nearly approaches the vicarious sacrifice of the Son of God in behalf of all mankind than any other work of which I am aware. . . . It is a service of the living in behalf of the dead. It is a service which is of the very essence of selflessness."[56] In short, "As the mission of the Church is to 'invite all to come unto Christ,' so I believe, in its clearest and loveliest sense, that this is also the mission of temples, where we not only undertake the sacred service of work for redemption of the dead, to open the door for them, but where the choicest of all opportunities exists to learn of Christ, and to come to know him and commune with him and to purify our own hearts."[57]

I sat at lunch some time ago with a dear friend of mine, an evangelical minister. On many occasions we had met to chat, to reflect on one another's faith, to ask hard questions, to seek to better understand one another. On this particular occasion, we were discussing grace and works. I had assured my friend that Latter-day Saints do in fact believe in, accept, and rely upon the saving mercy of Jesus. "But Bob," he said, "you folks believe you have to do so many things to be saved!" "Like what?" I asked. "Well," he continued, "let's just take baptism, for example. You believe that baptism is what saves you." "No we don't," I responded. "Yes you do," he followed up. "You believe baptism is essential for entrance into the celestial kingdom." "Yes," I said, "while baptism or other ordinances are necessary as channels of divine power and grace, they are not the things that save us. *Jesus* saves us!" While Latter-day Saints believe and teach that the highest form of salvation or exaltation comes to those who receive the blessings of the temple (D&C 131:1-4), we do not in any way believe that it is the temple, or the ordinances contained there, that saves us. Salvation is in Christ. We be-

---

56. *Teachings of Gordon B. Hinckley,* 635.

57. Marion D. Hanks, "Christ Manifested to His People," in *Temples of the Ancient World,* 16.

lieve the temple to be a house of learning, of communion and inspiration, of covenants and ordinances, of service, and of personal refinement. We believe the temple is the house of the Lord. But it is not the Lord. We look to Christ the Person for salvation.

The Glorification of Man

The final point I wish to make in this chapter is that Jesus Christ — the One we believe was and is the eternal Jehovah, as well as the Savior of the New Testament — is an unselfish being. While he is a glorified, exalted, perfected personage, he is also one who yearns to forgive our sins and purify our hearts, one who delights to honor those who serve him in righteousness and in truth (D&C 76:5). That is, he is not possessive of his powers, nor is he hesitant about dispensing spiritual gifts or sharing his divine attributes. In the words of Max Lucado, "God loves you just the way you are, but he refuses to leave you that way. He wants you to be just like Jesus."[58] Dallas Willard likewise noted that "Jesus offers himself as God's doorway into the life that is truly life. Confidence in him leads us today, as in other times, to become his apprentices in eternal living."[59]

Joseph Smith taught that all those who keep God's commandments "shall grow up from grace to grace, and become heirs of the heavenly kingdom, and joint heirs with Jesus Christ; possessing the same mind, being transformed into the same image or likeness." Truly, "As the Son partakes of the fulness of the Father through the Spirit, so the Saints are, by the same Spirit, to be partakers of the same fulness, to enjoy the same glory; for as the Father and Son are one, so, in like manner, the Saints are to be one in them. Through the love of the Father, the mediation of Jesus Christ, and the gift of the Holy Spirit, they are to be heirs of God, and joint heirs with Jesus Christ."[60]

God is the Father of the spirits of all men and women (Numbers 16:22; 27:16), the source of light and truth, the embodiment of all godly

---

58. *Just Like Jesus* (Dallas: W Publishing Group, 2003), 3.

59. *The Divine Conspiracy: Rediscovering Our Hidden Life in God* (San Francisco: Harper, 1998), 12.

60. *Lectures on Faith* (Salt Lake City: Deseret Book, 1985), 5:2-3.

attributes and gifts, the Father of lights, and the supreme power and intelligence over all things. On the one hand, we worship a divine Being with whom we can identify. That is to say, his infinity does not preclude either his immediacy or his intimacy. "In the day that God created man," LDS scripture attests, "in the likeness of God made he him; in the image of his own body, male and female, created he them" (Moses 6:8-9). We believe that God is not simply a spirit influence, a force in the universe, or the First Great Cause; when we pray "Our Father which art in heaven" (Matthew 6:9), we mean what we say. We believe God is comprehensible, knowable, approachable, and, like his Beloved Son, touched with the feeling of our infirmities (Hebrews 4:15).

On the other hand, our God is God. There is no knowledge of which the Father is ignorant and no power he does not possess (1 Nephi 7:12; 2 Nephi 9:20; Mosiah 4:9; Alma 26:35; Helaman 9:41; Ether 3:4). We feel that scriptural passages that speak of him being the same yesterday, today, and forever (e.g., Psalm 102:27; Hebrews 1:12; 13:8; 1 Nephi 10:18-19; 2 Nephi 27:23; Alma 7:20; Mormon 9:8-11, 19; Moroni 8:18; 10:7; D&C 3:2; 20:12, 17; 35:1) clearly have reference to his divine attributes — his love, justice, constancy, and willingness to bless his children.

We come to the earth to take a physical body, be schooled and gain experiences here that we could not have in the "first estate" (Jude 1:6), the premortal life. We then strive to keep the commandments and grow in faith and spiritual graces until we are prepared to go where God and Christ are. From the Doctrine and Covenants: "That which is of God is light; and he that receiveth light, and continueth in God, receiveth more light; and that light groweth brighter and brighter until the perfect day" (D&C 50:24). That "perfect day" is the resurrection, the day when spirit and body are inseparably united in immortal glory. That is, those "who are quickened by a portion of the celestial glory [in this life] shall then [in the resurrection] receive of the same, even a fulness" (D&C 88:29). In another place in the Doctrine and Covenants we are instructed that those who come unto Christ, follow his path to the Father, and thus realize the fruits of true worship, are empowered to "come unto the Father in my name, and in due time receive of his fulness" (D&C 93:19). This is what Latter-day Saints call gaining eternal life.

Let's define some terms at this point. *Salvation,* as we have said, is the greatest of all the gifts of God (D&C 6:13; 14:7). To be saved is to have eternal life and thus to be qualified to inherit the highest heaven. The word *salvation* lays stress upon one's saved condition, his or her state being one of deliverance from death and sin through the atoning sacrifice of Jesus Christ. "Eternal" is one of the names of God (D&C 19:11-12), and thus to possess *eternal life* is to enjoy God's life. More specifically, eternal life consists of (1) the continuation of the family unit into eternity, through compliance with the covenants and ordinances of the temple; and (2) inheriting, receiving, and possessing the fulness of the glory of the Father (D&C 132:19). To possess *exaltation* is to possess eternal life, to be entitled to the blessings of the highest degree of the celestial kingdom. The word *exaltation* lays stress upon the elevated and ennobled status of one who qualifies for the society of the redeemed and glorified. Essentially, salvation, exaltation, and eternal life, in their purest sense, are synonymous terms.[61]

Eternal life consists in being *with* God; in addition, it entails being *like* God. "People who live long lives together," Max Lucado observed, "eventually begin to sound alike, to talk alike, even to think alike. As we walk with God, we take on his thoughts, his principles, his attitudes. We take on his heart."[62] That is, we begin to be more and more like God. A study of Christian history reveals that the doctrine of the deification of man was taught at least into the fifth century by such notables as Irenaeus, Clement of Alexandria, Justin Martyr, Athanasius, and Augustine.[63] Latter-day Saints might not agree with some of what was taught about deification by such Christian thinkers, but it is clear that the idea was not foreign to the people of the early church.

All men and women, like Christ, are made in the image and likeness of God (Genesis 1:27; Moses 2:27), and so we feel it is neither audacity nor heresy for the children of God to aspire to be like God (Matthew 5:48; 1 John 3:2-3). Acquiring the attributes of godliness comes through overcoming the world through the Atonement (1 John 5:4-5; Revelation 2:7, 11; D&C 76:51-60), becoming heirs of God and joint-heirs with Christ, who is the natural Heir (Romans 8:17; Galatians 4:7), becoming

---

61. See Bruce R. McConkie, *The Promised Messiah*, 129-30.

62. *Just Like Jesus*, 61.

63. See Stephen E. Robinson, *Are Mormons Christians?* (Salt Lake City: Bookcraft, 1991), 60-61.

partakers of the divine nature (2 Peter 1:4), and thus inheriting all things, just as Jesus inherits all things (1 Corinthians 3:21-23; Revelation 21:7; D&C 76:55, 95; 84:38; 88:107). In that glorified state we will be conformed to the image of the Lord Jesus (Romans 8:29; 1 Corinthians 15:49; 2 Corinthians 3:18; 1 John 3:2; Alma 5:14), receive his glory, and be one with him and with the Father (John 17:21-23; Philippians 3:21).

Nor has the idea of the ultimate deification of man been completely lost from Christian thinking in our own time. "The Son of God became a man," C. S. Lewis pointed out, "to enable men to become sons of God."[64] Further, Lewis explained: God "said (in the Bible) that we were 'gods' and He is going to make good His words. If we let Him — for we can prevent Him, if we choose — He will make the feeblest and filthiest of us into a god or goddess, dazzling, radiant, immortal creature, pulsating all through with such energy and joy and wisdom and love as we cannot now imagine, a bright stainless mirror which reflects back to God perfectly (though, of course, on a smaller scale) His own boundless power and delight and goodness. The process will be long and in parts very painful; but that is what we are in for. Nothing less. He meant what He said."[65]

Lewis wrote elsewhere: "It may be possible for each to think too much of his own potential glory hereafter; it is hardly possible for him to think too often or too deeply about that of his neighbour. . . . It is a serious thing to live in a society of possible gods and goddesses, to remember that the dullest and most uninteresting person you can talk to may one day be a creature which, if you saw it now, you would be strongly tempted to worship. . . . There are no ordinary people."[66]

I honestly don't know what Lewis meant fully (and certainly what he understood or intended) by these statements. The doctrine of the deification of man did not originate with Lewis, nor with the Latter-day Saints; it is to be found throughout Christian history and within Orthodox Christian theology today. Whether Lewis would have agreed fully with the teachings of such notables as Irenaeus, Clement of Alexandria, Justin Martyr, Athanasius, and Augustine on deification — or, for that matter, with what the Latter-day Saints teach — I cannot tell.

64. *Mere Christianity,* 155.
65. *Mere Christianity,* 176.
66. *The Weight of Glory and Other Addresses* (New York: Touchstone, 1996), 39.

While Latter-day Saints certainly accept the teachings of Joseph Smith regarding man becoming like God, we do not fully comprehend all that is entailed by such a bold declaration. Subsequent or even current Church leaders have spoken very little concerning which of God's attributes are communicable and which are incommunicable. While we believe that becoming like God is entailed in eternal life (D&C 132:19-20), we do not believe we will ever, worlds without end, unseat or oust God the Eternal Father or his Only Begotten Son, Jesus Christ; those holy beings are and forever will be the Gods we worship. Even though we believe in the ultimate deification of man, I am unaware of any authoritative statement in LDS literature that suggests that men and women will ever worship any being other than the ones within the Godhead. Parley P. Pratt, early Mormon apostle, wrote one of the first theological treatises within Mormonism. In describing those who are glorified and attain eternal life, Parley stated: "The difference between Jesus Christ and another immortal and celestial man is this — the man is subordinate to Jesus Christ, does nothing in and of himself, but does all things in the name of Christ, and by his authority, being of the same mind, and ascribing all the glory to him and his Father."[67] We believe in "one God" in the sense that we love and serve one Godhead, one divine presidency, each of whom possesses all of the attributes of Godhood (Alma 11:44; D&C 20:28). While we do not believe that God and man are of a different species, we readily acknowledge that the chasm between a fallen, mortal being and an immortal, resurrected, and glorified Being is immense, almost infinite (see D&C 20:17; 109:77).

President Gordon B. Hinckley observed that "the whole design of the gospel is to lead us onward and upward to greater achievement, even, eventually, to Godhood. This great possibility was enunciated by the Prophet Joseph Smith in the King Follett sermon and emphasized by President Lorenzo Snow. . . . Our enemies have criticized us for believing in this. Our reply is that this lofty concept in no way diminishes God the Eternal Father. He is the Almighty. He is the Creator and Governor of the universe. He is the greatest of all and will always be so. But just as any earthly father wishes for his sons and daughters every success in life, so I believe our Father in Heaven wishes for his children that

67. *Key to the Science of Theology* (Salt Lake City: Deseret Book, 1978), 21-22.

they might approach him in stature and stand beside him resplendent in godly strength and wisdom."[68]

To summarize, Latter-day Saints teach that through the cleansing and transforming power of the blood of Jesus Christ, men and women may over time mature spiritually. That is, by and through his blood, we "have a forgiveness of sins, and also a sure reward laid up for [us] in heaven, even that of partaking of the fulness of the Father and the Son through the Spirit. As the Son partakes of the fulness of the Father through the Spirit, so the saints are, by the same Spirit, to be partakers of the same fulness, to enjoy the same glory; for as the Father and the Son are one, so, in like manner, the saints are to be one in them. Through the love of the Father, the mediation of Jesus Christ, and the gift of the Holy Spirit, they are to be heirs of God, and joint heirs with Jesus Christ."[69]

Some people have asked the following question: If the doctrine of theosis or the deification of man is a true part of Mormonism, why is it not found in the Book of Mormon? The Book of Mormon is said to contain "the fulness of the gospel of Jesus Christ" (D&C 20:9). This does not mean that it contains the fulness of gospel doctrine, or that it contains all of the doctrines within the faith. The Book of Mormon teaches the fulness of the gospel — the message of salvation in Christ — with simple plainness. The repetitive focus in the Book of Mormon is upon such principles as faith, repentance, baptism, the Holy Ghost, enduring to the end, the Atonement, bodily resurrection, and eternal judgment. Many of the more distinctive doctrines of Mormonism are found in the Doctrine and Covenants and Pearl of Great Price. Latterday Saints would not expect all of the principles and doctrines of the faith to be set forth within the pages of the Book of Mormon any more than traditional Christians would expect all of the doctrines of salvation to be articulated within the four Gospels.

Conclusion

In using language similar to that of the apostle Paul (see 1 Corinthians 15:25-26), Joseph Smith taught: "Salvation is nothing more nor less

---

68. Conference Report, October 1994, 64.
69. Joseph Smith, *Lectures on Faith* 5:3.

than to triumph over all our enemies and put them under our feet." That is, "Salvation is for a man to be saved from all his enemies; for until a man can triumph over death, he is not saved." In short, for a man to be saved means "being placed beyond the power of all his enemies."[70] Latter-day Saints believe and teach that Jesus Christ is Lord and Savior of all, the "prototype or standard of salvation; or, in other words, . . . a saved being. And if we should . . . ask how it is that he is saved? the answer would be — because he is a just and holy being." That just and holy Being, according to Joseph Smith, proposed to save the human family; that is, "he proposed to make them like unto himself, and he was like the Father, the great prototype of all saved beings; and for any portion of the human family to be assimilated into their likeness is to be saved." In this light, "salvation consists in the glory, authority, majesty, power and dominion which Jehovah possesses and in nothing else; and no being can possess it but himself or one like him."[71]

It is glorious and heartwarming to know that God our Father has a plan for his children, a plan of recovery, a plan of renewal and reconciliation, a plan of salvation, a plan by which those who wander — and that includes all of us — can pick ourselves up, dust ourselves off, and through the cleansing and enabling power of the Atonement, return home. No one of us is bright enough or powerful enough to do it alone; we must have help. And were it not for divine assistance, each of us would falter and fail, would lose the battle of life. "But thanks be to God, which giveth us the victory through our Lord Jesus Christ" (1 Corinthians 15:57). Our God offers us "so great salvation" (Hebrews 2:3) through the infinite intercession of the only completely pure and perfect being to walk the earth.

On 1 January 2000 the leaders of the highest councils of The Church of Jesus Christ of Latter-day Saints issued a statement entitled "The Living Christ" (see Appendix B). The document ends on a note of praise and witness by attesting that "Jesus is the Living Christ, the immortal Son of God. He is the great King Immanuel, who stands today on the right hand of the Father. He is the light, the life, and the hope of the world. His way is the path that leads to happiness in this life and eternal life in the world to come. God be thanked for the matchless gift of His divine Son."

70. TPJS, 297, 301, 305.
71. *Lectures on Faith* 7:9, 16.

6 Those Who Never Heard

Latter-day Saints take very seriously the obligation to do missionary work throughout the world, in order that every person might be invited to come unto Christ and be born of water and of the Spirit (John 3:5; Acts 2:37-38). And what of those who have died? What of those who never heard Jesus preach? What of those in the first century who never had occasion to hear the testimony of Peter or Nathaniel or Paul? And what of those before or since that day, men and women throughout the earth who have died ignorant of the gospel of Jesus Christ? Are they damned forever? Would God condemn a person to hell because they did not come unto a Christ they did not know or accept and receive laws or sacraments of which they were totally unaware?

The Soteriological Problem of Evil

Professor John Sanders has written: "What is the fate of those who die never hearing of the gospel of Christ? Are all the 'heathen' lost? Is there an opportunity for those who have never heard of Jesus to be saved?

"These questions raise one of the most perplexing, provocative and perennial issues facing Christians. It has been considered by philosophers and farmers, Christians and non-Christians. In societies where Christianity has had strong influence, just about everyone has either asked or been asked about the final destiny of those dying without knowledge of the only Savior, Jesus Christ. Far and away, this is the most-asked apologetic question on U.S. college campuses.

"During my freshman year at a large state university, several of my friends and I regularly practiced evangelism. On one of those occasions a thoughtful unbeliever asked me, 'if Jesus is the only way of salvation, then what about all those who have never heard about him?' At the time I had only been a Christian for a short while and consequently did not have an informed answer to give. Nevertheless, I acknowledged the importance of the question and later asked my pastor about it. He pointed me to some basic texts of scripture but did not, he said, have any firm opinion on the matter. In the years since that encounter, I have been asked the same question hundreds of times."

Sanders continues: "A large proportion of the human race has died without ever hearing the good news of Jesus. It is estimated that in A.D. 100 there were 181 million people, of whom 1 million were Christians. It is also believed there were 60,000 unreached people groups at that time. By the year 1000 there were 270 million people, 50 million of whom were Christians, with 50,000 unreached people groups. In 1989 there were 5.2 billion people, with 1.7 billion Christians and 12,000 unreached people groups. In addition we could think of all those who lived prior to [the birth of Christ] who never heard of the Israelites and God's covenant with them. Although there is no way of knowing exactly how many people died without ever hearing about Israel or the church, it seems safe to conclude that the vast majority of human beings who have ever lived fall into this category.

"In terms of sheer numbers, then, an inquiry into the salvation of the unevangelized is of immense interest. What may be said about the destiny of countless billions who have lived and died apart from any understanding of the divine grace manifested in Jesus?"[1]

This issue has been labeled by some as "the soteriological problem of evil." The problem of evil in philosophy and religion may be stated as follows: If God is all-powerful, all-knowing, and all-loving, how can he allow so much pain and suffering in the world? Soteriology is the study of salvation, and thus the soteriological problem of evil might be stated simply as follows: If in fact Christ is the only name by which salvation comes (Acts 4:12; Mosiah 3:17), and if, as we have seen, the majority of the human race will go to their graves without ever having heard

---

1. John Sanders, *What About Those Who Have Never Heard?* (Downers Grove, IL: InterVarsity, 1995), 7-8, 9; see also Clark Pinnock and Delwin Brown, *Theological Crossfire* (Grand Rapids: Zondervan, 1990), 227.

of Christ in this life, how could God be considered in any way to be a just or merciful Deity?

This is an ancient issue, one that dates back a long, long time. As early as the fourth century, St. Augustine attempted to respond to Porphyry, a philosopher who opposed Christianity. Porphyry asked: "If Christ declares himself to be the way of salvation, the grace and the truth, and affirms that in him alone, and only to souls believing in him, is the way of return to God, what has become of men who lived in the many centuries before Christ came? . . . What, then, has become of such an innumerable multitude of souls, who were in no wise blameworthy, seeing that he in whom alone saving faith can be exercised had not yet favored men with his advent?"[2]

Varied Responses

Efforts to respond to what is indeed a significant challenge to the Christian faith have been numerous. Some people readily adopt an agnostic position — we simply do not know what God intends to do with the unevangelized. Others tend to believe that those who remain true to the light they have here will somehow be rewarded with greater light, including the gospel itself, in the life to come. In Christendom these efforts to address the problem tend to fall into five main categories or camps: (1) what might be called exclusivism or restrictivism; (2) pluralism or universalism; (3) inclusivism; (4) universal evangelization before death; and (5) divine perseverance or postmortem evangelization.

Exclusivism

Exclusivism or restrictivism might be stated thusly: People are saved only if they accept the Lord Jesus Christ here and now, in this life. That includes a worship and practice of the only true God, a union with Christ through full acceptance of his saving grace and atonement, and a Christian walk that reflects one's membership in the body of Christ.

2. *Nicene and Post-Nicene Fathers,* 14 vols., ed. Philip Schaff (Grand Rapids: Eerdmans, 1983), 1:416.

All others will be damned. There is no chance for salvation or receipt of the gospel hereafter. Christians who believe in the election and predestination of souls would generally conclude that those who do not receive Christ here were not elected, in God's infinite wisdom, to do so. Besides, they might add, no one *deserves* to be saved; we ought to feel immense gratitude for those whom God foreknew and thus those foreappointed to salvation. In short, in this view "our destinies are sealed at death and no opportunity for salvation exists after that."[3]

Universalism

Pluralism or Universalism's response to the soteriological problem of evil is quite simple: There is goodness and morality in religions and religious practices throughout the world. Christians do not have a monopoly on morality and decency. The philosopher John Hick has written that "Coming to know both ordinary families, and some extraordinary individuals, whose spirituality has been formed by these different traditions and whose lives are lived within them, I have not found that the people of the other world religions are, in general, on a different moral and spiritual level from Christians. They seem on average to be neither better nor worse than are Christians." Hick further observes that "if we define salvation as being forgiven and accepted by God because of Jesus' death on the cross, then it becomes a tautology that Christianity alone knows and is able to preach the source of salvation. But if we define salvation as an actual human change, a gradual transformation from natural self-centeredness (with all the human evils that flow from this) to a radically new orientation centered in God and manifested in the 'fruit of the Spirit,' then it seems clear that salvation is taking place within all of the world religions — and taking place, so far as we can tell, to more or less the same extent." He thus argues "on Christian grounds for a doctrine of universal salvation."[4]

---

3. Sanders, *What About Those Who Have Never Heard?* 13.

4. John Hick, "A Pluralist View," in *Four Views on Salvation in a Pluralistic World,* ed. Dennis L. Okholm and Timothy R. Phillips (Grand Rapids: Zondervan, 1996), 39, 43, 45.

Inclusivism

The third approach to this difficult question is what some have called inclusivism. Justin Martyr, the early Christian apologist (ca. 100-165), explained that Christ "is the Word of whom every race of men were partakers; and those who lived reasonably are Christians, even though they have been thought atheists; as among the Greeks, Socrates and Heraclitus, and men like them."[5] Justin believed that all are partakers of a general revelation through the universal logos, though in Jesus Christ the logos was revealed in its fulness. Likewise Irenaeus (ca. 130-200) contended that God has never been completely unknown to any race of people, inasmuch as the universal Spirit of Christ is inherent in the minds of men and women of all times and places. "For it was not merely for those who believed on Him in the time of Tiberius Caesar that Christ came, nor did the Father exercise his providence for the men only who are now alive, but for all men altogether, who from the beginning, according to their capacity, in their generation have both feared and loved God, and practiced justice and piety towards their neighbors, and have earnestly desired to see Christ, and to hear His voice. Wherefore He shall, at His second coming . . . give them a place in His kingdom."[6]

C. S. Lewis wrestled with this question. Lewis explained that "Those who put themselves in [God's] hands will become perfect, as He is perfect — perfect in love, wisdom, joy, beauty, and immortality. The change will not be completed in this life, for death is an important part of the treatment." He also remarked: "Here is another thing that used to puzzle me. Is it not frightfully unfair that this new life [in Christ] should be confined to people who have heard of Christ and been able to believe in Him? But the truth is God has not told us what His arrangements about the other people are. We do know that no man can be saved except through Christ; we do not know that only those who know Him can be saved through Him."[7]

Further, Lewis taught that "Christ saves many who do not think

---

5. In *Ante-Nicene Fathers*, 10 vols., ed. Alexander Roberts and James Donaldson (Grand Rapids: Eerdmans, 1981), 1:178.

6. In *Ante-Nicene Fathers* 1:494.

7. *Mere Christianity* (New York: Touchstone, 1996), 174, 65.

they know Him. For He is (dimly) present in the good side of the inferior teachers they follow. In the Parable of the Sheep and the Goats (Matthew 25), those who are saved do not seem to know that they have served Christ."[8] Lewis also said: "There are people (a great many of them) who are slowly ceasing to be Christians but who still call themselves by that name: some of them are clergymen. There are other people who are slowly becoming Christians though they do not yet call themselves so. There are people who do not accept the full Christian doctrine about Christ but who are so strongly attracted by Him that they are His in a much deeper sense than they themselves understand. There are people in other religions who are being led by God's secret influence to concentrate on those parts of their religion which are in agreement with Christianity, and who thus belong to Christ without knowing it. . . . Many of the good Pagans long before Christ's birth may have been in this position."[9]

Lewis repeatedly taught that Jesus is the only way to salvation. But although "all salvation is through Christ, we need not conclude that He cannot save those who have not explicitly accepted Him in this life. And it should (at least in my judgment) be made clear that we are not pronouncing all other religions to be totally false, but rather saying that in Christ whatever is true in all religions is consummated and perfected."[10]

In the closing pages of C. S. Lewis's book, *The Great Divorce,* there is a fascinating conversation between Lewis and George MacDonald, a Scottish Congregational minister whose writings had deeply influenced Lewis. There Lewis is taught concerning Christ's descent into hell and told, "There is no spirit in prison to Whom He did not preach." Lewis then asks: "And some hear him?" MacDonald answers: "Aye." Lewis follows up: "In your own books, you were a Universalist. You talked as if all men would be saved. And St. Paul too." MacDonald then delivers a rather complex and difficult response, but one in which he seems to be saying, in essence, that everyone who desires to be saved will be saved. He continues by observing that although Christians speak rather categorically here of heaven and hell and formulate

---

8. Letter to a Mrs. Ashton, 8 November 1952, in *Letters of C. S. Lewis,* rev. ed., ed. Walter Hooper (New York: Harcourt, Brace & Co., 1993), 428.

9. *Mere Christianity,* 178.

10. *God in the Dock,* ed. Walter Hooper (Grand Rapids: Eerdmans, 1970), 102.

straightforward criteria for attaining each, from an eternal perspective, far more will be saved than we realize. Lewis does not attempt to correct MacDonald's doctrine for the reader.[11]

In short, while the inclusivist acknowledges that salvation is in Christ alone, he also notes that God is working through his Spirit to bring people to higher light, to that higher light we know as the gospel of Jesus Christ. Favorite passages of scripture for this group are Titus 2:11 ("For the grace of God that bringeth salvation hath appeared to all men") and 1 Timothy 2:3-4 ("For this is good and acceptable in the sight of God our Saviour; who will have all men to be saved, and to come unto the knowledge of the truth"). Scriptural illustrations of those who obviously exercised faith but were outside the purview of a traditional Christian reception of the gospel include people mentioned in Hebrews 11, such as Abel, Enoch, Noah, Job, Melchizedek, Jethro (those called by Clark Pinnock "holy pagans"), as well as premessianic Jews like Abraham and faithful Gentiles like Cornelius.[12]

From this perspective, "God saves people only because of the work of Christ, but people may be saved even if they do not know about Christ. God grants them salvation if they exercise faith in God as revealed to them through creation and providence." Further, "According to the inclusivist view, the Father reaches out to the unevangelized through both the Son and the Spirit via general revelation, conscience and human culture. God does not leave himself without witness to any people. Salvation for the unevangelized is made possible only by the redemptive work of Jesus, but God applies that work even to those who are ignorant of the atonement. God does this if people respond in trusting faith to the revelation they have."[13]

Universal Evangelization Before Death

In order to hold tenaciously to the notion that the gospel of Jesus Christ must be received in this life (that one's final destiny is fixed

11. *The Great Divorce* (New York: Macmillan, 1946), 124-25.

12. Cited in John Sanders, *What About Those Who Have Never Heard?* 36-42; *No Other Name* (Grand Rapids: Eerdmans, 1992), 259-60; see also Clark Pinnock, *Flame of Love* (Downers Grove, IL: InterVarsity, 1996), 185-214.

13. Sanders, *What About Those Who Have Never Heard?* 13, 36.

and established at death), and at the same time rely upon the tender mercies and justice of God in making that message available, some have concluded that the opportunity to learn of the gospel takes place just prior to or at the time of one's physical death.[14] Norman Geisler has written that "natural revelation is sufficient only to reveal the moral standard for man, but . . . it is not sufficient for man's salvation."[15]

Proponents of this view teach that the message may come at the hand of mortals, inspired dreams, angels, or even by open vision or revelation. One Roman Catholic view is that Jesus himself appears to each man or woman at the time of death and allows them to affirm or deny the faith. This is known as the "final option" theory. "Proponents of the theory maintain that the moment the soul is being separated from the body is the first time in an individual's existence that he or she has the ability to make a fully free personal act. . . . The soul is fully awake and aware of the seriousness of the situation. At this moment the soul ceases to act in a changeable way and acts rather with an unchangeable intent toward a particular end. Hence, the decision made at this moment is irreversible. The final distinguishing characteristic is that prior choices we have made deeply influence but do not determine our final decision. We may confirm to choose the way we have lived or we may reject it."[16] Should one not, then, wait until death to decide for or against Christ? No, comes the answer, for "who can assure me that I will wish to change my stand later?"[17]

One view of this perspective is similar to an inclusivistic view — that a person who would have received the gospel had it been presented to him or her in this life will be blessed as though they had indeed received it. That is, God will judge them by the intent of their hearts. God knows all things, including what people would have done under circumstance B, even though they lived under circumstance A. "God knows who would, under ideal circumstances, believe the gospel, and on the basis of his foreknowledge, applies that gospel even if the per-

14. The brief discussion that follows is based upon Sanders, *No Other Name*, 151-75.

15. *Options in Contemporary Christian Ethics* (Grand Rapids: Baker, 1981), 32; as cited in Sanders, *No Other Name*, 153.

16. Sanders, *No Other Name*, 164-65.

17. Roger Troisfontaines, *I Do Not Die,* trans. Francis Albert (New York: Desclee, 1963), 180, note 41; as cited in Sanders, *No Other Name*, 167.

son never hears the gospel during his lifetime."[18] In short, "To him who responds" to the light he receives in this life, "more light will be given."[19]

Postmortem Evangelism

A fifth position that has been taken by some Christians in regard to the soteriological problem of evil is what has variously been called future probation, second probation, eschatological evangelism, divine perseverance, and postmortem evangelism. According to this view, those who die without a knowledge of the gospel are not damned; they have an opportunity to receive the truth in the world to come. "God is resolute," one advocate of this position has pointed out, "never giving up on getting the Word out. In this world God will give us the power to spread the gospel far and wide. But the Word will also be declared to those we can't reach, even if it takes an eternity." He adds that "God's love is patient and persistent. It outlasts us. For the final victory of this powerful patience, however, we must await the end of the story. Only then will the kingdom come — the resurrection of the dead, the return of Christ, final judgment and everlasting life. In the end, God will settle accounts, vindicate the sufferer and validate the divine purposes."[20]

One respected evangelical, Donald Bloesch, has explained: "We do not wish to build fences around God's grace, . . . and we do not preclude the possibility that some in hell might finally be translated into heaven. The gates of the holy city are depicted as being open day and night (Isaiah 60:11; Revelation 21:25), and this means that access to the throne of grace is possible continuously. The gates of hell are locked, but they are locked only from within. C. S. Lewis has suggested in *The Great Divorce* that where there is a supposed transition from hell to heaven the person was never really in hell but only in purgatory. This, of course, is interesting speculation, and may be close to the truth. Yet we must maintain a reverent agnosticism concerning the workings of God's grace which are

18. Donald Lake, in *Grace Unlimited,* ed. Clark Pinnock (Minneapolis: Bethany, 1975), 43; cited in Sanders, *No Other Name,* 168.

19. Robertson McQuilken, *The Great Omission* (Grand Rapids: Baker, 1984), 44; as cited in Sanders, *No Other Name,* 156.

20. Gabriel Fackre, in *What About Those Who Have Never Heard?* 73, 78.

not revealed in Holy Scripture. We can affirm salvation on the other side of the grave, since this has scriptural warrant."[21]

Favorite passages of scripture for this group include 1 Peter 3:18-20 and 1 Peter 4:6, which refer to Christ teaching the gospel after his death; John 5:25, in which Jesus states that the dead will hear the voice of the Son of God; and Ephesians 4:8-9, which speaks of Christ descending to the "lower parts of the earth." One critic of the doctrine of postmortem evangelism declared that such a reading of 1 Peter 4:6 "is neither the only nor even the most plausible interpretation. Wise Christians do not base any important doctrine — especially one that is controversial and that might also contain heretical implications — on one single, highly debatable passage of Scripture. If this approach were applied by PME [Postmortem Evangelism] advocates to 1 Corinthians 15:29, it would lead Christians to follow a policy of baptizing living people as proxies for the unbaptized dead."[22] Indeed, it just might.

An Early Practice

Latter-day Saints believe that some time during or just following the mortal ministry of Jesus, the doctrine of salvation for the dead was revealed to the first-century Church. In the 15th chapter of his first epistle to the Corinthians, the apostle Paul testifies of the resurrection of the Lord. Paul presents the core of that supernal message known to us as the gospel, or the "glad tidings" that Christ suffered for our sins, died, rose again the third day, and ascended into heaven. Joseph Smith called these events "the fundamental principles of our religion," to which all other doctrines are but appendages.[23] Paul showed the necessity for the Savior's rising from the tomb and explained that the physical evidence of the divine Sonship of Christ is the resurrection. If Christ had not risen from the dead, Paul asserted, the preaching of the apostles and the faith of the Saints would be in vain. "If in this life only we have hope in Christ," he said, "we are of all men most miserable" (1 Corinthians 15:19).

---

21. *Essentials of Evangelical Theology*, 2 vols. (San Francisco: Harper, 1978), 2:226-27.

22. Ronald H. Nash, in Sanders, *What About Those Who Have Never Heard?* 130.

23. *Teachings of the Prophet Joseph Smith*, selected by Joseph Fielding Smith (Salt Lake City: Deseret Book Co., 1976), 121; cited hereafter as TPJS.

After establishing that the Lord has conquered all enemies, including death, Paul added: "And when all things shall be subdued unto him, then shall the Son also himself be subject unto him [the Father] that put all things under him, that God may be all in all. *Else what shall they do which are baptized for the dead, if the dead rise not at all? why are they then baptized for the dead?*" (1 Corinthians 15:28-29; emphasis added). Verse 29 has spawned a host of interpretations by biblical scholars of various faiths. Many consider the original meaning of the passage to be at best "difficult" or "unclear." One commentator stated that Paul here "alludes to a practice of the Corinthian community as evidence for Christian faith in the resurrection of the dead. It seems that in Corinth some Christians would undergo baptism in the name of their deceased non-Christian relatives and friends, hoping that this vicarious baptism might assure them a share in the redemption of Christ."[24] Some recent translations of the Bible have attempted to clarify this passage. The New King James Version has it: "Otherwise, what will they do who are baptized for the dead, if the dead do not rise at all? Why then are they baptized for the dead?" The Revised English Bible translates 1 Corinthians 15:29: "Again, there are those who receive baptism on behalf of the dead. What do you suppose they are doing? If the dead are not raised to life at all, what do they mean by being baptized on their behalf?"

One commentator noted that "it is difficult to imagine any circumstances under which Paul would think it permissible for living Christians to be baptized for the sake of unbelievers in general. Such a view, adopted in part by the Mormons, lies totally outside the NT understanding both of salvation and of baptism."[25] Many non-Latter-day-Saint scholars believe that in 1 Corinthians Paul was denouncing or condemning the practice of baptism for the dead as heretical.[26] This is a strange conclusion, since Paul uses the practice to support the doc-

24. Richard Kugelman, "The First Letter to the Corinthians," in *The Jerome Biblical Commentary*, 2 vols., ed. Raymond E. Brown, Joseph A. Fitzmyer, and Roland E. Murphy (Englewood Cliffs, NJ: Prentice-Hall, 1968), 2:273.

25. Gordon D. Fee, *The First Epistle to the Corinthians* (Grand Rapids: Eerdmans, 1987), 767.

26. For a summary of some of the alternative explanations see Fee, *The First Epistle to the Corinthians*, 763-77; see also a more recent proposal in Joel R. White, "'Baptized on Behalf of the Dead': The Meaning of 1 Corinthians 15:29 in Its Context," *Journal of Biblical Literature* 116, no. 3 (1997): 487-99.

trine of the resurrection. In essence, he says, "Why are we performing baptism in behalf of our dead, if, as some propose, there will be no resurrection of the dead? If there is to be no resurrection, would not such baptisms be a waste of time?"

On the subject of baptism for the dead, one non-Latter-day Saint scholar has recently observed: "Paul had no reason to mention baptism for the dead unless he thought it would be an effective argument with the Corinthians, so presumably he introduced what he thought was an inconsistency in the Corinthians' theology. In this case, some at Corinth might have rejected an afterlife but practiced baptism for the dead, not realizing what the rite implied." In addition, "Because his mention [of the practice] could imply his toleration or approval of it, many have tried to distance Paul from baptism for the dead or remove features regarded as offensive from it. Some maintain that Paul was arguing *ad hominem* or *ex concessu* in 1 Corinthians 15:29, so that he neither approved nor disapproved of the practice by referring to it. Yet it would have been unlike Paul to refrain from criticizing a practice he did not at least tolerate."[27] Or as an LDS New Testament scholar has pointed out: "Paul was most sensitive to blasphemy and false ceremonialism — of all people he would not have argued for the foundation truth of the resurrection with a questionable example. He obviously did not feel that the principle was disharmonious with the gospel."[28]

Latter-day Saints believe that the doctrine of salvation for the dead was known and understood by ancient Christian communities. Early commentary on the statement in Hebrews that "they without us should not be made perfect" (Hebrews 11:40) holds that the passage referred to the Old Testament Saints who were trapped in Hades awaiting the help of their New Testament counterparts and that Christ held the keys that would "open the doors of the Underworld to the faithful souls there."[29] It is significant that in his work, "Dialogue with Trypho," Justin Martyr cites an apocryphon which he charges had been deleted from the book of Jeremiah, but was still to be found in some

27. Richard E. DeMaris, "Corinthian Religion and Baptism for the Dead (1 Corinthians 15:29): Insights from Archaeology and Anthropology," *Journal of Biblical Literature* 114, no. 4 (1995): 678, 679.

28. Richard Lloyd Anderson, *Understanding Paul* (Salt Lake City: Deseret Book, 1983), 405.

29. J. A. MacCulloch, *The Harrowing of Hell* (Edinburgh: T&T Clark, 1930), 48-49.

synagogue copies of the text: "The Lord God remembered His dead people of Israel who lay in the graves; and He descended to preach to them His own salvation."[30] Irenaeus also taught: "The Lord descended to the parts under the earth, announcing to them also the good news of his coming, there being remission of sins for such as believe on him."[31]

One of the early Christian documents linking the writings of Peter on Christ's ministry in the spirit world (see 1 Peter 3:18-20; 4:6) with those of Paul on baptism for the dead is the *Shepherd of Hermas*, which states that "these apostles and teachers who preached the name of the Son of God, having fallen asleep in the power and faith of the Son of God, preached also to those who had fallen asleep before them, and themselves gave to them the seal of the preaching. *They went down therefore with them into the water and came up again,* but the latter went down alive and came up alive, while the former, who had fallen asleep before, went down dead but came up alive. *Through them, therefore, they were made alive, and received the knowledge of the name of the Son of God.*"[32] Similarly, another apocryphal New Testament document, the Gospel of Peter, speaks of the singular moment in Christian history when the tomb was opened at the time of the resurrection of our Lord. "When the soldiers saw these things, they woke up the centurion and the elders — for they were also there on guard. As they were explaining what they had seen, they saw three men emerge from the tomb, two of them supporting the other, with a cross following behind them. The heads of the two reached up to the sky, but the head of the one they were leading went up above the skies." Then we come to the following strange but fascinating account: "And they heard a voice from the skies, 'Have you preached to those who are asleep?' And a reply came from the cross, 'Yes.'"[33]

In a modern commentary on 1 Peter, the author observes that 1 Peter 3:19 and 4:6 are the only passages in the New Testament that

30. MacCulloch, *The Harrowing of Hell,* 84-85; also in *The Ante-Nicene Fathers* 1:235.

31. Irenaeus, *Against Heresies* 4.27.1, in J. B. Lightfoot, *The Apostolic Fathers* (Grand Rapids: Baker, 1962), 277-78.

32. *The Shepherd of Hermas,* similitude 9.16.2-4; cited in Anderson, *Understanding Paul,* 407-8, emphasis added.

33. Bart Ehrman, *Lost Scriptures: Books that Did Not Make It into the New Testament* (New York: Oxford, 2003), 33.

refer to the ministry of Christ to the postmortal spirit world. "But 1 Peter would not be able," he points out, "to make such brief reference to this idea if it were not already known in the churches as tradition. What 1 Peter says in regard to this tradition is, in comparison with the traditions of the second century, quite 'apostolic.'" Through this means, he points out, "The saving effectiveness of [the Lord's] suffering unto death extends even to those mortals who in earthly life do not come to a conscious encounter with him, even to the most lost among them."[34]

Tertullian, an early Christian apologist (ca. 160-240) who later seems to have opposed the practice of baptism for the dead, nevertheless taught that it was in fact a witness of the bodily resurrection. He quoted Paul's words to the Corinthians and said: "Do not then suppose that the apostle here indicates that some new god is the author and advocate of this practice. Rather, it was so that he could all the more firmly insist upon the resurrection of the body, in proportion of they who are baptized for the dead resorted to the practice from their belief of such a resurrection. We have the apostle in another passage defining 'only one baptism' [Ephesians 4:5]. Therefore, to be 'baptized for the dead' means, in fact, to be baptized for the body. For, as we have shown, it is the body that becomes dead. What, then, will they do who are baptized for the body, if the body does not rise again?"[35] Tertullian declared on another occasion: "Inasmuch as 'some are also baptized for the dead,' we will see whether there is a good reason for this. Now it is certain that they adopted this [practice] with a presumption that made them suppose that the vicarious baptism would be beneficial to the flesh of another in anticipation of the resurrection. For unless this is a bodily resurrection, there would be no pledge secured by this process of a bodily baptism."[36]

34. Leonhard Goppelt, *A Commentary on 1 Peter*, ed. Ferdinand Hahn, trans. John E. Alsup (Grand Rapids: Eerdmans, 1993), 263, 259.

35. Cited in David W. Bercot, ed., *A Dictionary of Early Christian Beliefs* (Peabody, MA: Hendrickson, 1998), 63.

36. Bercot, *A Dictionary of Early Christian Beliefs*, 63; see also Hugh Nibley, *Mormonism and Early Christianity* (Salt Lake City: Deseret Book and FARMS, 1987), 100-167.

An Ancient Practice Restored

Joseph Smith observed: "Aside from knowledge independent of the Bible, I would say that it [baptism for the dead] was certainly practiced by the ancient churches; . . . The Saints have the privilege of being baptized for those of their relatives who are dead, whom they believe would have embraced the Gospel, if they had been privileged with hearing it, and who have received the Gospel in the spirit [world], through the instrumentality of those who have been commissioned to preach to them."[37] On another occasion he said: "If we can, by the authority of the Priesthood of the Son of God, baptize a man in the name of the Father, of the Son, and of the Holy Ghost, for the remission of sins, it is just as much our privilege to act as an agent, and be baptized for the remission of sins for and in behalf of our dead kindred, who have not heard the Gospel, or the fullness of it."[38]

This practice is closely tied to another doctrinal belief of the Latter-day Saints — that the gospel is preached in the postmortal spirit world. The Saints believe this is what Peter meant when he wrote: "For Christ also hath once suffered for sins, the just for the unjust, that he might bring us to God, being put to death in the flesh, but quickened by the Spirit: by which also *he went and preached unto the spirits* in prison." Further: "For *for this cause was the gospel preached also to them that are dead,* that they might be judged according to men in the flesh, but live according to God in the spirit" (1 Peter 3:18-19; 4:6, emphasis added). In short, we feel that every person will have the opportunity, either in this life or the next, to receive the fulness of the gospel of Jesus Christ and enter into the everlasting covenant.

Frederic W. Farrar, writing in the nineteenth century, observed that "St. Peter has one doctrine that is almost peculiar to himself, and which is inestimably precious." This doctrine, Farrar adds, is a "much disregarded and, indeed, till recent times, half-forgotten article of the Christian creed; I mean the object of Christ's descent into Hades. In this truth is involved nothing less than the extension of Christ's redeeming work to the dead who died before his coming. Had the Epistle contained nothing else but this, it would at once have been raised

37. TPJS, 179.
38. TPJS, 201.

above the irreverent charge of being 'secondhand and commonplace.'" Farrar then quotes I Peter 3:18-20 and I Peter 4:6 and states: "Few words of Scripture have been so tortured and emptied of their significance as these." He notes that "every effort has been made to explain away the plain meaning of this passage. It is one of the most precious passages of Scripture, and it involves no ambiguity, except such as is created by the scholasticism of a prejudiced theology. It stands almost alone in Scripture. . . . For if language have any meaning, this language means that Christ, when His spirit descended into the lower world, proclaimed the message of salvation to the once impenitent dead." And then, in broadening our perspective beyond those of the days of Noah, Farrar writes: "But it is impossible to suppose that the antediluvian sinners, conspicuous as they were for their wickedness, were the only ones of all the dead who were singled out to receive the message of deliverance."

Continuing, the revered churchman pointed out: "We thus rescue the work of redemption from the appearance of having failed to achieve its end for the vast majority of those for whom Christ died. By accepting the light thus thrown upon 'the descent into Hell,' we extend to those of the dead who have not finally hardened themselves against it the blessedness of Christ's atoning work." Later Farrar writes that "we do not press the inference of Hermas and St. Clement of Alexandria by teaching that this passage implies also other missions of Apostles and Saints to the world of spirits."[39]

Between the time of Christ's death on the cross and his rise from the tomb, he went into the postmortal spirit world, preached his gospel, and organized the faithful, in order that the message of truth might be made available to all who are willing to receive it (see D&C 138). But because the sacraments or ordinances of the Church are earthly ordinances and must be performed on this side of the veil of death, Latter-day Saints go into temples to receive the sacraments in behalf of those who have died without them. "Every man," Joseph Smith pointed out, "that has been baptized and belongs to the kingdom has a right to be baptized for those who have gone before; and as soon as the law of the Gospel is obeyed here by their friends who act

39. *The Early Days of Christianity* (New York: Cassell, Petter, Galpin & Co., 1882), 139-42, 169.

as proxy for them, the Lord has administrators there [in the spirit world] to set them free."[40] He also taught: "Jesus Christ became a ministering spirit (while His body was lying in the sepulchre) to the spirits in prison, to fulfill an important part of His mission, without which He could not have perfected His work, or entered into his rest. . . . It is no more incredible that God should *save* the dead, than that he should *raise* the dead."[41] In that sense, Mormons feel the need to be anxiously engaged in the work of the ministry on both sides of the veil of death.

More often than not, baptism for the dead (together with other temple ordinances) is considered by traditional Christians to be an unnecessary, ill-advised, or even contemptible practice. In the 10 August 1998 issue of *Christianity Today,* a reader inquired: "I've heard Mormons criticized for getting 'baptized for the dead,' but in 1 Corinthians 15:29, Paul writes [she then quotes the verse]. Did Jews or early Christians practice this? Why do we believe it's wrong to practice it today?" D. A. Carson, a respected biblical scholar, responded briefly with familiar arguments against the practice: the doctrine is not taught in the Book of Mormon; it is mentioned in only one place in the Bible; Paul uses the word *they* (rather than *we*) in referring to the practice, thus implying that he was not associated with the practice; and, in short, "There is no good evidence for vicarious baptism anywhere in the New Testament or among the earliest apostolic fathers. . . . If the practice existed at all, it may have been tied to a few people or special cases — for example, when a relative died after trusting the gospel but before being baptized. We really do not know" (p. 63). In a Christian world where people are not persuaded that baptism in *the flesh* is necessary for entrance into the Lord's Church and thus essential to salvation (or where baptism is viewed as some type of extraneous and inessential work that somehow undercuts or compromises the saving grace of the Lord), we should not be surprised about some of the reactions to this doctrine and practice.

40. TPJS, 367.
41. TPJS, 191.

Conclusion

"Some things in Scripture are not perfectly clear," John MacArthur observed. "One notable example is the mention of 'baptism for the dead' in 1 Corinthians 15:29. There are at least forty different views about what that verse means. We cannot be dogmatic about such things."[42] J. I. Packer reminded the readers of *Christianity Today* that any notion of salvation beyond the grave "is nonscriptural speculation, and reflects an inadequate grasp of what turning to Christ involves." Further, he added, any idea of a person not receiving the gospel here in this life and then choosing to receive it hereafter is also unscriptural. He pointed out that "the unbeliever's lack of desire for Christ and the Father and heaven remains unchanged [after death]. So for God to extend the offer of salvation beyond the moment of death, even for thirty seconds, would be pointless. Nothing would come of it."[43]

Latter-day Saints believe that the good news or glad tidings of salvation in Christ is intended to lift our sights and bring hope to our souls, to "bind up the brokenhearted, to proclaim liberty to the captives, and the opening of the prison to them that are bound" (Isaiah 61:1). That hope in Christ is in the infinite capacity of an infinite Being to save men and women from ignorance, as well as from sin and death. The God of Abraham, Isaac, and Jacob is indeed the God of the living (Matthew 22:32), and his influence and redemptive mercies span the veil of death (1 Corinthians 15:19).

And so what of those who never have the opportunity in this life to know of Christ and his gospel; who never have the opportunity to be baptized for a remission of sins and for entrance into the kingdom of God; who never have the privilege of being bound in marriage and sealed in the family unit? In a world gripped by cynicism and strangled by hopelessness, the Latter-day Saints teach of a God of mercy and vision, of an Omnipotent One whose reach to his children is neither deterred by distance nor dimmed by death.

"There is never a time," Joseph Smith stated, "when the spirit is too

42. *Why One Way?* (Nashville: W Publishing Group, 2002), 61.

43. J. I. Packer, "Can the Dead Be Converted?" *Christianity Today*, vol. 43, no. 1 (11 January 1999), 82.

old to approach God. All are within reach of pardoning mercy, who have not committed the unpardonable sin. . . .

"This glorious truth [baptism for the dead] is well calculated to enlarge the understanding, and to sustain the soul under troubles, difficulties and distresses. For illustration, suppose the case of two men, brothers, equally intelligent, learned, virtuous and lovely, walking in uprightness and in all good conscience, so far as they have been able to discern duty from the muddy stream of tradition, or from the blotted page of the book of nature.

"One dies and is buried, having never heard the Gospel of reconciliation; to the other the message of salvation is sent, he hears and embraces it, and is made the heir of eternal life. Shall the one become the partaker of glory and the other be consigned to hopeless perdition? Is there no chance for his escape? Sectarianism answers 'none.' Such an idea is worse than atheism."[44]

As Jeffrey Trumbow has written, the Latter-day Saints "revived certain types of posthumous salvation, without necessarily being aware of the earlier history, save the one Pauline passage about baptism on behalf of the dead, 1 Cor. 15:29. This shows that the religious impulse to rescue the dead can arise any time there is enthusiasm for the new activity of God in the world. If the living can share in the new blessings bestowed by God, why should the dead be excluded? If the living can reorient themselves, repent, and/or benefit from the prayers of the living, why not the dead?"[45]

---

44. TPJS, 191-92.

45. *Rescue for the Dead: The Posthumous Salvation of Non-Christians in Early Christianity* (Oxford: Oxford University Press, 2001), 155.

7 Recurring Questions

It is simply impossible to cover, in a brief work of this sort, all of the aspects of the doctrine of The Church of Jesus Christ of Latter-day Saints that bear upon the work and ministry of Jesus Christ. In addition, there are numerous queries that arise from time to time about different aspects of the faith that deserve at least some mention. Consequently, this chapter will attempt to address some of the most frequently asked questions concerning Latter-day Saint Christianity.

Question (Q) 1: *Haven't the Latter-day Saints changed their doctrinal stance on Christ as a part of a public relations effort to persuade people that they really are Christians?*

Answer (A): Nothing in the LDS doctrine of Christ has changed in the last 175 years. To some extent, there has been a change in emphasis by Church leaders, and that change may be reflected in the Church's public affairs program. Let me suggest an analogy. Suppose a very devout Baptist minister, the only one in his community, were to encounter stiff opposition from a man who simply disliked Baptists. Suppose the critic began a smear campaign that took the form of brochures, booklets, books, and video presentations that stated in no uncertain terms that Baptists are not only not Christian but atheists! The Baptist minister might initially even smile at the ridiculous propaganda and dismiss it with a wave of the hand, concluding that no sane listener or viewer would give the anti-Baptist materials a moment's thought. But let's complicate the picture by suggesting further that after a decade of constant chants of "Baptists are not Christian!" or "Baptists are atheists!" a noticeable percentage of the public began to believe or at least attend to the propaganda. What then? What should the Baptist minister do? Would it be inappropriate or beneath his dignity to begin a similar campaign to set the record straight? Not at all.

In one sense, Latter-day Saints have been the target of anti-Mormon propaganda since 1830. This is nothing new. But in the last few decades the amount of polemical material has increased dramatically, some of it not only uncomplimentary but even blatantly false. One might be prone to dismiss my story above on the basis that the analogy does not hold — Mormons really aren't Christian. Well, this gets me to my point. The problem with saying that Latter-day Saints are not Christian is that such a statement is in many ways untrue and almost always misleading. While as we have pointed out in this work, there are certainly differences between the LDS conception of Jesus Christ and the more traditionally Christian view, to say that we are not Christian is to lead some who know very little of us to the conclusion that we are un-Christlike, anti-Christian, opposed to the teachings of Jesus, or that we do not accept the message of the New Testament. And this is false. The Church of Jesus Christ of Latter-day Saints has begun to emphasize its heartfelt acceptance of Jesus as the Christ, so that people in society may not misunderstand its fundamental and core beliefs. We believe what is in the New Testament, and we believe what God has revealed in the latter days concerning Christ. Such belief, such teachings (like the ones we have cited in this book) did not spring into existence within the last few years; they have been in the Book of Mormon, Doctrine and Covenants, Pearl of Great Price, and teachings of Church leaders from the beginning.

Let me illustrate the challenge the Church faces. Several years ago a colleague and I were asked if we would be willing to participate in an interview with representatives of a Christian organization. We were informed that they were preparing a video presentation on The Church of Jesus Christ of Latter-day Saints. My interview — which consisted basically of my response to a series of questions — lasted for about an hour and a half. We covered much ground, including the role of prophets, our views concerning the Bible, the person and nature of God the Father, and our teachings on Jesus Christ. For at least twenty or thirty minutes I described our understanding of the Atonement and of the necessity of the mercy and grace of Christ. When the video presentation was released several months later, I felt that it portrayed quite accurately, for the most part, our fundamental beliefs and, of course, the differences between LDS and other Christian beliefs. One part was, however, particularly troublesome to me: the narrator stated quite forthrightly that the Latter-day Saints do not believe in salvation by the grace of Christ.

Some months later, we met once again with representatives of this group. They were eager to know our feelings concerning the movie. We commented that it was nice that Latter-day Saints had been allowed to express themselves. But I also voiced my disappointment in what was said about our lack of belief in grace. I said, essentially, "If you want to say that the Latter-day Saints have an *unusual* view of grace, or a *different* view of grace, or a *deficient* view of grace, we can live with that, for we obviously have differences between our two faiths. But to say that we have *no* view of grace is a serious misrepresentation that confuses and misleads people."

One other point. When Ezra Taft Benson became the thirteenth president of the Church in 1985, he placed a strong emphasis upon the use of the Book of Mormon in the Church, stressing that the doctrines and teachings of the Book of Mormon should be studied and discussed and applied more regularly by the Latter-day Saints. As I have mentioned earlier in this work, the Book of Mormon is grounded in redemptive theology, and thus the stress by Church leaders of its teachings over a couple of decades would inevitably result in a more Christ-centered emphasis in the whole Church.

President Gordon B. Hinckley remarked: "Those who observe us say that we are moving into the mainstream of religion. We are not changing. The world's perception of us is changing. We teach the same doctrine. We have the same organization. We labor to perform the same good works. But the old hatred is disappearing; the old persecution is dying. People are better informed. They are coming to realize what we stand for and what we do."[1]

Q #2: How can the LDS claim to be Christian when they reject the doctrine of the Trinity?

A: To clarify, the Latter-day Saints believe in the three members of the Godhead — the Father, Son, and Holy Spirit. But they believe they are three distinct personages, three Beings, three separate Gods. Latter-day Saints believe that the doctrine of the Trinity, as taught throughout Christendom today, reflects more of the decisions of post-

---

1. Conference Report, October 2001, 3-4.

New Testament church councils than the teachings of the New Testament itself. Now to be sure, the scriptures, including Latter-day Saint scriptures, teach that the members of the Godhead are one; in fact, we believe they are infinitely more one than they are separate. As my colleague David Paulsen has written: "Latter-day Saints, like other Christians and New Testament writers, affirm that there is a plurality of divine persons. Yet, at the same time, we witness (as our scriptures repeatedly declare) that 'the Father, Son and Holy Ghost are one God' (2 Nephi 31:21; Alma 11:44; 3 Nephi 11:36; D&C 20:28). Given the plurality of divine persons, how can there be but one God? In at least three ways: (1) there is only one perfectly united, mutually indwelling, divine community. We call that community 'God' and there is only one such. (2) There is only one God the Father or fount of divinity (1 Corinthians 8:6). (3) There is only one divine nature or set of properties severally necessary and jointly sufficient for divinity."[2]

Q #3: *Isn't it true that The Church of Jesus Christ of Latter-day Saints is in reality a cult?*

A: The derisive label of *cult* frightens people and basically turns them off. It conjures up images of the bizarre, the unnatural, and even the demonic. The fact is, the first three definitions of cult in *Webster's Third International Dictionary* make no distinction between religion and cult. The fourth definition is the one, I suppose, most anti-Mormons have in mind: an unorthodox or spurious sect. Walter Martin, an evangelical Christian who spent much of his life denouncing what he perceived to be non-Christian faiths, proposed the following characteristics of cults: (a) they are started by strong and dynamic leaders; (b) they believe in additional scripture; (c) they have rigid standards for membership; (d) they proselyte new converts; (e) the leaders or officials of the cult are not professional clergymen; (f) they believe in ongoing and continual communication from God; and (g) they claim some truth not available to other individuals or groups.[3] By these standards of measure, the Latter-day Saints would certainly qualify as a cult. The problem for Rev. Martin is, of course, that the New Testament Christian Church would qualify also!

2. "Are Mormons Trinitarian?" in *Modern Reformation,* vol. 12, no. 6 (November/December 2003), 40-41.

3. *The New Cults* (Ventura, CA: Regal Books, 1980), 17-21.

Q #4: *Doesn't the Bible warn about those who seek to add to or take away from the scriptures? How can the Latter-day Saints then justify having additional books of scripture? Does this not disqualify them as Christians?*

A: First of all, it appears that the passages in the Old Testament that warn against such things (Deuteronomy 4:2; 12:32) are actually warning against adding to the books of Moses, the Pentateuch. This certainly could not have reference to adding to the Old Testament in general, or else we could not in good conscience accept the 34 books that follow the Pentateuch. Furthermore, the warning attached to the end of the Revelation of John is a warning against adding to or taking away from "the words of the prophecy of this book" (Revelation 22:18-19), namely, the Apocalypse. Most important, Latter-day Saints believe these warnings have to do with the condemnation associated with a man, an uninspired man, a man not called of God, taking upon himself the responsibility to add to or take from the canon of scripture. It is God's prerogative to speak beyond what he has spoken already (as he certainly did in the person and messages and works of Jesus himself), and God should be allowed to direct and empower his children as need arises. It is not for us to set up bounds and stakes for the Almighty. Nowhere in the Bible itself do we learn that God will no longer speak to his children or add to the canon.

Q #5: *Joseph Smith taught that man may become like God and that God was once a man. How can Latter-day Saints believe such ideas? Are they not blasphemous, and do they not lower the Almighty in the eternal scheme of things?*

A: I think that I have never opened myself to questions before a group of persons not of our faith that I have not been asked about our doctrine of God and the Godhead, particularly concerning the teachings of Joseph Smith and Lorenzo Snow. I generally do not have too much difficulty explaining our view of how through the Atonement man can eventually become like God, become more and more Christlike (as we discussed in chapter 5). For that matter, Orthodox Christianity, a huge segment of the Christian world, still holds to a view of human deification. The Bible itself teaches that men and women may become "partakers of the divine nature" (2 Peter 1:4), "joint heirs with Christ" (Romans 8:17), gain "the mind of Christ" (1 Corinthians 2:16), and become perfect, even as our Father in heaven is perfect (Matthew 5:48). The apostle John declared: "Beloved, now are we the [children] of

God, and it doth not yet appear what we shall be: but we know that, when he shall appear, we shall be like him; for we shall see him as he is" (1 John 3:2). In addition, this doctrine is taught clearly in modern revelation (D&C 76:58; 132:19-20).

The tougher issue for many Christians to deal with is the accompanying doctrine set forth in the King Follett Sermon[4] and the Lorenzo Snow couplet[5] — namely, that God was once a man. Latter-day scriptures state unequivocally that God is a man, a Man of Holiness (Moses 6:57) who possesses a body of flesh and bones (D&C 130:22). These concepts are clearly a part of what Mormons call the doctrinal restoration. We teach that man is not of a lower order or different species than God. This, of course, makes many of our Christian friends extremely nervous (if not angry), for it appears to them that we are pulling God down and thus attempting to bridge the Creator/creature chasm.

All we can say is that from our perspective the distance between God and man is still tremendous, almost infinite. Latter-day Saints worship "a God in heaven, who is infinite and eternal, from everlasting to everlasting, the same unchangeable God, the framer of heaven and earth, and all things which are in them" (D&C 20:17). Our Father in heaven is indeed omnipotent, omniscient, and, by the power of his Holy Spirit, omnipresent. He is a gloried, exalted, resurrected being, "the only supreme governor and independent being in whom all fullness and perfection dwell; . . . in him every good gift and every good principle dwell; . . . he is the Father of lights; in him the principle of faith dwells independently, and he is the object in whom the faith of all other rational and accountable beings center for life and salvation."[6] Modern revelation attests that the Almighty sits enthroned "with glory, honor, power, majesty, might, dominion, truth, justice, judgment, mercy, and an infinity of fulness" (D&C 109:77).

And what do we know beyond the fact that God is an exalted Man? What do we know of his mortal existence? What do we know of the time before he was God? Nothing! We really do not know more than what was stated by Joseph Smith, and that is precious little. Insights

---

4. *Teachings of the Prophet Joseph Smith,* selected by Joseph Fielding Smith (Salt Lake City: Deseret Book, 1976), 345-46; cited hereafter as TPJS.

5. *Teachings of Lorenzo Snow,* ed. Clyde J. Williams (Salt Lake City: Bookcraft, 1984), 1.

6. *Lectures on Faith* (Salt Lake City: Deseret Book, 1985), 2:2.

concerning God's life before Godhood are not found in the standard works, in official declarations or proclamations, in current handbooks or curricular materials, nor are doctrinal expositions on the subject delivered in general conference today. This topic is not what we would call a central and saving doctrine, one that must be believed (or understood) in order to hold a temple recommend or be in good standing in the Church.

Q #6: *How can Latter-day Saints believe in a God with a physical, flesh and bones body, when the scriptures clearly teach that "God is a spirit" (John 4:24)?*

A: The most direct answer to this question is, of course, that Latter-day Saints believe what they believe about the corporeal nature of God as a result of modern revelation. As early as 1830 Joseph Smith recorded the following, which is now in the Pearl of Great Price: "In the day that God created man, in the likeness of God made he him; in the image of his own body, male and female, created he them, and blessed them" (Moses 6:8-9). In 1841 he declared: "That which is without body, parts and passions is nothing. There is no other God in heaven but that God who has flesh and bones."[7] In April of 1843 Joseph taught that "The Father has a body of flesh and bones as tangible as man's; the Son also; but the Holy Ghost has not a body of flesh and bones, but is a personage of Spirit" (D&C 130:22). Two months later he explained: "As the Father hath power in Himself, so hath the Son power in Himself. . . . [S]o He has a body of His own; each one [God and Christ] will be in His own body; and yet the sectarian world believe the body of the Son is identical with the Father's."[8]

Secondly, the word "spiritual," as used in the New Testament and in LDS scripture, means immortal, not subject to death. Thus the mortal body is temporal and corrupt, while the resurrected, immortal body is incorruptible and spiritual, meaning that it is no longer subject to the pulls and passions of life and the ever-present reality of physical death (1 Corinthians 15:44). One Book of Mormon prophet affirmed that "this mortal body is raised to an immortal body, that is from death, even from the first death unto life, that they can die no more; their spirits uniting with their bodies, never to be divided; thus the

7. TPJS, 181.
8. TPJS, 312.

whole becoming spiritual and immortal, that they can no more see corruption" (Alma 11:44). Likewise a modern revelation, in speaking of the resurrection of men and women, pointed out that "notwithstanding they die, they also shall rise again, a spiritual body" (D&C 88:27). Bruce R. McConkie has written that the phrase "God is a spirit" has been "interpreted by the Christian world to mean that God is a spirit essence that fills all space, has no form or substance, and dwells in human hearts. It might properly be said that 'God is a spirit' if by that is meant that he has a spiritual or resurrected body in harmony with Paul's statement relative to the resurrection that the body 'is sown a natural body; it is raised a spiritual body.'"[9]

Finally, the correct translation of John 4:24 is not "God is a spirit," but rather "God is spirit" (NKJV, NIV, NRSV, NEB). That is to say, God is approached and known in spiritual ways, or he is known not at all; indeed, God stands revealed or he remains forever unknown. Because mortal men and women are made up of both body and spirit, and because the spirit is the real, inner, eternal part of man, a modern revelation teaches that "man is spirit" as well (D&C 93:33). "For what man knoweth the things of a man, save the spirit of man which is in him? Even so the things of God knoweth no man, but the Spirit of God" (1 Corinthians 2:11).

Q #7: *From an LDS point of view, was Jesus of Nazareth human or God?*

A: This was, of course, the object of centuries of discussion and debate within Christian history. Latter-day Saints believe that by inheritance as well as by perfect obedience, Jesus Christ was entitled to a fulness of the Spirit. Jesus spoke often of his divine inheritance. "Therefore doth my Father love me," John recorded, "because I lay down my life, that I might take it again. No man taketh it from me, but I lay it down of myself. I have power to lay it down, and I have power to take it again. This commandment have I received of my Father" (John 10:17-18). Herein is the fundamental truth to be believed if we are to accept the divine Sonship of Christ. Jesus was the son of Mary, a mortal woman, and from her inherited mortality, including the pull and passions of mortality (he "was in all points tempted like as we are, yet without sin," Hebrews 4:15), including the capacity to die. Jesus was the son of God, a glo-

---

9. McConkie, *A New Witness for the Articles of Faith* (Salt Lake City: Deseret Book, 1985), 61; see also 72-73.

rified immortal being, and from him inherited the capacity to rise up from the dead in resurrected immortality. In discoursing on the redemption of the Messiah, one Book of Mormon prophet stressed how vital it is to make these truths known "unto the inhabitants of the earth, that they may know that there is no flesh that can dwell in the presence of God, save it be through the merits, and mercy, and grace of the Holy Messiah, *who layeth down his life according to the flesh, and taketh it again by the power of the Spirit,* that he may bring to pass the resurrection of the dead, being the first that should rise" (2 Nephi 2:8, emphasis added). The Savior thus had "power given unto him from the Father" (Helaman 5:11; Mormon 7:5) to do what he was sent to earth to do.

In coming to earth, Jesus condescended and left his throne as the mighty Jehovah behind; in the process, he "humbled himself" (literally "emptied himself," see Philippians 2:8, NRSV). "After the humbling of incarnation, Jesus further humbled Himself in that He did not demand normal human rights, but subjected Himself to persecution and suffering at the hands of unbelievers."[10] Though the fulness of the glory and power of the Father would not be Christ's until after the resurrection (Matthew 28:18; D&C 93:16-17),[11] Jesus lived and moved and had his being in the Spirit of God and enjoyed that Spirit in its fulness. It was that fulness that enabled and empowered the lowly Nazarene to resist evil, dismiss Satan from his life, and enjoy constant communion with the Father. "Where is the man that is free from vanity?" Joseph Smith asked. "None ever were perfect but Jesus; and why was He perfect? Because *He was the Son of God, and had the fullness of the Spirit, and greater power than any man.*"[12] In speaking of becoming perfect, Elder Bruce R. McConkie observed: "We have to become perfect to be saved in the celestial kingdom. But nobody becomes perfect in this life. Only the Lord Jesus attained that state, and *he had an advantage that none of us has. He was the Son of God, and he came into this life with a spiritual capacity and a talent and an inheritance that exceeded beyond all comprehension what any of the rest of us was born with.*"[13]

10. John MacArthur, ed., *The MacArthur Study Bible* (Nashville: Word, 1997), 1823.

11. Joseph Fielding Smith, *Doctrines of Salvation* 2:269; Bruce R. McConkie, *Mormon Doctrine,* 2nd ed. (Salt Lake City: Bookcraft, 1966), 333.

12. TPJS, 187-88, emphasis added.

13. "Jesus Christ and Him Crucified," *1976 BYU Speeches of the Year* (Provo: BYU Publications, 1976), 399, emphasis added.

The Latter-day Saints teach, and the New Testament affirms, that the Beloved Son was in fact subordinate to his Father in mortality. Jesus came to carry out the will of the Father (John 4:34). He explained: "I seek not mine own will, but the will of the Father which hath sent me" (John 5:30; compare 6:38-40). In addition, the scriptures attest that the Father had power, knowledge, glory, and dominion that Jesus did not have at the time. Truly, "the Son can do nothing of himself, but what he seeth the Father do" (John 5:19). Even what the Son spoke was what the Father desired to be spoken. "For I have not spoken of myself; but the Father which sent me, he gave me a commandment, what I should say, and what I should speak. And I know that his commandment is life everlasting: whatsoever I speak therefore, even as the Father said unto me, so I speak" (John 12:49-50). How much more plainly could the Lord speak concerning his subordinate position than when he said, "If ye loved me, ye would rejoice, because I said, I go unto the Father: for my Father is greater than I" (John 14:28)?

On the other hand, the Father and the Son enjoyed much more than what we might call closeness; theirs was a divine indwelling relationship. Because he kept the law of God, Jesus was in the Father, and the Father was in Jesus (see John 14:10, 20; 17:21; 1 John 3:24). Though they were two separate and distinct beings, they were one. Their transcendent unity but epitomizes what ought to exist between God and all of his children. That is to say, we are under commission to seek the Spirit of God, to strive to be one with the Gods, to be, as Joseph Smith explained, "agreed as one,"[14] to have, as Paul wrote, "the mind of Christ" (1 Corinthians 2:16). "Hereby know we that we dwell in him, and he in us, because he hath given us of his Spirit" (1 John 4:13). We thus gain the mind of Christ as Christ gained the mind of the Father — through the power of the Spirit. In short, in the language of the Book of Mormon, Jesus was spirit and flesh, Father and Son, God and man. "And they" — spirit and flesh, Father and Son, God and man — "are one God, yea, the very Eternal Father of heaven and of earth" (Mosiah 15:1-4).

Q #8: *How can the Latter-day Saints continue to take seriously the Book of Mormon when there have been so few tangible evidences of its truthfulness?*

A: In the words of Terryl L. Givens, Professor of English at the Uni-

14. TPJS, 372.

versity of Richmond in Virginia, "The Book of Mormon is perhaps the most religiously influential, hotly contested, and, in the secular press at least, intellectually underinvestigated book in America."[15] Historian Nathan Hatch has observed, for example, that "For all the recent attention given to the study of Mormonism, surprisingly little has been devoted to the Book of Mormon itself. What are the patterns deep in the grain of this extraordinary work and what do they reveal about the perceptions and intentions of the prophet Joseph Smith? Mormon historians, of course, have been more interested in pointing out the ways in which the book transcends the provincial opinions of the man Joseph Smith, thus establishing its uniquely biblical and revelatory character. Mormon detractors, on the other hand, have attempted to reduce the book to an inert mirror of the popular culture of New York during the 1820s, thus overlooking elements that are unique and original. . . . Scholars have not taken seriously Joseph Smith's original rationale about the nature of his prophetic mission. The pivotal document of the Mormon church . . . still receives scant attention from cultural historians, while scholars rush to explore more exotic themes, such as the influence upon Joseph Smith of magic, alchemy, and the occult."[16]

Within the last few decades, much work has gone forward by LDS academicians, investigations into ancient literary devices, Hebraisms, name studies, treaty-covenant patterns, word print analyses that focus on single or multiple authorship within the Book of Mormon, warfare, and geography — all of which are intended to establish Book of Mormon antiquity and an ancient meso-American milieu for the narrative.[17] Latter-day Saints are also quick to suggest that time and patience

15. *By the Hand of Mormon* (New York: Oxford, 2002), 6.

16. *The Democratization of American Christianity* (New Haven: Yale University Press, 1989), 115.

17. See, for example, *Book of Mormon Authorship,* ed. Noel B. Reynolds and Charles D. Tate (Provo, UT: BYU Religious Studies Center, 1982); John W. Welch, *The Sermon at the Temple and the Sermon on the Mount* (Salt Lake City: Deseret Book and FARMS, 1990); *Reexploring the Book of Mormon,* ed. John W. Welch (Salt Lake City: Deseret Book and FARMS, 1992); Roger R. Keller, *Book of Mormon Authors* (Provo: BYU Religious Studies Center, 1996); John Sorenson, *An Ancient American Setting for the Book of Mormon* (Salt Lake City: Deseret Book and FARMS, 1996); *Book of Mormon Authorship Revisited,* ed. Noel B. Reynolds (Provo, UT: FARMS, 1997); Richard Rust, *Feasting on the Word: The Literary Testimony of the Book of Mormon* (Salt Lake City: Deseret Book and FARMS, 1997); *King Benjamin's Speech,* ed. John W. Welch and Stephen D. Ricks (Provo, UT: FARMS, 1998).

are needed when it comes to "proving" Book of Mormon historicity. Biblical scholars have had centuries to establish the historical veracity of the people and events of the Old and New Testaments, and some things have only been corroborated within very recent years. Should people of the Book have hesitated to believe in the man Abraham until sufficient archaeological evidence existed? Should Christians have refused to accept the resurrection itself until physical evidence was uncovered that substantiated it? Joseph Smith's golden plates are not available for scholarly examination, nor are the Urim and Thummim. Mormons are not, however, rushing forward in great numbers to toss their copies of the Book of Mormon into a bonfire.

Interestingly enough, almost all attacks on the Book of Mormon take the form of questioning or undermining its origins and coming forth. Precious little attention has been given to the doctrinal content of the Book of Mormon by its critics, except for an occasional comment to the effect that King James language is used here and there. Latter-day Saints believe that spiritual realities are investigated and confirmed first and foremost in a spiritual way, that, as the apostle Paul wrote, the things of God are known only in and through the power of the Spirit of God (1 Corinthians 2:11-14). People can indeed "know" of the truthfulness of a spiritual reality, can possess "an inward conviction that is perfectly valid to [those] in whom it arises." The decision to accept a spiritual matter without current physical evidence can "carry with it an incontrovertible inner endorsement that is worth any amount of argument."[18] While there must be an actual physical referent upon which faith is built (a moment in real time, an event such as the resurrection of Jesus, or a set of golden plates), to exercise faith is to believe in the reality of the unseen and to accept as evidence the hope in that which cannot, for the time being, be proven empirically.

Joseph Smith referred to the Book of Mormon as the "keystone of our religion."[19] The keystone of the Roman arch was, of course, the stone at the top of the arch that holds the entire structure together. A Latter-day Saint lecturer at London University, Joseph Hamstead, spoke of the LDS faith, including its youth and family programs. One of those in attendance responded as follows: "I like all of this, what is

18. J. B. Phillips, *Your God Is Too Small* (New York: Touchstone, 1997), 83, 86.
19. TPJS, 194.

being done for families, etc. If you could take out that bit about an angel appearing to Joseph Smith, I could belong to your church." Hamstead retorted: "Ah, but if you take away the angel appearing to the Prophet Joseph, then I couldn't belong to the Church because that is its foundation."[20]

Jeffrey R. Holland, former president of Brigham Young University and now a member of the Quorum of the Twelve Apostles, has written: "To consider that everything of saving significance in the Church stands or falls on the truthfulness of the Book of Mormon and, by implication, the Prophet Joseph Smith's account of how it came forth is as sobering as it is true. It is a 'sudden death' proposition. Either the Book of Mormon is what the Prophet Joseph said it is, or this Church and its founder are false, a deception from the first instance onward. . . . Joseph Smith must be accepted either as a prophet of God or else as a charlatan of the first order, but no one should tolerate any ludicrous, even laughable middle ground about the contours of a young boy's imagination or his remarkable facility for turning a literary phrase. This is an unacceptable position to take — morally, literarily, historically, or theologically."

Elder Holland went on to say: "If Joseph Smith did not translate the Book of Mormon as a work of ancient origin, then I would move heaven and earth to meet the 'real' nineteenth-century author. After one hundred and fifty years, . . . surely there must be someone willing to step forward — if no one else, at least the descendants of the 'real' author — claiming credit for such a remarkable document and all that has transpired in its wake. After all, a writer than can move millions can make millions. Shouldn't someone have come forth then or now to cashier the whole phenomenon?"[21] Perhaps the reader can appreciate why Joseph Smith stated simply: "Take away the Book of Mormon and the revelations, and where is our religion? We have none."[22]

Church leaders have been unruffled in the midst of criticism. Neal A. Maxwell, a modern apostle, stated: "It is the author's opinion that all the scriptures, including the Book of Mormon, will remain in the realm of faith. Science will not be able to prove or disprove holy

20. Personal correspondence to James E. Faust; cited in Faust, "Lord, I Believe; Help Thou Mine Unbelief," *Ensign*, November 2003, 19-20.

21. Holland, *Christ and the New Covenant* (Salt Lake City: Deseret Book, 1997), 345-47.

22. *History of the Church of Jesus Christ of Latter-day Saints*, 7 vols., ed. B. H. Roberts (Salt Lake City: Deseret Book, 1957), 2:52; cited hereafter as HC.

writ. However, enough plausible evidence will come forth to prevent scoffers from having a field day, but not enough to remove the requirement of faith. Believers must be patient during such unfolding."[23] "We do not have to prove the Book of Mormon is true," Ezra Taft Benson declared. "The book is its own proof. All we need to do is read it and declare it. The Book of Mormon is not on trial — the people of the world, including the members of the Church, are on trial as to what they will do with this second witness for Christ."[24]

Gordon B. Hinckley likewise affirmed: "I can hold [the Book of Mormon] in my hand. It is real. It has weight and substance that can be physically measured. I can open its pages and read, and it has language both beautiful and uplifting. The ancient record from which it was translated came out of the earth as a voice speaking from the dust. . . .

"The evidence for its truth, for its validity in a world that is prone to demand evidence, lies not in archaeology or anthropology, though these may be helpful to some. It lies not in word research or historical analysis, though these may be confirmatory. The evidence for its truth and validity lies within the covers of the book itself. The test of its truth lies in reading it. It is a book of God. Reasonable individuals may sincerely question its origin, but those who read it prayerfully may come to know by a power beyond their natural senses that it is true, that it contains the word of God, that it outlines saving truths of the everlasting gospel, that it came forth by the gift and power of God."[25] Another LDS leader, James E. Faust, spoke of the reality of "knowing" of things unseen: "I testify through the sure conviction that springs from the witness of the Spirit that it is possible to know things that have been revealed with greater certainty than by actually seeing them. We can have a more absolute knowledge than eyes can perceive or ears can hear. God Himself has put His approval on the Book of Mormon, having said, 'As your Lord and your God liveth it is true' [D&C 17:6]."[26]

It is worth attending to the perspective of perhaps the greatest Latter-day Saint apologist, Hugh Nibley. "The words of the prophets," he stated, "cannot be held to the tentative and defective tests that men

23. *Plain and Precious Things* (Salt Lake City: Deseret Book, 1983), 4.
24. *A Witness and a Warning* (Salt Lake City: Deseret Book, 1988), 13.
25. *Faith: The Essence of True Religion* (Salt Lake City: Deseret Book, 1989), 10-11.
26. "The Keystone of Our Religion," *Ensign,* January 2004, 6.

have devised for them. Science, philosophy, and common sense all have a right to their day in court. But the last word does not lie with them. Every time men in their wisdom have come forth with the last word, other words have promptly followed. The last word is a testimony of the gospel that comes only by direct revelation. Our Father in heaven speaks it, and if it were in perfect agreement with the science of today, it would surely be out of line with the science of tomorrow. Let us not, therefore, seek to hold God to the learned opinions of the moment when he speaks the language of eternity."[27]

In writing of faith in the unseen, Luke Timothy Johnson explained: "Belief in the existence of God is already an act by which one 'entrusts' oneself to a world that is not entirely defined by what can be seen and counted, heard, and accounted for." Further: "Christians need to begin by insisting, first of all to themselves, then to each other, and finally to the world, that faith itself is a way of knowing reality. They need to insist that faith establishes contact with reality in a way different from, but no less real than, the very limited (though, in their fashion, extremely impressive) ways of knowing by which the wheels of the world's empirical engine are kept spinning." As an illustration, "If religion can hold as true only what is 'within the bounds of reason,' and if 'reason' is defined in terms of the empirically verifiable, then the resurrection is excluded by definition. But if the resurrection is excluded, why should Christians continue to revere Jesus, who is then only one of many figures from antiquity worthy of attention and honor?"[28]

Q #9: *Doesn't recent DNA research prove that the Book of Mormon could not be an actual history of an ancient Hebrew people?*

A: The specific question posed by critics of the Book of Mormon is to the effect that Native Americans have been shown to be of Asiatic ancestry, whereas the Book of Mormon claims its peoples came from the Middle East in 600 B.C. and would thus have a different genetic signature. This is an extremely complex issue, well beyond my own capacity to respond intelligently. I will therefore make a few comments and then provide sources for the reader for a more detailed treatment.

Brigham Young University Biology Professor Michael F. Whiting, a

27. *The World and the Prophets* (Salt Lake City: Deseret Book and FARMS, 1987), 134.
28. *The Creed: What Christians Believe and Why It Matters* (New York: Doubleday, 2003), 45, 101, 180.

specialist in molecular systematics who frequently evaluates proposals for the National Science Foundation, has offered the following ideas for consideration:

- DNA analysis has proven a remarkable tool in recent years but cannot properly address itself to a faith claim, which the Book of Mormon certainly is. To begin with, then, the truthfulness of the message of the Book of Mormon, or even its origins, cannot really be fully explained, explained away, supported, or dismissed by scientific proofs, any more than we could prove scientifically many of the faith claims (miraculous events) in the New Testament that Jesus healed the sick, raised the dead, multiplied fish and loaves, or was resurrected himself.
- The reader needs to understand clearly that the "evidence" put forward by Tom Murphy, a doctoral candidate in anthropology, is not based upon a particular study he conducted; there is no study here, only interpolations of and extrapolations from others' work that had nothing to do with testing Book of Mormon truth claims.
- Murphy's statements presuppose a kind of "global colonization" of the Book of Mormon peoples, that they remained a separate and distinct people for over a thousand years and thus that no kind of "genetic drift" occurred during that millennium. The problem with his approach is that many if not most Book of Mormon scholars believe in a "local colonization" process, that when the colony of Lehi came to America there were already indigenous peoples in the land (with unknown genetic origin), peoples whom the Nephites identified as the "other guys" or the Lamanites, peoples with whom over time they intermarried and mixed, thus precluding a single Lehite DNA strain to be identified, isolated, followed, and studied carefully.
- Whiting declared that "I would be just as critical of someone who rose up and said, 'I now have DNA evidence proving the Book of Mormon is true.' The science is tough, and the answers do not come unambiguously."[29]

29. This brief response is based upon a report of a lecture and presentation by Michael Whiting; as reported in FARMS "Insights," vol. 23, no. 2 (2003), 1, 4-5; for a detailed treatment of this issue, the reader is referred to *Journal of Book of Mormon Studies,* vol. 12, no. 1 (2003).

Q #10: *Do not recent translations of the so-called "Joseph Smith papyri" by experts demonstrate that the Book of Abraham is a hoax?*

A: In the summer of 1835 members of the Church purchased from Michael Chandler four mummies and two or more papyrus scrolls that had been discovered in Egypt by a man named Antonio Lebolo. Joseph Smith showed little interest in the mummies but was fascinated by the papyri. Through the use of the Urim and Thummim, Joseph began to translate the scrolls, with W. W. Phelps and Oliver Cowdery as scribes. "I commenced the translation of some of the characters or hieroglyphics, and much to our joy found that one of the rolls contained the writings of Abraham, another the writings of Joseph of Egypt, etc., — a more full account of which will appear in its place, as I proceed to examine or unfold them. Truly we can say, the Lord is beginning to reveal the abundance of peace and truth."[30]

Note that in the Prophet's 1 October 1835 journal entry he stated that "during the research, the principles of astronomy as understood by Father Abraham and the ancients unfolded to our understanding."[31] Early on Oliver Cowdery reported that "When the translation of these valuable documents will be completed, I am unable to say; *neither can I give you a probable idea how large volumes they will make;* but judging from their size, and the comprehensiveness of the language, one might reasonably expect to see a sufficient to develop much upon the mighty acts of the ancient men of God, and of his dealing with the children of men when they saw him face to face."[32] In 1838 Anson Call visited the Prophet in Far West. Joseph invited him in and said, "'Sit down and we will read to you from the translations of the Book of Abraham.' Oliver Cowdery then read until he was tired when Thomas Marsh read" — now note this comment — "*making altogether about two hours.* I was much interested in the work."[33] The Book of Abraham and the three facsimiles, as we now have them in our Pearl of Great Price, were published in the *Times and Seasons* in March of 1842. In the 1 February 1843 issue of

30. HC 2:236.

31. HC 2:286.

32. *Messenger and Advocate,* 2, December 1835, 236, emphasis added.

33. Anson Call Manuscript, 9, Church Historian's Office, Salt Lake City, emphasis added; cited in Duane D. Call, "Anson Call and His Contributions toward Latter-day Saint Colonization," unpublished master's thesis, Brigham Young University, 1956, 33.

the *Times and Seasons,* editor John Taylor encouraged the Saints to renew their subscriptions to the paper, adding the following intriguing detail: "We would further state that *we had the promise of Br. Joseph, to furnish us with further extracts from the Book of Abraham.*"[34]

The history of the papyri after the death of the Prophet in 1844 is somewhat sketchy. The Egyptian relics were kept by Lucy Mack Smith, Joseph's mother, until her death and then sold by Emma Smith Bidamon (Joseph's widow who remarried), to a Mr. A. Combs. Combs sold two of the mummies with some papyri to the St. Louis Museum in 1856, and later in 1863 they were sold to the Chicago Museum (later renamed the Woods Museum). It has generally been assumed that all of the papyri were destroyed in the great Chicago fire in 1871. However, in 1967 an announcement was made that Dr. Aziz Atiya, a professor of Middle Eastern Studies at the University of Utah, had found eleven papyrus fragments, including Facsimile #1 in the New York Metropolitan Museum of Art. Not being a Latter-day Saint himself (he was a Coptic Christian) but being somewhat familiar with LDS culture and the Pearl of Great Price, Dr. Atiya recognized Facsimile #1 and made contact with Church leaders, who eventually took possession of the papyri fragments.

When the announcement was made that the papyrus fragments had been acquired, both committed Latter-day Saints and critics of the faith were intrigued by what would come of the find. The latter group exulted that once and for all the Book of Abraham could be exposed for what it was — a figment of Joseph Smith's fertile imagination. The translation of the eleven fragments and the facsimile by trained Egyptologists revealed parts of the ancient Egyptian Book of Breathings, an excerpt of the larger Book of the Dead, which are actually funerary texts, material associated with the burial and future state of the dead. In other words, the fragments presumably had nothing to do with the person and work of Abraham. In response, the late H. Donl Peterson, professor of Ancient Scripture at BYU and serious student of the Book of Abraham, replied: "The Book of Abraham and Joseph papyri were described as 'Beautifully written on papyrus, with black, and a small part red, ink or paint, in perfect preservation.' The eleven frag-

---

34. *Times and Seasons,* 6 vols. (Nauvoo: The Church of Jesus Christ of Latter-day Saints, 1839-46), 4:95, emphasis added.

ments recovered from the Metropolitan Museum of Art in New York City do not fit that description at all. What was discovered was Facsimile One and some other fragments unrelated to the published account of the present Book of Abraham. They were part of the original scrolls once owned by Joseph Smith but not directly related to the Abrahamic text. The partial text of the Book of Breathings returned to the Church in 1967 was not the text for the Book of Abraham."

Professor Peterson went on to say: "It [the Book of Abraham] was not finished. In fact, it was hardly begun. The Book of Abraham was a lengthy record. . . . Oliver Cowdery spoke of volumes necessary to contain it. Only two short installments were published during Joseph Smith's lifetime, although more was promised. Had not Joseph Smith's last 16 months been so turbulent, no doubt more of the translation would have been forthcoming, as he had promised. We have but a small fraction of a rather lengthy record."[35] "Is the Book of Abraham true?" Elder Bruce R. McConkie asked. "Yes," he answered, "but it is not complete; it stops almost in midair. Would that the Prophet had gone on in his translation or revelation, as the case may be."[36]

Q #11: *Why does Joseph Smith play such a prominent role in Mormonism? If the Saints believe that salvation is in Christ, why such a strong emphasis upon the person and work of a mortal man?*

A: Latter-day Saints worship God and the Godhead. They do not worship any mortal man. But they revere and deeply appreciate the work and contribution of Joseph Smith. They revere him in the same way believers revered Abraham two millennia before Christ, the way ancient Israel respected Moses centuries later, and the way the early Christians looked to Peter and Paul after the death of Jesus. These men were prophets, divinely called spokesmen. The revelations and divine direction that came from them were received as God's own words. The LDS concept of "Christ's eternal gospel" discussed in chapter 1 — that Christian prophets have declared Christian doctrine and administered Christian sacraments since the beginning of recorded time — is linked

35. "The History and Significance of the Book of Abraham," in *Studies in Scripture, Volume 2: The Pearl of Great Price*, ed. Robert L. Millet and Kent P. Jackson (Salt Lake City: Randall Book, 1985), 173, 174; citing HC 2:348.

36. "The Doctrinal Restoration," in *The Joseph Smith Translation: The Restoration of Plain and Precious Things*, ed. Monte S. Nyman and Robert L. Millet (Provo: BYU Religious Studies Center, 1985), 21.

to the prominent place of the prophet. The prophet is called to be the preeminent revealer of Christ and the plan of salvation. Thus as Peter taught, to Christ "give all the prophets witness" (Acts 10:43).

The bearing of testimony is an important part of LDS culture. In their worship services Latter-day Saints can be heard to say, often at the conclusion of a sermon or lesson, "I bear my testimony that I know that God lives. I know that Jesus is the Christ." And then, almost in the same breath, the person may say: "I know that Joseph Smith was called of God to restore the truths of salvation." They may then bear a like testimony of the current president of the Church as God's prophet. Thus the foundational truths are that God lives and his Son Jesus Christ is the Savior and Redeemer of all humankind. Of next importance is that God has revealed himself anew in our time through latter-day spokesmen.

Q #12: *I find much of Mormonism appealing and am fascinated by many of your distinctive doctrines. A few of my Christian friends and I have commented to one another that we would even consider joining your church if it weren't for Joseph Smith. How would you react to that?*

A: On the surface, one could view Joseph Smith just as he or she might view a Martin Luther, a John Calvin, a Roger Williams, an Alexander Campbell — as the leader of a new religious group, as one who recognized errors in Christianity and sought through divine assistance to address them. At the same time, it is in reality not possible to accept fully the revelation — the doctrine and teachings, the way of life, the fruits of the faith — and yet reject the revelator. This would be like saying: "I appreciate the value and importance of the ten commandments but just cannot accept the fact that Moses was a prophet and received them from God." Or: "I am deeply committed to Christianity and love the teachings of the New Testament but have a real problem with the apostolic callings of Peter, John, and Paul."

Heber J. Grant, the seventh president of the Church, stated: "In many places I have met people who have studied our faith. Some of them would say: 'I could accept everything that you people teach were it not for this man Joseph Smith. If you would only eliminate him!'

"The day can never come when we could do that. As well might we undertake to leave out Jesus Christ, the Son of the living God. Either Joseph Smith *did* see God and *did* converse with Him, and God Himself *did* introduce Jesus Christ to the boy Joseph Smith, and Jesus Christ *did* tell Joseph Smith that he would be the instrument in the hands of God of establishing again upon the earth the true gospel of Jesus Christ — or Mormonism, so-called, is a myth. And Mormonism is not a myth! It is the power of God unto salvation."[37]

Q #13: *None of the LDS churches or temples have crosses on them. Further, Latter-day Saints do not seem to wear crosses. Do Mormons not believe in the cross of Christ?*

A: We believe the Atonement of Jesus Christ to be the central act of all history, just as Christians around the world do. Because Jesus was crucified, the cross has become for LDS, as well as other Christians, associated with the Atonement (1 Corinthians 1:17-18; Galatians 6:12-14; Philippians 2:5-9; 3:18; Hebrews 12:2; 3 Nephi 12:30; Moses 7:55). According to LDS teachings, however, Jesus' suffering in the garden was not just the awful anticipation of the cross. Instead, the atoning sacrifice was performed in the Garden of Gethsemane and on the cross of Calvary. That is, the suffering and shedding of Christ's blood that began in Gethsemane was completed on Golgotha the next day. Thus for Latter-day Saints the acceptance of the Atonement is not symbolized by the cross, whether on or in buildings, on religious vestments, or on church literature. One Church leader noted that "the cross is the symbol of the dying Christ, while our message is a declaration of the living Christ." He explained further that "the lives of our people must become the only meaningful expression of our faith and in fact, therefore, the symbol of our worship."[38]

Q #14: *Do the Latter-day Saints believe people must be "born again" to be saved?*

A: Before I respond directly to this question, let me relate an experience that may prove interesting to the reader. Several years ago, I received a phone call from the religion editor of one of the Salt Lake City newspapers. We exchanged niceties for a moment and then she asked: "Bob, have you seen the results of a recent Barna study on Christian beliefs in America?" I indicated that I had not. She then explained that thousands of persons from various Christian groups, including the Latter-day Saints, had been asked a series of questions about their per-

---

37. *Gospel Standards* (Salt Lake City: Deseret Book, 1976), 3, emphasis in original.

38. Gordon B. Hinckley, *Be Thou An Example* (Salt Lake City: Deseret Book, 1981), 85-86.

sonal beliefs and religious lifestyle. One of the questions was, essentially: "Do you consider yourself to be a 'born again' Christian?" She then read the percentages, by denomination, of those who had answered Yes. Then, with a measure of excitement in her voice, she exulted: "Guess what! Twenty-six percent of Latter-day Saints stated that they had been born again. Isn't that exciting?" I wondered what part of the report was exciting to her: Was it that Latter-day Saints had been included in the survey? Was it that 26 percent spoke affirmatively? "What exactly excites you about this?" I asked. "That such a high percentage of Mormons should express that they had been born again!" she responded. I went silent but thought to myself: "What about the other 74 percent?"

I pondered over the matter for a number of days, wondering why so few LDS folks had answered as they did. Spiritual rebirth is fundamental to our faith and a central doctrine in the Book of Mormon, Doctrine and Covenants, and Pearl of Great Price. It has been written about and spoken about hundreds of times through the years by Church leaders. After about five days of reflection, it occurred to me that many Latter-day Saints probably responded as they did because they perceived the question to be something like the following: "Are you a born again Christian, like many of your Protestant neighbors?" My guess is that a much higher percentage of Mormons would have said Yes to questions like the following, all of which are descriptive of the new birth: Do you believe that Jesus is the Christ, the Promised Messiah? (1 John 5:1). Have you accepted Jesus Christ as your Savior? Is Christ the Lord of your life, and have you given yourself to him? Have you enjoyed a remission of your sins through faith in Christ and repentance? Have you undergone a change in your heart, such that you no longer feel a desire to engage in sinful behavior? (1 John 3:9; 5:18). Have you enjoyed the love of God in your heart, and have you felt spiritually impelled to share that love with others? (1 John 4:7).

Now, to the question: Do we believe in being born again? Yes. In addition to the receipt of the sacrament of water baptism, LDS scripture teaches that all accountable persons "must be born again; yea, born of God, changed from their carnal and fallen state, to a state of righteousness, being redeemed of God, becoming his sons and daughters; and thus they become new creatures; and unless they do this, they can in nowise inherit the kingdom of God" (Mosiah 27:25-26;

compare Alma 7:14). The Christian world is largely divided over this matter of the new birth. A large segment of Christianity today believes that being born again consists of having a personal spiritual experience with Jesus, of receiving him as Lord and Savior. A large segment of Christianity believes that being born again takes place through receiving the sacraments (ordinances) of the church. Joseph Smith stated simply that "Being born again, comes by the Spirit of God through ordinances."[39]

Although the new birth is made possible through the atoning blood of our Lord and Savior, the Holy Ghost is vital in bringing about change. The Holy Ghost is a revelator, a comforter, a teacher, a sanctifier. Parley P. Pratt wrote that the Spirit "quickens all the intellectual faculties, increases, enlarges, expands, and purifies all the natural passions and affections, and adapts them, by the gift of wisdom, to their lawful use. It inspires, develops, cultivates, and matures all the fine-toned sympathies, joys, tastes, kindred feelings, and affections of our nature. It inspires virtue, kindness, goodness, tenderness, gentleness, and charity. It develops beauty of person, form, and features. It tends to health, vigor, animation, and social feeling. It invigorates all the faculties of the physical and intellectual man. It strengthens and gives tone to the nerves. In short, it is, as it were, marrow to the bone, joy to the heart, light to the eyes, music to the ears, and life to the whole being."[40] We would agree with John Stackhouse who wrote that conversion "denotes both the moment of new birth and the lifetime of transformation that follows as the Holy Spirit prepares us for eternity with God."[41]

Q #15: *Because the LDS believe in a universal apostasy or falling away of the primitive Christian church, do they therefore believe they are the only true Christians on earth?*

A: In the Doctrine and Covenants, one of the books within the LDS scriptural canon, the restored Church is referred to as "the only true and living church upon the face of the whole earth" (D&C 1:30). That is, we believe that The Church of Jesus Christ of Latter-day Saints

39. TPJS, 162.
40. *Key to the Science of Theology* (Salt Lake City: Deseret Book, 1978), 61.
41. *Evangelical Landscapes: Facing Critical Issues of the Day* (Grand Rapids: Baker, 2002), 164.

is the custodian of the fulness of the gospel of Jesus Christ and the only church on earth possessing the power to act in the name of God. This position — one, by the way, that is extremely unpopular, at least in the Christian world — is fundamental to who the Latter-day Saints are and why they are.

Latter-day Saints believe that truth is to be found throughout the earth — among men and women in all walks of life, among sages and philosophers, and among persons of differing religious persuasions. But they do claim that through the call of Joseph Smith and his successors, and through the establishment of The Church of Jesus Christ of Latter-day Saints, the *fulness* of the gospel of Jesus Christ has been restored to earth. They value the truths had among the children of God everywhere but believe that theirs is the "only true church" in the sense that the same divine authority and the same doctrines of salvation had from the beginning are now to be found *in their fulness* in the LDS faith. Although Latter-day Saints do believe that the fulness of the gospel, including the proper authority to administer the ordinances (sacraments) of salvation, are contained within their church, they readily acknowledge that any man or woman who believes in the divinity of Jesus Christ and seeks to live in the manner Christ has prescribed, is a Christian.

Q #16: *Latter-day Saints seem to place a great deal of emphasis upon emotion and feelings. They are famous, for example, for suggesting that a person pray about their message and then follow their feelings. Isn't that a risky proposition?*

A: A few years ago my Baptist minister friend, Greg Johnson, and I were driving through Boston in an effort to get to the LDS Institute of Religion at Cambridge. As has been my custom most every time I have been there, I was absolutely lost and had no idea where we were. During our scavenger hunt of sorts, we chatted. My colleague commented on a matter that we had discussed several times, namely the idea that Latter-day Saints are more prone to rely upon feelings than tangible evidence for truth of religious claims. Being just a bit frustrated, I asked: "Do you believe in the literal bodily resurrection of Jesus Christ?" The look he gave me was similar to that which a sixteen-year-old would give to someone who had asked what the teenager felt to be an inane question. "Of course I believe in the resurrection, Bob; I'm an ordained minister." I followed up: "Why do you believe in the resurrection? How do you know it really happened?" He answered: "Because the New Testament teaches of the resurrection of Jesus." I shot right back "But how do you know that the New Testament accounts are true? How do you know the Bible can be trusted? Maybe someone just made all of this up. Maybe the Bible is a giant hoax."

"No," he said, "there is strong evidence to support the truthfulness of the Bible." "Like what?" I asked. "Well, there are archaeological, historical, and cultural evidences that what is being described actually happened." I then queried: "And so that's how you know the resurrection is real?" "Yeah, I suppose so," he said. At this point my mind began to race. I found myself saying something I hadn't planned to say. "You know, I feel a great sense of sadness right now." My evangelical friend was surprised and said: "Sadness? Why are you sad?" "I was just thinking of a good friend of mine, an older woman in Montgomery, Alabama." My partner asked: "What about her?" I then said, "Well, I was thinking of how sad it is that this wonderful and devoted Christian, a person who has given her life to Jesus and cherished and memorized Bible passages like few people I know, a woman whose life manifests her complete commitment to the Savior, is not really entitled to have a witness of the truthfulness of the Bible." "Why is that?" he followed up. "Well, she knows precious little about archaeology or languages or culture or history or manuscripts, and so I suppose she can't know within her heart that the Bible really is the word of God."

"Of course she can," he said. "She can have her faith, her personal witness that the Bible is true." I turned to him, smiled, and stated: "Do you mean that she can have the power of the Holy Spirit testify to her soul that her Bible is completely trustworthy and can be relied upon as God's word?" "Yes, that's what I mean." My smile broadened as I added: "Then we've come full circle." "What do you mean by that?" he asked. "You're telling me that this good woman, one who has none of the supposed requisite background or knowledge of external evidence, can have a witness of the Spirit, including deep personal feelings about the Bible and that those feelings are genuine and heaven-sent." At that point my friend looked into my eyes and he smiled. "I see where you're going with this." We then engaged in one of the most productive conversations of our time together as friends. We agreed between us that it is so easy to yield to the temptation to categorize and pigeonhole and stereotype persons whose faith is different than our own. It is so easy to overstate, to misrepresent, to create and then dismantle "straw men" in an effort to establish our own point.

We agreed that evangelical Christians and Latter-day-Saint Christians both base their faith upon evidence — both seen and unseen. While, as we observed earlier, saving faith is always built upon that which is true, upon an actual historical moment in time, upon something that really existed in the past, true believers will never allow their faith to be held hostage by what science has or has not found at a given time. I know, for example, that Jesus fed the 5,000, healed the sick, raised the dead, calmed the storm, and rose from the dead — not just because I have physical evidence for each of those miraculous events (because I do not), nor even because I can read of these things in the New Testament, which I accept with all my heart. But I know these things actually happened because the Spirit of the Living God bears witness to my spirit that the Lord of Life did all the scriptures say he did, and more.

Religious historian Randall Balmer has written: "I believe because of the epiphanies, small and large, that have intersected my path — small, discrete moments of grace when I have sensed a kind of superintending presence outside of myself. I believe because these moments . . . are too precious to discard, and I choose not to trivialize them by reducing them to rational explanation. I believe because, for me, the alternative to belief is far too daunting. I believe because, at the turn of the twenty-first century, belief itself is an act of defiance in a society still enthralled by the blandishments of Enlightenment rationalism. . . .

"Somehow, I don't think Jeffrey [who asks how he can know there is a God] wants me to rehearse the ontological, the teleological, and the cosmological arguments for the existence of God. . . . So instead of dusting off the teleological argument, I think I'll remind Jeffrey about Karl Barth, arguably the most important theologian of the twentieth century. Toward the end of his life, after he had written volume after volume on the transcendence of God and the centrality of Jesus, Barth was asked to sum up his work. The good doctor paused for a minute and no doubt looked out the window and played with the stubble on his chin before responding with the words of a Sunday school ditty: "Jesus loves me, this I know, for the Bible tells me so."[42]

42. *Growing Pains: Learning to Love My Father's Faith* (Grand Rapids: Brazos Press, 2001), 34, 42-43, 44-45, 61-62.

Q #17: *Do the Latter-day Saints believe in the Second Coming of Jesus Christ? What are they doing to prepare for it?*

A: *Eschatology*, or the study of "end times," is an important dimension of the life and theology of members of The Church of Jesus Christ of Latter-day Saints. What the Latter-day Saints believe about the events to come impacts significantly how they now live and conduct themselves. Without a knowledge of what lies ahead, one cannot have the proper perspective of the overall plan of God to save his children. LDS scriptures are thus filled with references to the last days, to both great and dreadful things that lie ahead. A knowledge of the glories and the trials does much to motivate individuals and congregations to greater fidelity and devotion, to "hold on" to the iron rod, the word of God. The growing fascination in today's world with such phenomena as the Near Death Experience, angels, miracles, etc. attests to men and women's deepest desires to make sense out of what would otherwise be a chaotic existence, a yearning to know that there is a God, that there is life after death, that there is purpose to some of the ironies and challenges of today's world.

Latter-day Saints believe that God can and does speak to men and women through inspiration. They believe the Almighty can make his will known for the world through prophets, and that those prophets have the capacity not only to speak for the present but also to predict future occurrences. The LDS therefore accept wholeheartedly the predictive prophecies in the scriptures. Church leaders have counseled the members of the Church to take a wholesome and sane approach to prophecy, to study and be aware of the prophetic word but to live each day with confidence and conviction that God is in his heaven and will bring to pass his purposes in process of time. Church leaders have therefore counseled against what might be called either *eschatomania* (an unhealthy obsession with signs of the times) and *eschatophobia* (an unhealthy fear of what lies ahead).

Mormons have been counseled for decades to prepare for what lies ahead, and each family has been encouraged to work toward having a year's supply of food and fuel, as well as a moderate amount of money in savings. Although there are always those who tend to react and overreact to such counsel through doomsday living, through crying out that "The sky is falling," Latter-day Saints have been encouraged to engage in provident living, to take the future seriously but to live in the world. Church leaders continue to advise against rumor, speculation, and in general the kind of frenzied attitudes that both evidence and perpetuate emotional and spiritual instability. In short, we try not to take counsel from our fears.

As Christians, Latter-day Saints do believe that Jesus Christ will come again in glory to reign as King of kings and Lord of lords. That is, we believe in the Second Coming of Christ: that it is a fixed time, and that we are obviously closer to that great or dreadful day than were the people who lived in the first century. The very name of the church, The Church of Jesus Christ of Latter-day Saints, epitomizes our belief that these are in fact the last days. We do not, however, believe that the Second Coming will take place right away or that our preparations for that day should be any different than if it were five hundred years from now. As Jesus pointed out in the Parable of the Ten Virgins, there are some things — like years of personal devotion and meaningful service — that one cannot borrow from a neighbor on the spur of the moment. Reservoirs of faith and spiritual depth must be built gradually. We believe that the way to peace and preparation is not through spiritual marathons at the last hour, but rather through consistent and steady spiritual progress throughout our lives. Those who are prepared need not fear.

Q #18: *Do you feel your answers are consistent with traditional Mormonism? That is, is this work an accurate statement of the LDS faith? Would the average Mormon on the street — such as my neighbor down the road or the two missionaries who show up at my door regularly — explain things as you have?*

A: This an excellent question, one I receive quite regularly. I have tried my very best in this work to be true to the central teachings of The Church of Jesus Christ of Latter-day Saints, that is, to reflect what is taught in scripture and by living apostles and prophets. I have no desire whatsoever to compromise or concede one whit on doctrine in order to minimize differences or court favor in any way. I cannot, however, assure the reader that every Latter-day Saint in the world would answer questions or explain principles in exactly the same way I do.

I recently read of a Barna study in which only 50 percent of those who identified themselves as Bible-believing persons felt there were absolute truths to be relied upon in making decisions. Further, of those who identified themselves as born again Christians, some 61 percent believed that the greater responsibility for their attainment of heaven rested with them and their good works.[43] Sometimes what the established doctrine is and what individuals within the faith understand are two different things.

Q #19: *What is the appeal of Mormonism? Why are people choosing to leave their old faiths and join yours?*

A: For one thing, many in our day are weary of the shifting sands of secularity and the ever-mobile standards of society. They long for a return to time-honored values and absolute truths. Because wickedness is widening, honest truth seekers yearn for something to hold on to, something of substance, something that will stand when all else is falling. At the same time, they long to be a part of a religious organization that requires something of them. In fact, recent sociological studies attest that the churches that tend to be growing in our day are those that demand the most of their membership. Latter-day Saints do not apologize, for example, for our position on chastity and virtue, nor do we hesitate to teach the need to pay our tithes and offerings. We know that persons remain steadfast and immovable in the faith to the degree that they invest themselves in the faith.

There is another significant appeal of the Church, as attested by converts. It is our doctrine. It is comforting for people to know that God our Heavenly Father has a plan, and that there is purpose to struggles and suffering, and even death. As an illustration of what we're here discussing — why the Church appeals to so many — let's consider the LDS doctrine on life after death. The idea of a divine plan — including that which deals with heaven and the hereafter — is especially appealing to those who encounter Mormonism. "Expressions of the eternal nature of love and the hope for heavenly reunion," Colleen McDannell and Bernhard Lang have written, "persist in contemporary Christianity."

They continue: "Such sentiments, however, are not situated within a theological structure. Hoping to meet one's family after death is a wish and not a theological argument. While most Christian clergy would not deny that wish, contemporary theologians are not interested in articulating the motif of meeting again in theological terms. The motifs of the modern heaven — eternal progress, love, and fluidity between earth and the other world — while acknowledged by pastors in their funeral sermons, are not fundamental to contemporary Chris-

43. George Barna, *Think Like Jesus* (Nashville: Integrity Publishers, 2003), 21, 29, 123-24.

tianity. Priests and pastors might tell families that they will meet their loved ones in heaven as a means of consolation, but contemporary thought does not support that belief as it did in the nineteenth century. There is no longer a strong theological commitment.

"The major exception to this caveat is the teaching of The Church of Jesus Christ of Latter-day Saints, whose members are frequently referred to as the Mormons. The modern perspective on heaven — emphasizing the nearness and similarity of the other world to our own and arguing for the eternal nature of love, family, progress, and work — finds its greatest proponent in Latter-day Saints' (LDS) understanding of the afterlife. While most contemporary Christian groups neglect afterlife beliefs, what happens to people after they die is crucial to LDS teachings and rituals. Heavenly theology is the result not of mere speculation, but of revelation given to past and present church leaders. . . .

". . . There has been . . . no alteration of the LDS understanding of the afterlife since its articulation by Joseph Smith. If anything, the Latter-day Saints in the twentieth century have become even bolder in their assertion of the importance of their heavenly theology. . . . In the light of what they perceive as a Christian world which has given up belief in heaven, many Latter-day Saints feel even more of a responsibility to define the meaning of death and eternal life."[44]

A people's conduct and way of life cannot be separated from their doctrine, for what they believe empowers and directs what they do. A number of years ago an article appeared in *Christianity Today* entitled "Why Your Neighbor Joined the Mormon Church." Five reasons were given:

1. The Latter-day Saints show genuine love and concern by taking care of their people.
2. They strive to build the family unit.
3. They provide for their young people.
4. Theirs is a layman's church.
5. They believe that divine revelation is the basis for their practices.

After a brief discussion of each of the above, the author of the article concluded: "In a day when many are hesitant to claim that God has

44. *Heaven: A History* (New Haven: Yale, 1988), 313, 322.

said anything definitive, the Mormons stand out in contrast, and many people are ready to listen to what the Mormons think the voice of God says. It is tragic that their message is false, but it is nonetheless a lesson to us that people are many times ready to hear a voice of authority."[45] The Savior taught of the importance of judging things — prophets, for example — by their fruits, by the results of their ministry and teachings, by what their teachings produce (Matthew 7:15-20). He also explained that "Every plant, which my heavenly Father hath not planted, shall be rooted up" (Matthew 15:13).

Q #20: *Why do the Latter-day Saints send their missionaries out into the world, especially into Christian nations? What do they hope to accomplish?*

A: Before The Church of Jesus Christ of Latter-day Saints was even organized, a spirit of enthusiasm and zeal was evident among those who encountered the message of Joseph Smith, the Book of Mormon, and the idea that God had chosen to restore biblical truths and authorities to earth. That spirit intensified after the formal organization of the Church. Many of the revelations recorded in the Doctrine and Covenants instruct the Latter-day Saints to travel, to preach, and to make converts. Because the Latter-day Saints believe what they have to share with others represents a *fulness* of the gospel of Jesus Christ, and that the fulness is not found elsewhere, they feel a responsibility to make the message available to all who will hear. The Great Commission given to the apostles when Jesus ascended into heaven, a commission to make disciples of all nations (Matthew 28:19-20; Mark 16:15-18), has been repeated and renewed to the Latter-day Saints: "Go ye into all the world, preach the gospel to every creature, acting in the authority which I have given you, baptizing in the name of the Father, and of the Son, and of the Holy Ghost" (D&C 68:8). Those who are content with what they have are perfectly free to express the same to LDS missionaries or members. Those who are curious, unsatisfied with their present faith or way of life, or those who may be seeking for answers to some of life's puzzling questions, may find an encounter with the Latter-day Saints worth their time and attention.

Because the LDS believe that peace and happiness here and hereafter are to be found only in and through the person and powers of Jesus

---

45. Donald P. Shoemaker, "Why Your Neighbor Joined the Mormon Church," *Christianity Today*, 19 (11 October 1974), 11-13.

Christ, they also believe the only hope for the world is to come unto Christ. The answer to the world's problems — the vexing dilemmas of starvation, famine, disease, crime, inhumanity, and the dissolution of the nuclear family — is ultimately not to be found in more extravagant social programs or stronger legislation. They acknowledge and value the good that is done by so many to bring the message of Jesus from the New Testament to a world that desperately needs it. At the same time, they long to say to a drifting world that there is more truth to be known, more power to be exercised, and more profound fulfillment to be had. As a twentieth-century Church leader pointed out, "We seek to bring all truth together. We seek to enlarge the circle of love and understanding among all the people of the earth. Thus we strive to establish peace and happiness, not only within Christianity but among all mankind."[46] In that same spirit, in 1907 the First Presidency of The Church of Jesus Christ of Latter-day Saints made the following declaration: "Our motives are not selfish; our purposes not petty and earth-bound; we contemplate the human race, past, present and yet to come, as immortal beings, for whose salvation it is our mission to labor; and to this work, broad as eternity and deep as the love of God, we devote ourselves, now, and forever."[47]

Q #21: *Given the major differences between the beliefs of Latter-day Saints and other more traditional Christians, is it appropriate to refer to them as a Christian faith?*

A: This really is the question of questions, isn't it? Given that there are meaningful differences between the Latter-day Saints and other Christians, the Church has begun to speak of being "Christian but different." If an acceptance of the divinity of Jesus of Nazareth makes one a Christian, then Latter-day Saints are Christian. If an acceptance of the writings and witness of the New Testament makes one a Christian, then Latter-day Saints are Christian. If an acceptance of the atoning sacrifice, willing substitutionary offering, and literal bodily resurrection of Jesus makes one a Christian, then Latter-day Saints are Christian. If striving to live in the manner that Jesus taught us, according to

46. Howard W. Hunter, *That We Might Have Joy* (Salt Lake City: Deseret Book, 1994), 59.

47. Conference Report, April 1907, appendix, 16; cited in Hunter, *That We Might Have Joy*, 59.

his matchless example, makes one a Christian, then Latter-day Saints are Christian.

If, however, being in the historical line of Christian churches — either Catholic or Protestant — makes one a Christian, then clearly Latter-day Saints are not Christian, for they believe that a restoration of divine truth and power were necessary. If a belief in the sufficiency and inerrancy of the Bible makes one a Christian, then obviously Latter-day Saints are not Christian, for while they accept and love the Bible they welcome the call of modern prophets and additional scripture. If an acceptance of the doctrine of the Trinity makes one a Christian, then of course Latter-day Saints are not Christian, for they believe the doctrine of the Trinity as expressed in modern Protestant and Catholic theology is the product of the reconciliation of Christian theology with Greek philosophy.

On one occasion, President Gordon B. Hinckley said to the Latter-day Saints: "We are met to worship the Lord, to declare his divinity and his living reality. We are met to reaffirm our love for him and our knowledge of his love for us. No one, regardless of what he or she may say, can diminish that love.

"There are some who try. For instance, there are some of other faiths who do not regard us as Christians. That is not important. How we regard ourselves is what is important. We acknowledge without hesitation that there are differences between us. Were this not so, there would have been no need for a restoration of the gospel. . . .

"I hope we do not argue over this matter. There is no reason to debate it. . . . We must not become disagreeable as we talk of doctrinal differences. There is no place for acrimony. But we can never surrender or compromise that knowledge which has come to us through revelation. . . .

"We can respect other religions and must do so. We must recognize the great good they accomplish. We must teach our children to be tolerant and friendly toward those not of our faith. We can and do work with those of other religions in the defense of those values which have made our civilization great and our society distinctive."[48]

CONCLUSION:
Revisiting the Question

So often people of different religious persuasions simply talk past one another when they converse on matters religious. They may even use the same words, but they bring a different mindset and an entirely different perspective to the encounter. In other situations we employ a different vocabulary but intend to convey the same message. Misperception and misrepresentation inevitably follow. If there is anything needed in this confused world, it is understanding. While Latter-day Saints readily acknowledge that not all who learn of their doctrine will accept what they teach, it is very important to them that others understand what they say and what they mean.

"Disagreeing with one another need not, and should not, be scary and divisive," Gregory Boyd has written, "so long as we keep our hearts and minds focused on the person of Jesus Christ. Indeed, when our hearts and minds are properly focused, our dialogues with one another, however impassioned they may be, become the means by which we lovingly help each other appreciate aspects of God's word we might otherwise overlook or fail to understand."[1] Persons can possess what my friend Richard Mouw calls "convicted civility" — they can be completely committed to their own faith and way of life but also eager to learn and grow in understanding and thus to treat those with differing views with the dignity and respect they deserve as a son or daughter of God.[2] President Gordon B. Hinckley

---

1. *God of the Possible* (Grand Rapids: Baker, 2000), 20.
2. See *Uncommon Decency: Christian Civility in an Uncivil World* (Downers Grove, IL: InterVarsity, 1992).

said of the Latter-day Saints: "We want to be good neighbors; we want to be good friends. We feel we can differ theologically with people without being disagreeable in any sense. We hope they feel the same way toward us. We have many friends and many associations with people who are not of our faith, with whom we deal constantly, and we have a wonderful relationship. It disturbs me when I hear about any antagonisms. . . . I don't think they are necessary. I hope that we can overcome them."[3]

In a 1997 teleconference with religion writers, former President Jimmy Carter, a Southern Baptist himself, called upon others within Christianity to exercise a greater measure of Christian charity and tolerance when it comes to dealing with persons of other faiths. He chastised the leaders of the Southern Baptist Convention for characterizing Mormons as non-Christian. "Too many leaders now, I think, in the Southern Baptist Convention and in other conventions, are trying to act as the Pharisees did, who were condemned by Christ, in trying to define who can and who cannot be considered an acceptable person in the eyes of God. In other words, they're making judgments on behalf of God. I think that's wrong."

President Carter added that "among the worst things we can do, as believers in Christ, is to spend our time condemning others who profess faith in Christ and try to have a very narrow definition of who is and who is not an acceptable believer and a child of God.

"I think this is one of the main reasons that Christ not only said once, but repeated on other occasions, that we should not judge others, we should let God be the judge of the sincerity of a human mind or a human heart, and let us spend our time trying to alleviate suffering, opening our hearts to others, learning about the needs of others, being generous, being compassionate and so forth."

The former President reminded us that the Great Commission — to take the gospel of Jesus Christ to all the world (Matthew 28:19-20; Mark 16:15-16) — is "a mandate that has guided Baptists as well as members of The Church of Jesus Christ of Latter-day Saints and others all down through the centuries. I think that . . . part of my own life commitment is to tell others about Christ, and to offer them, at least, the

---

3. Cited in Sheri L. Dew, *Go Forward with Faith: The Biography of Gordon B. Hinckley* (Salt Lake City: Deseret Book, 1996), 576.

word of God, and to let the Holy Spirit decide, or ordain the results of those intercessions."[4]

"As a Church we have critics, many of them," President Hinckley stated. "They say we do not believe in the traditional Christ of Christianity. There is some substance to what they say. Our faith, our knowledge is not based on ancient tradition, the creeds which came of a finite understanding and out of the almost infinite discussions of men trying to arrive at a definition of the risen Christ. Our faith, our knowledge comes of the witness of a prophet in this dispensation who saw before him the great God of the universe and his Beloved Son, the resurrected Lord Jesus Christ. . . . It is out of that knowledge, rooted deep in the soil of modern revelation, that we, in the words of [a Book of Mormon prophet named] Nephi, 'talk of Christ, we rejoice in Christ, we preach of Christ, we prophesy of Christ, and we write according to our prophecies, that [we and] our children may know to what source [we] may look for a remission of our sins.'"[5] "Are we Christians?" President Hinckley asked on another occasion. "Of course we are Christians. We believe in Christ. We worship Christ. We take upon ourselves in solemn covenant his holy name. The Church to which we belong carries his name. He is our Lord, our Savior, our Redeemer through whom came the great Atonement with salvation and eternal life."[6]

If I may be pardoned, let me now speak a bit personally and share some thoughts and feelings that enter upon this question of who and what we worship. I cannot guarantee that every Latter-day Saint would describe their faith and way of life exactly as I have, but I have tried, to the best of my ability, to be true to the scriptures (for us, those ancient and modern) and to the teachings of latter-day prophets. In short, *I* sincerely believe that this is what *we* believe. To paraphrase the apostle Paul, the Spirit bears witness with my spirit (Romans 8:16) that Jesus is the Christ, the Son of the Living God, and that he was crucified for the sins of the world. Knowing what we know, feeling what we feel, and having experienced what we have in regard to the person and power of the Savior, it is sometimes difficult for us to be patient to-

---

4. Reported in *Deseret News,* 15 November 1997; see also *The Personal Beliefs of Jimmy Carter* (New York: Three Rivers Press, 1997), 185-99.

5. Conference Report, April 2002, 107-8.

6. Gordon B. Hinckley, Conference Report, October 1998, 91.

ward those who denounce us as non-Christian or cultists. But we are constrained to do so in the spirit of Him who also was misunderstood and misrepresented. While it would be a wonderful thing to have others acknowledge our Christianity, we do not court favor, nor will we compromise our distinctiveness in order to gain acceptance or popularity.

Richard Mouw pointed out that "while I am no universalist, my own inclination is to emphasize the 'wideness of God's mercy' rather than the 'small number of the elect' motif that has often dominated the Calvinist outlook. I take seriously the Bible's vision of the final gathering-in of the elect, of that 'great multitude that no one could count, from every nation, from all tribes and peoples and languages,' who shout the victory cry, 'Salvation belongs to our God who is seated on the throne, and to the Lamb' (Revelation 7:9-10). For all I know — and for all any of us can know — much of what we now think of as common grace may in the end time be revealed to be saving grace. But in the meantime, we are obligated to serve the Lord in accordance to patterns that he has made clear to us."[7]

A short time ago a colleague and I sat at lunch with two prominent theologians. This was not our first visit together, as we had met two years earlier and had had a sweet and delightful discussion of Jesus Christ, the centrality of his Atonement, the lifting and liberating powers of his grace, and how our discipleship is and should be lived out day by day. In that initial meeting there was no defensiveness, no pretense, no effort to put the other down or prove him wrong. Instead, there was that simple exchange of views, an acknowledgement of our differences, and a spirit of rejoicing in those central features of the doctrine of Christ about which we were in complete agreement, a sobering spirit of gratitude for the incomparable blessings that flow from the life and death and transforming power of the Redeemer.

Now, two years later, we picked up where we had left off, almost as if no time had passed at all. Many things were said, diagrams were drawn on napkins, and a free flow of ideas took place. At about the midpoint of our meeting, one of our friends turned to me and said: "Okay Bob, here's the question of questions, the one thing I would like

7. *He Shines in All That's Fair: Culture and Common Grace* (Grand Rapids: Eerdmans, 2001), 100.

to ask in order to determine what you really believe." I indicated that I thought I was ready for his query, though I readily admit that his preface to the question was a bit unnerving. He continued: "You are standing before the judgment bar of the Almighty, and God turns to you and asks: 'Robert Millet, what right do you have to enter heaven? Why should I let you in?'" It was not the kind of question I had anticipated. (I had assumed he would be asking something more theologically theoretical. This question was theological, to be sure, but it was poignant, practical, and extremely penetrating.) For about thirty seconds I tried my best to envision such a scene, searched my soul, and sought to be as clear and candid as possible. Before I indicate exactly what I said, I want to take us forward twenty-four hours in time.

The next day I spoke to a large group of LDS single adults from throughout New England who had gathered for a conference in Boston. My topic was "Hope in Christ." Two-thirds of the way through my address I felt it would be appropriate to share our experience from the day before. I posed to the young people the same question that had been posed to me. There was a noticeable silence in the room, an evidence of quiet contemplation upon a singularly significant question. I allowed them to think about it for a minute or so and then walked up to one of the young women on the front row and said: "Let's talk about how we would respond. Would I say something like the following to God? 'Well, I should go to heaven because I was baptized into the church, I served a full-time mission, I married in the temple, I attend worship services regularly, I read my scriptures daily, I pray in the morning and at night. . . .' At that point the young woman cut me off with these words: "Wait . . . Wait . . . I don't feel right about your answer. In fact, it makes me very uncomfortable." "Why should it make you uncomfortable?" I responded. "I've done all of those things, haven't I? Shouldn't I provide for the Lord a complete list of my good deeds?" She then wisely answered: "I think he knows what you've done with your life. Your answer sounds like you're reading God your resume."

Several hands then went up. One young man blurted out: "How did you answer the question? Tell us what you said!" I thought back upon the previous day, recalled to mind many of the feelings that swirled in my heart at the time, and told the single adults how I had answered. "I looked my friend in the eye and replied: 'I would say to God: I claim the right to enter heaven because of my complete trust in and reliance upon the merits and mercy and grace of the Lord Jesus Christ.'" My questioner stared at me for about ten seconds, smiled gently, and said: "Bob, that's the correct answer to the question."

Now, for the benefit of the reader, it matters very much to me that you know that I sincerely feel what I said. I believe a person's good works are necessary in the sense that they indicate what we are becoming through the powers of the gospel of Jesus Christ; they manifest who and what we are. But I also know that there will never be enough good deeds on my part — prayers, hymns, charitable acts, financial contributions, or thousands of hours of church service — to save myself. The work of salvation requires the work of a God. Unaided man is and will forevermore be lost, fallen, and unsaved. It is only in the strength of the Lord that we are able to face life's challenges, handle life's dilemmas, engage life's contradictions, endure life's trials, and eventually defeat life's inevitable foe — death.

I know of the power that is in Christ, power not only to create the worlds and divide the seas but also to still the storms of the human heart, to right life's wrongs, to ease and eventually even remove the pain of scarred and beaten souls. There is no bitterness, no anger, no fear, no jealousy, no feelings of inadequacy that cannot be healed by the Great Physician. He is the Balm of Gilead. He is the One sent by the Father to "bind up the brokenhearted, to proclaim liberty to the captives, and the opening of the prison to them that are bound" (Isaiah 61:1) True followers of Christ learn to trust in him more, in the arm of flesh less. They learn to rely on him more, on man-made solutions less. They learn to surrender their burdens to him more. They take their discipleship seriously but seek that grace or enabling power that will make up the difference, that sacred power that makes all the difference! Because of who Christ our Lord is and what he has done, there is no obstacle to peace and joy here or hereafter too great to face or overcome. Because of him, our minds can be at peace. Our souls may rest.

Afterword

On several occasions I have called publicly for evangelical Christians to tone down the rhetoric in order to take a fresh and honest look at what Mormons really believe. And each time I have received angry responses from evangelicals who see me as calling for ungodly compromises with a religion that is fundamentally and unalterably opposed to biblical Christianity. Before looking specifically at what Robert Millet has said in these pages, then, I want to explain briefly why I am convinced that those of us who profess the teachings of the historic Christian tradition should wrestle seriously with what he has written here.

My interest in getting clear about these matters goes back to a Sunday night in the 1950s when I sat as a teenager in a fundamentalist church in northern New Jersey. Walter Martin, the well-known evangelical "cult expert," was doing a series of weekly talks in that church, and on this particular evening his subject was Mormonism. The session had been widely advertised, and the small church was packed. A dozen or so Mormons were in attendance, seated as a group near the front of the auditorium. We had seen them walking in, carrying their copies of the Book of Mormon. Martin was well known to both Mormons and evangelicals as an itinerant lecturer, and he soon would become even better known from "counter-cult" books that he would author, especially his influential *The Kingdom of the Cults*.

Martin was a highly effective public speaker and debater, and I was captivated by the way he made his case against non-Christian groups. He had a fine one-liner, for example, about Christian Science: just as Grape Nuts are neither grapes nor nuts, he said, so Mary Baker Eddy's system of thought is neither Christian nor science. On this particular evening it was clear that the LDS contingent had come armed for debate, and Martin was eager to mix it up with them. During the discussion period, one young man was quite articulate as he argued that Martin misunderstood the Mormon teachings regarding atonement and salvation. Martin was not willing to yield an inch, and what began as a reasoned exchange ended in a shouting match. The young Mormon finally blurted out with deep emotion: "You can come up with all of the clever arguments you want, Dr. Martin, but I know in the depths of my heart that Jesus is my Savior, and it is only through his blood that I can go to heaven!" Martin dismissed him with a knowing smile as he turned to his evangelical audience: "See how they love to distort the meanings of words?" I am paraphrasing from a memory reaching back over about four decades, but I can still hear in my mind what the Mormon said next, in an anguished tone: "You are not even *trying* to understand!"

I came away from that encounter strongly convinced that Martin's theological critique of Mormonism was correct on many of the basic points at issue. But I also left the church that night with the nagging sense that there was more to be said, and that the way to let it be said was captured in the young Mormon's complaint: both sides had to *try* to understand each other. And I vowed to myself that someday I would make an effort to facilitate that kind of effort.

I have tried over the decades since then to pay some attention to LDS thought, but it is only in the past five years that I have had the opportunity to delve seriously into the subject — an investigation greatly facilitated by regular meetings that I have helped to convene between LDS and evangelical scholars. I have studied Mormon writings and questioned my LDS friends at length on key topics. I have made an effort to listen very carefully; my goal has not been so much to win arguments as to be sure that I have understood as best I can what they really believe.

There are two general points that I want to be very clear about here. One is that I am no closer to accepting the historical claims of Mormonism than I was the night that I listened to Walter Martin make the case against Mormon teachings. I do not accept the Book of Mormon as divine revelation, nor do I believe that Joseph Smith was a prophet called by God to restore ancient teachings and practices that had long been lost to the traditional Christian churches.

The second point is that I have absolutely no suspicions that my friend Bob Millet is deceiving us in this book about his own deepest convictions. This has to be said, because many of my fellow Christians view the things that Mormons say with much cynicism about what they "really" mean. The most common charges along these lines are that LDS leaders are so eager to be accepted as a mainstream religion that they are deliberately misleading us about their actual beliefs and that when Mormons utter Christian-sounding words, such as that "Jesus died for our sins," they are using the words in very different ways than do we in the Christian tradition.

I believe that I know Bob Millet well enough to say that these suspicions should be set aside in evaluating the case he has made here. He has made every effort to provide as clearly as he can an honest and frank account of what the LDS believe about the person and work of Jesus Christ. He has shown earlier drafts to me and to other evangelical friends, and he has always responded willingly and enthusiastically to all of our suggestions about how he can best explain his position. This book is a sincere statement of faith by an honest man.

The question of whether he really does mean what, say, an evangelical means when he uses the same words that we employ is, of course, a more complicated matter. In a very important sense, I think that he *does* mean what we mean on some very basic points. For example, take his story — one that I find very moving — about what he replied when he was asked by an evangelical theologian about what he would say to God about why he, Bob Millet the Mormon, ought to be allowed into heaven. I believe that Bob means in his testimony the same thing that I mean when I say that my only plea before the judgment seat of God is that I am covered by the mercy and merits of Jesus Christ. My question is not about the adequacy of his reply to this all-important question. My continuing worry is whether his *other* LDS beliefs can properly *sustain* him in — whether they provide a solid theological *grounding* for — his deep and sincere conviction that his only hope for eternal life is the substitutionary work of Jesus Christ that was completed for his salvation on Calvary. And this is why energetic and sustained — and mutually respecting — arguments between Mormons and traditional Christians have to keep going!

Three things about this book make me hopeful that we can make some progress together in keeping at those arguments. One is the way

Bob Millet makes it clear that we are at least developing a shared under-standing of some basic theological terms. In his groundbreaking book-length dialogue with evangelical theologian Craig Blomberg, Ste-phen Robinson, Bob Millet's colleague at Brigham Young University, made the important observation that "LDS terminology often seems naive, imprecise and even sometimes sloppy by evangelical standards, but evangelicals have had centuries in which to polish and refine their terminology," and besides, he added, "we have no professional clergy to keep our theological language finely tuned." In this present discussion Bob Millet gives much evidence of having read many evangelical au-thors carefully — John Stott, Cornelius Plantinga, John MacArthur, and others — and in a way that brings considerable clarification of the intent of some key LDS doctrines.

Second, reading this book has made it even clearer to me that many — not all, but many — of the arguments that I as a Calvinist evan-gelical have with Mormons are not too far removed from the argu-ments that I have pursued with theologians who represent traditions that are clearly in the Christian mainstream. We evangelicals argue at length with Roman Catholics about whether the Bible is our only au-thority or whether there are additional sources of revealed truth that must be taken as equally authoritative. The question of "divinization" — of how we must think about the apostle John's promise that, while we are already God's children, "it does not yet appear what we shall be," but we can be assured that someday "we will be like Him" — has been much discussed between Christians of the Western churches and the Eastern Orthodox. And Bob Millet's insistence that the "good work" that we must perform in order to gain saving grace is the act of having faith — well, this is not unlike a claim that I regularly argue about with my friends in the Arminian tradition.

Of course, we will have to see whether the Mormon "spin" on these matters means that the apparent similarities with admittedly intra-Christian perspectives are deceptive. But the recognition that some-thing like these and other teachings have been long debated within mainstream Christianity can give us some new handles for assessing the unique "spin" that Mormons put on them.

A third hopeful sign is the kind of interpretations that Millet of-fers for what many of us have taken to be very harsh-sounding LDS claims. Not the least of these is the insistence by Joseph Smith that the "creeds" that many of us profess are an "abomination." To be sure, my own reaction to this kind of rhetoric in Mormonism has long been tempered by an awareness of a similar harshness in my own tradition; the historic Reformed confessional documents that I subscribe to depict, for example, Catholics as "accursed idolators" and Mennonites as people whom we Calvinists must "detest." But Bob Millet helpfully shows that Joseph Smith himself says things about mainstream Christians that do not fit well with a thoroughly nasty interpretation of his "abomination" statement.

For all of that, though, there is still what Millet rightly sets forth as the "more" of Mormonism. Baptism for the dead. The importance of the temple rites. Multiple heavenly realms. The restoration of the ancient offices of prophet and apostle. Golden plates. New revelations.

This is not the place to rehearse the standard — and, I am convinced, the compelling — Christian objections to these and other "more" teachings of the Latter-day Saints. These uniquely Mormon beliefs have to be kept in mind as reminders that the divide between many LDS doctrines and some key beliefs of Christian orthodoxy is still wide indeed. And I will continue to be deeply bothered by this divide, even as I nervously stick to what I have said by way of appreciation for what my good friend has written.

At the heart of our continuing disagreements, I am convinced, are very basic worldview issues. Judaism and Christianity have been united in their insistence that the Creator and the creation — including God's human creatures — are divided by an unbridgeable "being" gap. God is the "Wholly Other" — eternal and self-sufficient — who is in a realm of existence that is radically distinct from the creation that was brought into being out of nothing by God's sovereign decree. On this view of things, to confuse the Creator's being with anything in his creation is to commit the sin of idolatry. Mormons, on the other hand, talk about God and humans as belonging to the same "species." Inevitably, then, the differences are described, not in terms of an unbridgeable gap of being, but in the language of "more" and "less."

This kind of disagreement has profound implications for our understanding of who Jesus Christ is. In traditional Christianity, the question of Christ's saving power cannot be divorced from how we understand his "being." If we believe that we are, in our fallenness, totally incapable of earning our own salvation, then the crucial questions are:

What would it take to save us? What would a Savior have to *be* in order to pay the debt for our sin? And, faced with answers given to these questions by teachers who saw Jesus as less than fully God, the church leaders gathered at the Council of Nicea set forth, in A.D. 325, this profound confession of who Jesus is. "We believe," they wrote,

> in one Lord Jesus Christ,
> the only Son of God,
> begotten from the Father before all ages,
> God from God,
> Light from Light,
> true God from true God,
> begotten, not made;
> of the same essence as the Father.
> Through him all things were made.

And only when we acknowledge all of this about him, the Council stipulated, can we move confidently to this bold and amazing proclamation:

> For us and for our salvation
> he came down from heaven.

As an evangelical Christian I want more than anything else that people — whatever disagreements I might have with them on other matters — know Jesus personally, as the heaven-sent Savior who left heaven's throne to come to the manger, and to Gethsemane, and to Calvary, to do for us what we could never do for ourselves. I also know that having a genuine personal relationship with Jesus Christ does not require that we have all our theology straight. All true Christians are on a journey, and until we see the Savior face-to-face we will all see through a glass darkly.

But I also believe with all my heart that theology is important. There is a real danger for all of us that we will define Jesus in such a way that we cannot adequately claim the full salvation that he alone can provide. I think that an open-minded Christian reader of this book will sense that Bob Millet is in fact trusting in the Jesus of the Bible for his salvation. That is certainly my sense. And this is why I find it especially exciting to be in dialogue with him and other LDS friends about what it means to have a theologically adequate understanding of the person and work of the One who alone is mighty to save. I hope that reading this book will inspire many people — traditional Christians as well as Latter-day Saints — with a new motivation for engaging in that eternally significant conversation.

RICHARD J. MOUW

The Articles of Faith of
The Church of Jesus Christ of Latter-day Saints

1. We believe in God, the Eternal Father, and in His Son, Jesus Christ, and in the Holy Ghost.
2. We believe that men will be punished for their own sins, and not for Adam's transgression.
3. We believe that through the Atonement of Christ, all mankind may be saved, by obedience to the laws and ordinances of the Gospel.
4. We believe that the first principles and ordinances of the Gospel are: first, Faith in the Lord Jesus Christ; second, Repentance; third, Baptism by immersion for the remission of sins; fourth, Laying on of hands for the gift of the Holy Ghost.
5. We believe that a man must be called of God, by prophecy, and by the laying on of hands by those who are in authority, to preach the Gospel and administer in the ordinances thereof.
6. We believe in the same organization that existed in the Primitive Church, namely, apostles, prophets, pastors, teachers, evangelists, and so forth.
7. We believe in the gift of tongues, prophecy, revelation, visions, healing, interpretation of tongues, and so forth.
8. We believe the Bible to be the word of God as far as it is translated correctly; we also believe the Book of Mormon to be the word of God.
9. We believe all that God has revealed, all that He does now reveal, and we believe that He will yet reveal many great and important things pertaining to the Kingdom of God.
10. We believe in the literal gathering of Israel and in the restoration of the Ten Tribes; that Zion (the New Jerusalem) will be built upon

the American continent; that Christ will reign personally upon the earth; and, that the earth will be renewed and receive its paradisiacal glory.

11. We claim the privilege of worshiping Almighty God according to the dictates of our own conscience, and allow all men the same privilege, let them worship how, where, or what they may.

12. We believe in being subject to kings, presidents, rulers, and magistrates, in obeying, honoring, and sustaining the law.

13. We believe in being honest, true, chaste, benevolent, virtuous, and in doing good to all men; indeed, we may say that we follow the admonition of Paul — We believe all things, we hope all things, we have endured many things, and hope to be able to endure all things. If there is anything virtuous, lovely, or of good report or praiseworthy, we seek after these things.

JOSEPH SMITH

APPENDIX B:
The Living Christ

The First Presidency and Council of the Twelve Apostles
The Church of Jesus Christ of Latter-day Saints
January 1, 2000

As we commemorate the birth of Jesus Christ two millennia ago, we offer our testimony of the reality of His matchless life and the infinite virtue of His great atoning sacrifice. None other has had so profound an influence upon all who have lived and will yet live upon the earth.

He was the Great Jehovah of the Old Testament, the Messiah of the New. Under the direction of His Father, He was the creator of the earth. "All things were made by him; and without him was not any thing made that was made" (John 1:3). Though sinless, He was baptized to fulfill all righteousness. He "went about doing good" (Acts 10:38), yet was despised for it. His gospel was a message of peace and goodwill. He entreated all to follow His example. He walked the roads of Palestine, healing the sick, causing the blind to see, and raising the dead. He taught the truths of eternity, the reality of our premortal existence, the purpose of our life on earth, and the potential for the sons and daughters of God in the life to come.

He instituted the sacrament as a reminder of His great atoning sacrifice. He was arrested and condemned on spurious charges, convicted to satisfy a mob, and sentenced to die on Calvary's cross. He gave His life to atone for the sins of all mankind. His was a great vicarious gift in behalf of all who would ever live upon the earth.

We solemnly testify that His life, which is central to all human history, neither began in Bethlehem nor concluded on Calvary. He was the

Firstborn of the Father, the Only Begotten Son in the flesh, the Redeemer of the world.

He rose from the grave to "become the firstfruits of them that slept" (1 Cor. 15:20). As Risen Lord, He visited among those He had loved in life. He also ministered among His "other sheep" (John 10:16) in ancient America. In the modern world, He and His Father appeared to the boy Joseph Smith, ushering in the long-promised "dispensation of the fulness of times" (Eph. 1:10).

Of the Living Christ, the Prophet Joseph wrote: "His eyes were as a flame of fire; the hair of his head was white like the pure snow; his countenance shone above the brightness of the sun; and his voice was as the sound of the rushing of great waters, even the voice of Jehovah, saying:

"I am the first and the last; I am he who liveth, I am he who was slain; I am your advocate with the Father" (D&C 110:3-4).

Of Him the Prophet also declared: "And now, after the many testimonies which have been given of him, this is the testimony, last of all, which we give of him: That he lives!

"For we saw him, even on the right hand of God; and we heard the voice bearing record that he is the Only Begotten of the Father —

"That by him, and through him, and of him, the worlds are and were created, and the inhabitants thereof are begotten sons and daughters unto God" (D&C 76:22-24).

We declare in words of solemnity that His priesthood and His Church have been restored upon the earth — "built upon the foundation of . . . apostles and prophets, Jesus Christ himself being the chief corner stone" (Eph. 2:20).

We testify that He will someday return to earth. "And the glory of the Lord shall be revealed, and all flesh shall see it together" (Isa. 40:5). He will rule as King of Kings and reign as Lord of Lords, and every knee shall bend and every tongue shall speak in worship before Him. Each of us will stand to be judged of Him according to our works and the desires of our hearts.

We bear testimony, as His duly ordained Apostles — that Jesus is the Living Christ, the immortal Son of God. He is the great King Immanuel, who stands today on the right hand of His Father. He is the light, the life, and the hope of the world. His way is the path that leads to happiness in this life and eternal life in the world to come. God be thanked for the matchless gift of His divine Son.

Glossary

Aaronic Priesthood   The Aaronic Priesthood is called the "lesser priest-hood" or the preparatory priesthood. It consists of four offices: deacon, teacher, priest, and bishop. Worthy young men may be ordained a deacon at the age of twelve, a teacher at the age of fourteen, and a priest at the age of six-teen. A bishop, who is the local pastor of the congregation, presides over the Aaronic Priesthood, as well as over the adult congregation. Joseph Smith ex-plained that John the Baptist appeared to him and Oliver Cowdery on 15 May 1829 and conferred upon them the Aaronic Priesthood.

Adam and Eve   Adam and Eve are the parents of the whole human family. They were real people in real time. Their act of partaking of the "forbidden fruit" is viewed in Mormonism, not as an act of rebellion against God but as a means of bringing mortality into being. Latter-day Saint scripture teaches that Adam and Eve were taught the gospel by God and angels, were baptized and re-ceived the Holy Ghost, and had a knowledge of the coming of Jesus Christ. They were earth's first Christians.

Agency   "Moral agency" is the capacity to choose, a gift of God provided to man as a part of the Plan of Salvation. In this sense, man has a significant role to play, with God, in gaining his own salvation.

Angel   An angel of God is a heavenly messenger, sent to comfort, counsel, warn, instruct, or confer divine authority. Angels are men and women, human beings, sons and daughters of God, personages of the same type as we are. Angels are per-sons who have lived or will live at some time on this earth as a mortal being.

Apostasy   An apostasy is a falling away from the truth, generally entailing a loss of divine power and/or correct doctrine. Latter-day Saints often speak of the "great apostasy" as the period of time following the crucifixion of Christ and subsequent deaths of the original apostles.

Apostle   An apostle is one of the offices of the Melchizedek or Higher Priesthood. Apostles are chosen as special witnesses of the name of Christ in all the world. They are called upon to teach, testify (particularly of the ministry, death, and resurrection of the Savior), and to build up the Church and regulate all the affairs of the same in all nations. Twelve men constitute the Quorum of the Twelve Apostles, one of the highest councils of the Church.

Articles of Faith   The Articles of Faith are thirteen statements of LDS doctrine and practice written by Joseph Smith in 1842. They are now contained in the Pearl of Great Price (see Appendix A).

Atonement   The Atonement of Jesus Christ is the most significant event in human history. It is the means by which our Lord's substitutionary offering makes forgiveness of sins, renewal and transformation of human nature, and resurrection from the dead available to all humankind. It reconciles finite and fallen man with an infinite and eternal God.

Baptism   Baptism is a covenant and an ordinance (sacrament) required for salvation, one that evidences a person's acceptance of the atoning sacrifice of Christ. It is performed by immersion for accountable persons by one holding proper priesthood authority. The immersion in water symbolizes the death, burial, and resurrection of the Master.

Baptismal Covenant   In being baptized a person agrees to take upon him or her the name of Jesus Christ, keep his commandments, and always remember him. God promises that the initiate will always have His Spirit to be with them.

Baptism for the Dead   Jesus commanded that all men and women should be born of water and of the Spirit, to be baptized. Those who do not have the opportunity to learn of Christ and his gospel in this life will have that opportunity in the postmortal spirit world. An authorized baptism may be performed for that individual in a temple on earth, thus making the blessings of baptism available to all who accept the gospel, here or hereafter.

Bible   The Bible is the word of God, scripture, a significant part of the LDS canon. Latter-day Saints also believe in other books of scripture: the Book of Mormon, Doctrine and Covenants, and Pearl of Great Price.

Birth   Birth is the process whereby the children of God pass from their premortal existence as spirits into mortality as physical beings.

Body, Physical   While passions and appetites of the flesh are to be bridled and controlled, the physical body is looked upon as the temple of God in that it houses the Holy Spirit. It is only through the inseparable union of body and spirit in the resurrection that men and women will receive a fulness of joy hereafter.

Book of Abraham   The Book of Abraham is a part of the Pearl of Great Price, one of the books within the LDS "standard works" or canon. Joseph Smith explained that it is a translation of some Egyptian papyri that came into the possession of the Church in 1835. It deals with Abraham's journey from Ur to Canaan, threats upon his life by wicked priests, a vision by Abraham of the cosmos, and an account of the creation of the earth.

Book of Mormon   The Book of Mormon is one of the books within the LDS canon of scripture, known to the Latter-day Saints as "Another Testament of Jesus Christ." It is a translation of a record kept by prophets and kings on golden plates by two civilizations of people living in America from approximately 2200 B.C. to 400 A.D. These people had the fulness of the gospel of Jesus Christ, were led by inspired prophets, and had the opportunity to be visited by Jesus as a part of his "other sheep."

Book of Moses   The Book of Moses is one of the sections of the Pearl of Great Price and thus part of the LDS canon. It represents Joseph Smith's revelatory translation of the early chapters of Genesis. It provides extra-biblical details concerning the premortal war in heaven; Adam, Eve, and the Fall; the conspiracy of Cain and murder of Abel; the ministry, teachings, and ultimate translation of Enoch; and God's dealings with Noah prior to the flood.

Born Again   To be born again is to be changed, through the Atonement of Christ, from a carnal and fallen state to a state of righteousness, to be renewed in spirit, to come alive to things of righteousness. It is to be adopted into the family of Jesus Christ.

Callings   Callings are assignments, duties, and responsibilities that one receives as a member of the Church — to minister to others' needs, to teach, to work with children, youth, or adults, all as a part of the mission of the Church to invite all to "come unto Christ."

Canon of Scripture   Latter-day Saints refer to the Bible, Book of Mormon, Doctrine and Covenants, and Pearl of Great Price as the "standard works," a standard against which doctrine and practice are measured. The standard works are the canon of scripture. One of the tenets of Mormonism is that the canon is not closed to new revelation and new scripture. Additional scripture is added to the canon or standard works by a vote of the members of the Church assembled in conference. An addition to the canon took place in April 1976.

Celestial Kingdom   Jesus taught that in his Father's house are "many mansions." The celestial kingdom is the highest heaven hereafter, made up of people who received the gospel of Jesus Christ and were valiant in their testimony of Jesus.

Charity   Charity is the highest and holiest form of love, the pure love of Christ. It is a gift and fruit of the Spirit.

Chastity   Latter-day Saints believe in sexual purity before marriage and in complete fidelity and devotion to one's spouse after marriage.

Christmas   Latter-day Saints celebrate Christmas with the rest of the Christian world and rejoice in the Incarnation, the coming of a God to earth — Jesus of Nazareth.

Commandments   Commandments are divine rules, laws, statutes, and judgments given by a gracious Lord to enable and assist his people to keep themselves unspotted from the sins of the world. While no one, save Jesus only, will live the laws of God perfectly, men and women who have come unto Christ by covenant are expected to "keep the commandments," to do all in their power to manifest their faith through faithfulness.

Communion   (See Sacrament of the Lord's Supper.)

Condescension of God   The condescension of God is the Incarnation, the coming of the God of the ancients to earth to dwell among his people. God so loved the world that he allowed his Son to leave his throne divine to assume a physical body and face challenges, taunts, rejection, and even death at the hands of those who spurned the Light.

Confirmation   Baptism is a two-part ordinance (sacrament): by water and by the Spirit. After a person has been immersed in water, hands are then laid upon his or her head and he or she is a confirmed member of The Church of

Jesus Christ of Latter-day Saints and instructed: "Receive the Holy Ghost." We speak of this latter ordinance — the laying on of hands associated with and following baptism — as confirmation.

Conversion   Conversion is the process by which one is changed, repents, literally turns away from sin and toward a new life in Christ.

Covenant   A gospel covenant is a two-way promise — between God and man. It is a binding and solemn agreement, initiated and specified by the Almighty.

Creeds   Latter-day Saints believe that the post–New Testament creeds of Christendom, though a well-intentioned effort to better understand the relationship between the members of the Godhead, represent a superimposition of Greek philosophy upon Christian theology and thus do not represent the simple gospel of the New Testament.

Cross   The cross symbolizes the atoning work of Jesus Christ, and thus it is not unusual to hear Latter-day Saints speak, like other Christians, of Jesus dying for our sins on the cross. Inasmuch as the Saints focus strongly upon the risen and glorified Lord (not just the suffering Savior), they do not adorn their churches with crosses or wear them as a symbol of their Christian devotion.

Cult   In its simplest form, the word *cult* refers merely to an organized group of people with shared beliefs. In this sense, the early Christians were considered by both the Jews and the Romans as a cult. The word has over time taken on a negative connotation, used to speak derisively of any religious group outside popular mainstream religious traditions.

Death   Death has two forms: (1) physical death, which is the separation of the spirit from the body, and (2) spiritual death, which is separation from the presence of God and from things of righteousness. Both deaths are overcome through the Atonement of Jesus Christ.

Degrees of Glory   Joseph Smith learned by vision that because of the varied levels of righteousness and wickedness of all humankind, there is more than a heaven and a hell hereafter. He taught that there are three degrees of glory: celestial, terrestrial, and telestial.

Deification of Man   Latter-day Saints believe that God desires to assist and enable his children to achieve all that they are capable of achieving in and beyond this mortal life. Through obedience to the Lord's commandments, and, most important, through the divine mercy and grace of an all-loving God, men and women may acquire the gifts and fruit of the Spirit, may become partakers of the divine nature, and eventually acquire those divine attributes that make them more and more like God. Notwithstanding man's noble possibilities, God and Christ will always be the object of our devotion and our worship.

Devil   (See Satan.)

Discipleship   Latter-day Saints do not believe that a mere acceptance of Jesus as Savior is sufficient for salvation. Accepting him as Lord of our lives demands dedicated discipleship. Discipleship is the fruit of one's conversion, the faithfulness that manifests one's faith or acceptance of Christ and his gospel.

Dispensation   A dispensation is a period of time in which the knowledge of God and his plan of salvation is dispensed or revealed anew through living prophets. While there have been many dispensations from the beginning, Latter-day Saints often speak of such major dispensations as the dispensations of Adam, Enoch, Noah, Abraham, Moses, Jesus Christ, and Joseph Smith.

Dispensation of the Fulness of Times   The dispensation of the fulness of times is the final dispensation, the one from which there will be no apostasy or falling away of the church and kingdom of God. It is the dispensation in which all of the truths, doctrines, powers, and divine authorities of days past are restored to earth. It began with the calling of Joseph Smith in the First Vision in the spring of 1820.

Doctrine   Doctrines are teachings, inspired declarations, and proclamations that come from holy scripture or from the mouths of living prophets. An acceptance of true doctrine leads to salvation. Doctrine is foundational to ethical behavior and defines why we do and do not do certain things; that is, we learn the nature of God (that he is pure and holy), come to understand true principles (the importance of morality and chastity), and then teach his precepts (thou shalt not commit adultery).

Doctrine and Covenants   The Doctrine and Covenants is one of the books within the LDS scriptural canon. It contains revelations, visions, and inspired instruction given mostly through Joseph Smith (with a few revelations directed to subsequent Church leaders). It is divided into 138 sections with two Official Declarations.

Earth The planet on which we live plays a significant role in God's eternal plan of salvation. It was created by God as a place on which Adam, Eve, and their posterity could learn, grow, develop, be tested, repent, and come to worship and know God through divine disclosure. Latter-day Saints believe that the earth now exists in a telestial condition, will be elevated to a terrestrial condition at the time of Christ's Second Coming in glory (in which the Millennium is initiated), and will, after a new heaven and a new earth have been created, eventually become the abode of those who inherit the celestial or highest heaven.

Easter Latter-day Saints celebrate Easter with the rest of the Christian world and rejoice in the rise from the tomb of death by Jesus. His resurrection makes the resurrection and a glorious reunion with departed loved ones available to all others.

Elohim Elohim is the name-title of God the Eternal Father, the Father of the spirits of all men and women. God the Father is the ultimate object of our worship.

Endowment The temple endowment consists of instruction, the receipt of ordinances (sacraments), and the making of covenants to live lives of virtue and morality, to pattern one's life after our great Exemplar, Jesus Christ.

Eternal Life Eternal life is salvation, the greatest of all the gifts of God. It consists of (1) acquiring the attributes and qualities of God, and (2) the continuation of the family unit into eternity.

Eternal Marriage Marriages in LDS temples are performed by men holding the "sealing power," the same power given by Jesus to Peter, James, and John to bind and seal on earth, with the assurance that their actions would have efficacy and force in heaven. These marriages are not performed "until death do you part" but rather "for time and all eternity." Such a marriage seals husband and wife, parents and children, together forever, contingent upon continued faithfulness to their covenants. Eternal marriage is sometimes called the new and everlasting covenant of marriage.

Exaltation Exaltation is salvation. It is eternal life. The word *exaltation* lays stress upon the exalted and ennobled status of one who inherits the highest degree of heaven hereafter.

Faith To have faith in Christ is to accept him as Lord and Savior, to have complete confidence, trust, dependence, and reliance upon him. It is to know that salvation comes in and through his atoning blood and in no other way.

Fall   For Latter-day Saints, the Fall of Adam and Eve was a "fortunate fall," one that introduced mortality and helped to put the Father's plan for the salvation of his children into operation. It was a fall downward but forward.

Family   The family is the most important unit in time and in eternity. All church organizations, programs, and auxiliaries exist as service agencies to assist individuals and families to gain eternal life. Families may be bound together forever through the sealing ordinances of the temple.

First Estate   The premortal life as spirits was our first estate. Latter-day Saints believe that those who kept their first estate qualified to come to earth as mortals and thus participate in the second estate. Those who followed Lucifer or Satan in the war in heaven did not qualify for life in the second estate and thus forfeit their right to have a physical body. Those who keep this second estate will have glory added upon them forever and ever. In our first estate we grew and developed in understanding and power, all in preparation for life on earth. At the time we enter mortality through physical birth, a veil of forgetfulness is placed upon our minds in order that we might in this life walk by faith.

First Presidency   The First Presidency is the highest governing council in the Church. It consists of the President of the Church (the living prophet) and his two counselors.

First Principles and Ordinances of the Gospel   The Atonement of Jesus Christ is appropriated into the lives of men and women through their participation in the first principles and ordinances of the gospel: faith in the Lord Jesus Christ; repentance; baptism by immersion for the remission of sins; and the laying on of hands for the gift of the Holy Ghost.

First Resurrection   The first resurrection is the resurrection of the just, the resurrection of the righteous; it began with the resurrection of Jesus Christ. The scriptures inform us that at the time the Lord came forth from his tomb many bodies of the Saints who had been dead were raised from the grave as well. Latter-day Saints believe that the first resurrection will resume when Jesus returns in glory and will continue throughout the Millennium. Both celestial and terrestrial persons will have part in the first resurrection.

196

First Vision   Joseph Smith's First Vision took place in the spring of 1820. Joseph explained that God the Father and his Son Jesus Christ instructed him concerning the restoration of the gospel of Jesus Christ.

Foreordination   Persons who were faithful in their first estate (the premortal life) were foreordained to perform certain ministerial labors and receive designated blessings on earth. These foreordained promises were delivered, however, on a conditional basis; they would come to pass only as the individuals exercised their moral agency wisely and thus proved true and faithful to their gospel covenants. Thus Latter-day Saints do not accept the doctrine of the unconditional election to eternal life (predestination).

Fulness of the Gospel   Truth is to be found in religious bodies throughout the world, but The Church of Jesus Christ of Latter-day Saints claims to have received the fulness of the gospel of Jesus Christ, in that divine authority and saving truths have been restored in these last days through modern prophets. The Book of Mormon is said to contain the fulness of the gospel, not in the sense that it contains all doctrines within the corpus of LDS theology, but in that it teaches powerfully the gospel in its fulness — the glad tidings of the redemption to be found in and through Christ.

Gethsemane   Jesus' Atonement began in the Garden of Gethsemane and was consummated on the cross of Calvary. The suffering in the Garden described in the Gospels was the beginning of his suffering for the sins of all humankind.

Gift of the Holy Ghost   While each person may enjoy the influence of the Holy Ghost as he or she responds to the power of God's word or to divine influences in his or her life, the gift of the Holy Ghost comes only through the ordinance of confirmation, through the laying on of hands following water baptism. That gift entitles one to a more constant and intense manifestation of the Spirit of God.

Gifts of the Spirit   The gifts of the Spirit are those signs and wonders and divine manifestations — e.g., prophecy, healing, tongues, wisdom, knowledge — that are to be found in the lives of the followers of Christ. The people of God come together to meet and to worship, and each contributes to the strength and power of the body of Christ (the church), just as the eye, the hand, and the foot — though they have separate functions — contribute to the overall functioning of the human body.

God   God is the ultimate object of our worship, an independent being who is omnipotent, omniscient, and, by the power of his Spirit, omnipresent. He possesses every godly attribute in perfection. Latter-day Saints teach that he is our Heavenly Father, the Father of the spirits of all men and women, and that he possesses a body of flesh and bones.

Godhead   The Godhead consists of three distinct personages and three Gods — the Father, Son, and Holy Spirit. The Father and Son have bodies of flesh and bones, while the Holy Spirit is a spirit personage.

Gold Plates   The Book of Mormon is a record of a people who inhabited ancient America and who etched their secular and religious histories onto metal plates having the appearance of gold. The gold plates were delivered to Joseph Smith in 1827, and he translated them into English by the gift and power of God.

Grace   Divine grace is God's unmerited favor, his unearned divine assistance to his children. It is not only that final boost into glory that must come to each of us who seek salvation in Christ, but also the enabling power needed by every person daily to accomplish what he or she could never do on his or her own.

Heaven   In a broad sense, Latter-day Saints believe in a type of universal salvation — not that each person will live with God in heaven hereafter, but rather that each person will inherit some degree of heaven. (See Degrees of Glory.)

Hell   The word *Hell* has two meanings for Latter-day Saints: (1) that realm within the postmortal spirit world now inhabited by men and women who lived wicked and depraved lives on earth; and (2) the final state of the sons of perdition, those who have known God, known the truth, and have then denied and defied the faith.

Holy Ghost   The Holy Ghost, also known as the Holy Spirit, is a male spirit personage. He is the third member of the Godhead and is often referred to as the Comforter. His mission is to bear witness of the Father and the Son, to teach and convey divine truth, to confirm one's witness, to sanctify and cleanse human hearts, and to strengthen and empower.

Hope   The hope of which the scriptures speak is not merely worldly wishing. Hope in Christ follows from one's faith in Christ and represents anticipation, expectation, assurance, and security that the blessings promised by the Lord are sure and certain.

Immortality   The work and glory of God is to bring to pass the immortality and eternal life of man. To possess immortality is to live forever, to rise from the dead in the resurrection and then to never die again. It is a free gift that comes to all mortal men and women through the mediation of Jesus Christ.

Inerrancy of Scripture   Joseph Smith did not believe in the inerrancy of the Bible, nor do Latter-day Saints today. To be sure, the essential message of the Bible is true and from God; it is "God's word." But in addition to written scripture, it is the spirit of revelation, the living, vibrant, and current word of God, upon which the Saints lean for support and direction and to which they turn for doctrinal understanding.

Jehovah   Yahweh or Jehovah is the God of the Old Testament, the God of the antediluvians, the God of Abraham, Isaac, and Jacob. Under the direction of Elohim, the Eternal Father, Jehovah became the creator of worlds without number. To answer man's needs brought on by the Fall of Adam and Eve, Jehovah condescended and came to earth as Jesus of Nazareth.

Jesus Christ   Jesus' name means literally "Jehovah saves." His title is the Christ, meaning "the anointed one." He is the Son of God, the Redeemer and Savior of all humankind, and his is the only name by which salvation can come. He lived, taught his gospel, organized his Church, performed miracles (such as healing the sick, casting out devils, and raising the dead), and suffered and died as a substitutionary offering for the sins of all. After his body had lain in the tomb for three days, he rose from the dead in glorified immortality and thus broke the bands of death. He dwells with his Father in heaven today, answers prayers, directs the affairs of his Church, and will one day return to earth in the fulness of his glory, to reign as King of kings and Lord of lords.

Joseph Smith's Translation of the Bible   In June of 1830 Joseph Smith began a serious study of the King James Bible (KJV), a work that has come to be known as Joseph Smith's Translation of the Bible. Acting under divine authority in what Joseph called "this branch of my calling," he made inspired corrections and clarifications to over 3400 verses in the KJV. Portions of this work have been canonized (the Book of Moses and Joseph Smith-Matthew in the Pearl of Great Price) and hundreds of the changes are reflected in textual notes in the 1979 LDS edition of the KJV.

Judgment   Latter-day Saints believe, with the Christian world, in a great day of judgment when all men and women will be held accountable for the degree to which they accepted the gospel of Jesus Christ and devoted their lives to him.

Justification   When one comes unto Christ by covenant (including baptism and reception of the Holy Spirit), he is justified by and through his faith in Christ. That is, he is declared innocent, pronounced guiltless and free from sin, and, in addition, has imputed to him the righteousness of Christ. He is thus a participant in what many have called the "great exchange": the sin and guilt of man are transferred to the Lord, while the righteousness of God is transferred to the individual.

Keys of the Priesthood   Keys are the directing power, the right of presidency. Ordinances (sacraments) are only valid if performed by one having proper authority, under the direction of one holding the keys.

Last Resurrection   The last resurrection (often identified by LDS as the second resurrection) will take place at the end of the Millennium and will entail the resurrection of the telestial and of the sons of perdition.

Melchizedek   According to LDS teachings, Melchizedek, the king of Salem, was a righteous high priest whose faithful ministry led to the conversion of his people. He was also the man who conferred the priesthood upon Abraham.

Melchizedek Priesthood   The Melchizedek Priesthood is also called the higher priesthood. Anciently it was called the Holy Priesthood after the Order of the Son of God. It has within it the power of the holy apostleship and contains the right to confer the gift of the Holy Ghost and perform certain ordinances (sacraments). There are five offices within the Melchizedek Priesthood: elder, high priest, patriarch, seventy, and apostle. Joseph Smith explained that in 1829 Peter, James, and John appeared and conferred upon him and Oliver Cowdery the Melchizedek Priesthood.

Meridian of Time   The period of time known to much of the world as the Christian era is known to the Latter-day Saints as the meridian of time. Because it was the time in which the Son of God would come to earth and perform his work of divine intercession, it is the high point, the apex of salvation history.

Messiah   Jesus is the Messiah, the anointed one, the one sent by God to bind up the broken-hearted and proclaim liberty to the captives. Since the testimony of Jesus is the spirit of prophecy, Latter-day Saints believe that all the prophets, from the beginning, bore witness of the coming of the Messiah.

Millennium   The Savior's second coming in glory initiates the Millennium. The Millennium is a thousand-year period of light and love and peace in which the Christ will reign on earth. Evil will have been done away and the Master will dwell once again among his people.

Mormon   Mormon was the master editor-writer of the gold plates, the one charged to continue the history of the inhabitants of the people in ancient America and also to abridge the record. It is for this reason that the record itself is known as the Book of Mormon. He lived toward the very end of the Book of Mormon story. Because of the Saints' acceptance of the Book of Mormon, they were labeled by their critics as Mormons.

Moroni   Moroni, the son of Mormon, was the final writer and abridger of the gold plates. In 421 A.D. he buried the plates in a hill called Cumorah in upstate New York and later returned, as a resurrected being, an angel, to deliver them to Joseph Smith.

New and Everlasting Covenant   The sum of all covenants and ordinances associated with the gospel of Jesus Christ is called the new and everlasting covenant. It is *everlasting* in the sense that it has been on earth from the beginning of time. It is *new* in the sense that it is restored anew, generally following a time of apostasy.

New and Everlasting Covenant of Marriage   (See Eternal Marriage.)

Omnipotence, Omniscience, Omnipresence of God   God possesses all power (he is omnipotent). He possesses all knowledge (he is omniscient). Because Latter-day Saints believe that God is a corporeal being, has a physical body, he can be in only one place at a time. Thus God is omnipresent by means of his Holy Spirit, which is in and through all things.

Ordinance (sacrament)   In the broadest sense, ordinances are laws, commandments, and statutes of God. In a more narrow sense, ordinances (here also called sacraments) are rites and ceremonies associated with membership in the Church and with the receipt of all its blessings. Certain ordinances (such as baptism, confirmation, the Sacrament of the Lord's Supper) are known as ordinances of salvation, for they are required for entrance into the highest heaven. Others (such as the blessing of children, administration of the sick, the dedication of graves) are known as ordinances of comfort and are not required for salvation. Joseph Smith taught that ordinances of salvation are forever the same — they have existed from the beginning of time and are to be performed in divinely designated ways.

Original Sin   Because Latter-day Saints do not believe that Adam and Eve "sinned" in partaking of the forbidden fruit; because they feel that the Fall was as much a part of the foreordained plan of the Father as the very Atonement; and because they believe that Christ's Atonement covers and thus forgives Adam and Eve's act of disobedience, they do not believe in an original sin on the part of our first parents or that such a taint is answered upon the heads of their posterity. Thus from an LDS perspective while each of us must answer for our own sins, no one of us is responsible for what took place in Eden. At the same time, to say that we are not responsible is not to suggest that we are unaffected by the Fall; sin, bodily decay, and death are all by-products of the Fall that impact each of us and with which we must grapple as long as we live. Deliverance comes only through Christ.

Paradise   There are two uses of the word *paradise* in LDS literature: (1) Life in Eden was paradisiacal — no death, decay, or sin. (2) One dimension of the postmortal spirit world where all go who have been true to the light within them and true to the gospel covenant, is known as paradise. Paradise is a state of rest, a state of peace and joy, where men and women continue to grow, learn, and develop until the time of their resurrection.

Pearl of Great Price   The Pearl of Great Price is one of the books within the LDS canon of scripture, the "standard works." It contains Joseph Smith's translation of the early chapters of Genesis and the 24th chapter of Matthew (the Book of Moses and Joseph Smith-Matthew), his translation of some Egyptian papyri that pertains to the early life of Abraham (the Book of Abraham), a brief history of the Church (Joseph Smith-History), and thirteen statements of belief known as the Articles of Faith.

Perfection   No person, save Jesus only, walks the paths of life without committing sin. And yet we are charged to become perfect, even as our Father in heaven is perfect. On the one hand, that entails a serious effort to keep the commandments of God as best we can. More directly, however, we become "perfect in Christ" as we enter into his gospel covenant and allow him to become the Author and Finisher of our faith. To be perfect is to be whole, fully formed, complete. Thus we exercise perfect faith in Christ to the extent that we rely wholly, rely alone upon his merits, mercy, and grace.

Plan of Salvation   God's plan for the blessing and ultimate glorification of his children has many names: the great plan of the eternal God; the great plan of happiness; the merciful plan of the great Creator; the plan of redemption; the eternal plan of deliverance; the plan of restoration, etc. At the center of

God's plan of salvation is Jesus Christ, the Redeemer. His atoning sacrifice is the key to happiness and joy here and eternal reward hereafter.

Plural Marriage   During the ministry of Joseph Smith and continuing for over fifty years, plural marriage was practiced. Latter-day Saints believe that God commanded them to do so. Plural marriage was a religious principle, and this is the only valid explanation as to why the practice was maintained, in spite of decades of opposition and persecution. Latter-day Saints believe that whatever God commands is right, and that plural marriages, when properly performed by authorized persons, were both legal and acceptable to God. Men and women within a plural marriage family were expected to demonstrate loyalty and devotion to spouse and to observe the highest standards of fidelity and morality. A Manifesto was issued in 1890 by Wilford Woodruff, fourth president of the Church, and the practice was officially discontinued.

Predestination   (See Foreordination.)

Preexistence, Premortal Life   (See First Estate.)

Priesthood   In its broadest sense, priesthood is the power of God by which the cosmos was organized and the worlds were framed. In a more limited sense, priesthood is the power and authority of God, delegated to man on earth, to act in all things for the salvation of humankind. It is the authority by which the ordinances of salvation and comfort are performed and by which the Church is led and directed.

Prophet   In the broadest sense, a prophet is anyone who possesses the testimony of Jesus, since the testimony of Jesus is the spirit of prophecy (Revelation 19:10). More specifically, a prophet is a mouthpiece for God, a covenant spokesman whose charge is to lead, direct, and warn God's people, and also, as a legal administrator, to oversee the work of the ministry. Fifteen men are called to serve as prophets, seers, and revelators for the entire Church (the First Presidency and the Quorum of the Twelve Apostles).

Reformation, the   Latter-day Saints believe the Reformation was God-ordained, preparatory, and that it laid the foundation for a more complete restoration in later years. Protests against the abuses of the mother church set in motion a mindset, a worldview in which the people welcomed the translation of the scriptures for the common man and delighted in a greater reliance upon the mercy and grace of Christ.

Repentance   To repent is to turn away from sin and turn toward God. It is to undergo a transformation of the will such that the sinner experiences a "change of mind" and thus a new way of thinking. Latter-day Saints believe that godly sorrow for sin and sincere repentance precede divine forgiveness.

Resurrection   Resurrection is the inseparable union of body and spirit. All who have taken a physical body will one day be raised from the dead in immortality and inherit the appropriate kingdom of glory, or in the case of sons of perdition, no glory.

Revelation for the Church   Joseph Smith taught that it is contrary to the economy of heaven for any person to receive revelation for those in authority higher than themselves. Revelation for the entire Church will come only through the apostles and prophets charged to direct the Church.

Revelation, Personal   Every person who has received the gift of the Holy Ghost (and the Holy Ghost is a revelator) is entitled to divine guidance for him- or herself and for those directly within his or her own sphere of responsibility.

Sacrament of the Lord's Supper   The administration of the Sacrament of the Lord's Supper (generally called "the Sacrament" by Latter-day Saints or "Communion" by other Christians) follows the pattern established in the New Testament. Baptized members partake of bread and water in remembrance of the broken body and spilt blood of our Savior. The sacramental service is a time for reflection, introspection, and prayerful re-commitment. It provides an occasion for members of the Church to remember and renew their baptismal covenants (see Baptismal Covenant) and enjoy the cleansing and lifting influence of God's Spirit for the coming week. The Sacrament is administered in sacrament meeting, the main worship service held every Sabbath.

Saints   Saints are baptized members of the Church, the "sanctified ones" — or at least they are striving to be so — those who are set apart, distinct from worldliness and waywardness, those who have come out of darkness into the marvelous light of Christ.

Salvation   Salvation is eternal life, the greatest of all the gifts of God. The word *salvation* lays stress upon being saved from death and sin through the Atonement. While the fulness of salvation cannot be enjoyed in this life, the peaceful assurance that one's life is acceptable to God may be known by the power of the Holy Spirit.

Sanctification   While justification describes one's legal *standing* before God — innocent, pure, free from sin, through the Atonement — sanctification describes the gradual purification of one's nature, one's *state,* through the ongoing and everyday work of the Holy Spirit upon the human soul.

Satan   Latter-day Saints believe in a literal devil, an actual spirit being from the unseen world who is bent upon our destruction and the overthrow of the Father's plan of salvation. In the premortal world he was known as Lucifer, but many today speak of him as Satan. His pride led him to wage war against the forces of God in the premortal war in heaven, as a result of which he was cast to the earth, together with one-third of the spirit sons and daughters of God who followed him. Satan and his minions continue to tempt, allure, entice, and take possession of men and women on earth. Eventually the forces of God and the forces of Satan will meet again, and Satan and his followers will then be banished to outer darkness forever.

Scripture   Scripture is that which is spoken or written by the power of the Holy Ghost; it is the will, mind, word, and voice of God. Canonized scripture is that which has been received by vote of a constituent assembly of Saints to be a part of the standard works. It then becomes binding upon the Saints, in terms of belief and practice.

Sealing   (See Eternal Marriage.)

Second Estate   Earth life is our second estate. Those who keep their second estate qualify for glory, honor, and eternal life hereafter. The purposes of this second estate include receiving a physical body, learning to discipline the body and bridle the passions, learning to face and overcome obstacles in life, and developing meaningful relationships.

Sin   Sin is violation of God's law. It entails either acting against the expressed will of God (sin of commission) or failing to do what God has called upon us to do (sin of omission). One cannot have sin removed from his or her heart through a change in behavior alone; a remission of sins comes through repentance and forgiveness by God, by virtue of the atoning blood of Christ.

Sons of Perdition   A son of perdition is one who commits the "unpardonable sin," the sin that will not be forgiven in this world or the world to come. One guilty of such an offense has enjoyed major revelation from God and yet has come out in open rebellion and opposition to the faith and thereby "sinned against the Holy Ghost." They inherit hereafter a kingdom of no glory.

Soul   The strictest definition of the soul in LDS literature is the spirit joined with the body. Much of the time, however, the word *soul* as used in scripture refers to the spirit of man.

Spirit World   Latter-day Saints speak of two types of spirit world: (1) the premortal spirit world, inhabited by spirits who have not yet been born (unembodied spirits); and (2) the postmortal spirit world, inhabited by those who have died and await the resurrection (disembodied spirits).

Standard Works   (See Canon of Scripture.)

Telestial Kingdom   The telestial kingdom of glory is the lowest of the three kingdoms, made up of those who were guilty in this life of such things as lying, stealing, sorcery, immorality, and murder. They received neither the testimony of Jesus nor the gospel covenant in this life. These will suffer in the postmortal spirit world as they are forced to confront who and what they have become. They will not come forth from the grave until the last resurrection.

Temple   The temple is the house of the Lord. Ordinances (sacraments) are performed in temples that do not take place in chapels or meetinghouses. These include the sealing of husbands, wives, and children for time and eternity, as well as baptism for the dead for those who never had the opportunity in this life to learn the gospel and participate in its saving ordinances (see also Endowment).

Terrestrial Kingdom   The terrestrial kingdom of glory will be made up of good people, honorable people of the earth, people who received the testimony of Jesus in this life but were not valiant in that testimony. Thus they are not entitled in eternity to enjoy a close association with God the Father.

Unpardonable Sin   (See Sons of Perdition.)

Virgin Birth   Mary was a virgin, a precious and chosen daughter of God. Jesus was the Son of God, while his siblings (James, Joses, Juda, and Simon, as well as his sisters) were born later to Mary and Joseph. Latter-day Saints do not accept the doctrine of the immaculate conception or the perpetual virginity of Mary.

War in Heaven   (See Satan.)

Works   The works of righteousness are the fruits of one's conversion to Christ, those acts of Christian service, devotion, and involvement in the work of the ministry that characterize a disciple. True faith always manifests itself in faithfulness. Latter-day Saints believe that works are *necessary* for salvation; they evidence our commitment to the Lord, our desire to do our part in working with God toward the salvation of our soul. Our works are *not sufficient* to save us, however. In the end, after all we can do on our own, we are saved by the merits and mercy of the Holy Messiah.

Worship   We worship the Lord in a myriad of ways — through prayer, praise, scripture study and daily devotions, the singing of hymns, and an ever-present acknowledgement of the hand of God in all that is good in our lives. And perhaps the highest form of worship is emulation, our desire to have our minds and hearts transformed to such extent that we are conformed to the image of Christ; we gain "the mind of Christ" and act in ways that evidence who we are and Whose we are.

Zion   In the Book of Mormon one encounters a concept of Zion that is much broader than Jerusalem or the Holy Mount. Zion is a holy community, the city of God, a fortification of the Saints against evil. For a number of years specific locations like Kirtland, Ohio, or Independence, Missouri — sites where the headquarters of the Church were established — became known as Zion. In the Doctrine and Covenants, however, the concept of Zion is expanded to include "the pure in heart," both the place as well as the people who are striving to become pure in heart. Thus Zion does not refer solely to Salt Lake City, the present headquarters of The Church of Jesus Christ of Latter-day Saints, but rather to faithful individuals, devoted homes, and congregations of pure-hearted people found throughout the earth. Zion is where the covenant people have gathered to worship Christ, the King of Zion.

Bibliography

Anderson, Richard Lloyd. *Understanding Paul.* Salt Lake City: Deseret Book, 1983.

Ante-Nicene Fathers, 10 vols. Edited by Alexander Roberts and James Donaldson. Grand Rapids, Michigan: Eerdmans, 1981.

Backman, Milton V., Jr. *American Religions and the Rise of Mormonism.* Salt Lake City: Deseret Book, 1965.

————. "Awakenings in the Burned-Over District: New Light on the Historical Setting of the First Vision." *Brigham Young University Studies* 9, no. 3 (Spring 1969).

————. *Joseph Smith's First Vision.* 2nd ed. Salt Lake City: Bookcraft, 1980.

Balmer, Randall. *Mine Eyes Have Seen the Glory: A Journey into the Evangelical Subculture in America.* 3rd ed. New York: Oxford University Press, 2000.

————. *Growing Pains: Learning to Love My Father's Faith.* Grand Rapids, Michigan: Brazos, 2001.

Barna, George. *Think Like Jesus.* Nashville: Integrity Publishers, 2003.

Benson, Ezra Taft. *Come Unto Christ.* Salt Lake City: Deseret Book, 1983.

————. *The Teachings of Ezra Taft Benson.* Salt Lake City: Bookcraft, 1988.

Bercot, David, ed. *A Dictionary of Early Christian Beliefs.* Peabody, Massachusetts: Hendrickson, 1998.

————. *Will the Real Heretics Please Stand Up: A New Look at Today's Evangelical Church in the Light of Early Christianity.* 3rd ed. Tyler, Texas: Scroll Publishing, 1999.

Bloesch, Donald. *Essentials of Evangelical Theology.* 2 vols. San Francisco: Harper, 1978.

Blomberg, Craig L., and Stephen E. Robinson. *How Wide the Divide? A Mormon and an Evangelical in Conversation.* Downers Grove, Illinois: InterVarsity Press, 1997.

Boyd, Gregory A. *God of the Possible.* Grand Rapids, Michigan: Baker Books, 2000.

Bruce, F. F. *The Books and the Parchments.* Westwood, New Jersey: Fleming H. Revell Co., 1963.

———. *The New Testament Documents: Are They Reliable?* Grand Rapids, Michigan: Eerdmans, 1974.

Bushman, Richard. *Joseph Smith and the Beginnings of Mormonism.* Urbana: University of Illinois Press, 1984.

Callister, Tad R. *The Infinite Atonement.* Salt Lake City: Deseret Book, 2000.

Christofferson, D. Todd. "Justification and Sanctification." *Ensign of The Church of Jesus Christ of Latter-day Saints,* June 2001.

Collins, Raymond F. *Introduction to the New Testament.* New York: Doubleday, 1983.

Conference Report of The Church of Jesus Christ of Latter-day Saints. April 1907 through April 2004.

Curran, Charles E. "Creative Fidelity: Keeping the Religion a Living Tradition." *Sunstone,* July 1987.

Davies, Douglas. *Private Passions: Betraying Discipleship on the Journey to Jerusalem.* Norwich: Canterbury Press, 2000.

DeMaris, Richard E. "Corinthian Religion and Baptism for the Dead (1 Corinthians 15:29): Insights from Archaeology and Anthropology." *Journal of Biblical Literature* 114, no. 4 (1995).

Dew, Sheri L. *Go Forward with Faith: The Biography of Gordon B. Hinckley.* Salt Lake City: Deseret Book, 1996.

Ehrman, Bart D. *Lost Scriptures: Books that Did Not Make It into the New Testament.* New York: Oxford, 2003.

———. *Lost Christianities: The Battles for Scripture and the Faiths We Never Knew.* New York: Oxford, 2003.

———. *The Orthodox Corruption of Scripture.* New York: Oxford, 1993.

Erickson, Millard. *Making Sense of the Trinity.* Grand Rapids, Michigan: Baker, 2000.

Farrar, Frederic W. *The Early Days of Christianity.* New York: Cassell, Petter, Galpin & Co., 1882.

Fee, Gordon D. *The First Epistle to the Corinthians.* Grand Rapids, Michigan: Eerdmans, 1987.

Fortman, Edward J. *The Triune God: A Historical Study of the Doctrine of the Trinity.* Philadelphia: Westminster Press, 1972.

Funk, Robert W., Roy W. Hoover, et al. *The Five Gospels: What Did Jesus Really Say?* New York: Macmillan, 1993.

Gaustad, Edwin, and Leigh Schmidt. *The Religious History of America: The Heart of the American Story from Colonial Times to Today.* San Francisco: Harper, 2002.

Goppelt, Leonhard. *A Commentary on 1 Peter.* Edited by Ferdinand Hahn. Translated by John E. Alsup. Grand Rapids, Michigan: Eerdmans, 1993.

Grant, Heber J. *Gospel Standards.* Selected by G. Homer Durham. Salt Lake City: Deseret Book, 1976.

Greenlee, J. Harold. *Scribes, Scrolls, and Scripture.* Grand Rapids, Michigan: Eerdmans, 1985.

Grenz, Stanley J., David Guretzki, and Cherith Fee Nordling. *Pocket Dictionary of Theological Terms.* Downers Grove, Illinois: InterVarsity Press, 1999.

Guthrie, Donald. "The Historical and Literary Criticism of the New Testament." In *Biblical Criticism: Historical, Literary and Textual,* edited by R. K. Harrison, B. K. Waltke, D. Guthrie, and G. D. Fee. Grand Rapids, Michigan: Zondervan, 1978.

Hanks, Marion D. "Christ Manifested to His People." In *Temples of the Ancient World,* edited by Donald W. Parry. Salt Lake City: Deseret Book and F.A.R.M.S., 1994.

Harper's Bible Dictionary. Edited by Paul J. Achtemeier. San Francisco: Harper & Row, 1985.

Hatch, Edwin. *The Influence of Greek Ideas on Christianity.* Gloucester, Massachusetts: Peter Smith Publishers, 1970.

Hick, John. "A Plurist View." In *Four Views on Salvation in a Pluralistic World,* edited by Dennis L. Okholm and Timothy R. Phillips. Grand Rapids, Michigan: Zondervan, 1996.

Hinckley, Gordon B. *Be Thou An Example.* Salt Lake City: Deseret Book, 1981.

———. *Faith: The Essence of True Religion.* Salt Lake City: Deseret Book, 1989.

———. "Meeting with Religion Newswriters Association." Albuquerque, New Mexico, 14 September 1997.

———. *Teachings of Gordon B. Hinckley.* Salt Lake City: Deseret Book, 1997.

History of The Church of Jesus Christ of Latter-day Saints. 7 vols. Edited by B. H. Roberts. Salt Lake City: Deseret Book, 1957.

Hopkins, Richard R. *How Greek Philosophy Corrupted the Christian Concept of God.* Bountiful, Utah: Horizon, 1998.

Hunter, Howard W. *That We Might Have Joy.* Salt Lake City: Deseret Book, 1994.

———. *The Teachings of Howard W. Hunter.* Edited by Clyde J. Williams. Salt Lake City: Bookcraft, 1997.

Jackson, Kent P. "Latter-day Saints: A Dynamic Scriptural Process." In *The Holy Book in Comparative Perspective,* edited by Frederick M. Denny and Rodney L. Taylor. Columbia, South Carolina: University of South Carolina Press, 1985.

Journal of Discourses. 26 vols. Liverpool: F. D. Richards & Sons, 1851-86.

Kimball, Spencer W. *The Teachings of Spencer W. Kimball.* Edited by Edward L. Kimball. Salt Lake City: Bookcraft, 1982.

Kugelman, Richard. "The First Letter to the Corinthians." In *The Jerome Biblical Commentary.* 2 vols. Edited by Raymond E. Brown, Joseph A. Fitzmyer, and Roland E. Murphy. Englewood Cliffs, New Jersey: Prentice-Hall, 1968.

Lee, Harold B. LDS Student Association fireside, Utah State University, 10 October 1971.

———. *The Teachings of Harold B. Lee.* Edited by Clyde J. Williams. Salt Lake City: Bookcraft, 1996.

Lewis, C. S. *Christian Reflections.* London: Fount/Harper Collins, 1981.

———. *Christian Reunion and Other Essays.* London: William Collins Sons & Co., 1990.

———. *God in the Dock.* Edited by Walter Hooper. Grand Rapids, Michigan: Eerdmans, 1970.

———. *The Great Divorce.* New York: Macmillan, 1946.

———. *Letters of C. S. Lewis.* Rev. ed. Edited by Walter Hooper. New York: Harcourt, Brace & Co., 1993.

———. *Letters to Malcolm: Chiefly on Prayer.* San Diego: Harcourt, Brace & Co., 1964.

———. *Mere Christianity.* New York: Touchstone, 1996.

———. *The Problem of Pain.* New York: Touchstone, 1996.

———. *The Weight of Glory and Other Addresses.* New York: Touchstone, 1996.

Lightfoot, J. B. *The Apostolic Fathers.* Grand Rapids, Michigan: Baker Book House, 1962.

———. Lundwall, N. B., compiler. *The Vision.* Salt Lake City: Bookcraft, n.d.

MacArthur, John F. *Faith Works: The Gospel According to the Apostles.* Dallas: Word, 1993.

———. *Hard to Believe. The High Cost and Infinite Value of Following Jesus.* Nashville: Thomas Nelson, 2003.

———. *The Murder of Jesus.* Nashville: Word, 2000.

———. *Why One Way?* Nashville: W Publishing, 2002.

MacCulloch, J. A. *The Harrowing of Hell.* Edinburgh: T&T Clark, 1930.

Madsen, Truman G. "The Temple and the Atonement." In *Temples of the Ancient World,* edited by Donald W. Parry. Salt Lake City: Deseret Book and F.A.R.M.S, 1994.

Martin, Walter. *The New Cults.* Ventura, California: Regal Books, 1980.

Maxwell, Neal A. *Things As They Really Are.* Salt Lake City: Deseret Book, 1978.

McConkie, Bruce R. *A New Witness for the Articles of Faith.* Salt Lake City: Deseret Book, 1985.

———. *Mormon Doctrine.* 2nd ed. Salt Lake City: Bookcraft, 1966.

———. *The Promised Messiah.* Salt Lake City: Deseret Book, 1978.

McConkie, Joseph. *Sons and Daughters of God.* Salt Lake City: Bookcraft, 1994.

McKay, David O. *Gospel Ideals.* Salt Lake City: The Improvement Era, 1953.

McKnight, Scot. "Who Is Jesus? An Introduction to Jesus Studies." In *Jesus Under Fire: Modern Scholarship Reinvents the Historical Jesus,* edited by Michael J. Wilkins and J. P. Moreland. Grand Rapids, Michigan: Zondervan, 1995.

Meir, John. *A Marginal Jew: Rethinking the Historical Jesus.* 3 vols. New York: Doubleday, 1991.

Metzger, Bruce M. *The New Testament: Its Background, Growth, and Content.* 2nd ed. Nashville: Abingdon, 1983.

Millet, Robert L. *Alive in Christ: The Miracle of Spiritual Rebirth.* Salt Lake City: Deseret Book, 1997.

———. *Getting at the Truth: Responding to Difficult Questions about LDS Beliefs.* Salt Lake City: Deseret Book, 2004.

———. *Grace Works.* Salt Lake City: Deseret Book, 2003.

———, ed. *Joseph Smith: Selected Sermons and Writings.* New York: Paulist Press, 1989.

———. *The Mormon Faith: A New Look at Christianity.* Salt Lake City: Shadow Mountain, 1998.

Montgomery, John Warwick. *History and Christianity.* San Bernardino, California: Here's Life Publishers, 1983.

Mouw, Richard J. *He Shines in All That's Fair: Culture and Common Grace.* Grand Rapids: Eerdmans, 2001.

———. *Uncommon Decency: Christian Civility in an Uncivil World.* Downers Grove, Illinois: InterVarsity Press, 1992.

Muggeridge, Malcolm. *Jesus: The Man Who Lives.* New York: Harper & Row, 1975.

Neuhaus, Richard John. *Death on a Friday Afternoon.* New York: Basic Books, 2000.

Nicene and Post-Nicene Fathers. 14 vols. Edited by Philip Schaff. Grand Rapids: Eerdmans, 1983.

Noll, Mark. *America's God: From Jonathan Edwards to Abraham Lincoln.* New York: Oxford University Press, 2002.

Packer, J. I. "Can the Dead Be Converted?" *Christianity Today,* vol. 43, no. 1, 11 January 1999.

Paulsen, David L. "Are Mormons Trinitarian?" *Modern Reformation* 12, no. 6 (November/December 2003).

———. "Early Christian Belief in a Corporeal Deity: Origen and Augustine as Reluctant Witnesses." *Harvard Theological Review* 83, no. 2 (1990).

Penrose, Charles W. "Mormon Doctrine." Salt Lake City: George Q. Cannon & Sons, 1897.

Pinnock, Clark H. *Flame of Love.* Downers Grove, Illinois: InterVarsity Press, 1996.

————. *Most Moved Mover: A Theology of God's Openness.* Grand Rapids, Michigan: Baker, 2001.

Pinnock, Clark H., Richard Rice, John Sanders, William Hasker, and David Basinger. *The Openness of God: A Biblical Challenge to the Traditional Understanding of God.* Downers Grove, Illinois: InterVarsity Press, 1994.

Pinnock, Clark H. and Delwin Brown. *Theological Crossfire.* Grand Rapids, Michigan: Zondervan, 1990.

Plantinga, Cornelius. *Not the Way It's Supposed to Be: A Breviary of Sin.* Grand Rapids: Eerdmans, 1995.

Pratt, Orson. *Orson Pratt's Works.* Salt Lake City: Deseret News Press, 1945.

————. "The True Faith." In *A Series of Pamphlets.* Liverpool: Franklin D. Richards, 1852.

Pratt, Parley P. *Key to the Science of Theology.* Salt Lake City: Deseret Book, 1978.

Prothero, Stephen. *American Jesus: How the Son of God Became a National Icon.* New York: Farrar, Straus and Giroux, 2003.

Proust, Marcel. In Gabriel Marcel, *Homo Viator.* New York: Harper & Row, 1963.

Rahner, Karl. *The Trinity.* New York: Herder and Herder, 1970.

Remini, Robert. *Joseph Smith.* New York: Penguin, 2002.

Richards, LeGrand. *A Marvelous Work and a Wonder.* Salt Lake City: Deseret Book, 1950.

Roberts, B. H. *The Gospel and Man's Relationship to Deity.* Salt Lake City: Deseret Book, 1966.

Robinson, Stephen E. *Are Mormons Christians?* Salt Lake City: Bookcraft, 1991.

————. "The 'Expanded' Book of Mormon?" In *Second Nephi: The Doctrinal Structure,* edited by Monte S. Nyman and Charles D. Tate, Jr. Provo: BYU Religious Studies Center, 1989.

Sanders, John. *The God Who Risks.* Downers Grove, Illinois: InterVarsity Press, 1998.

————. *No Other Name.* Grand Rapids, Michigan: Eerdmans, 1992.

————, ed. *What About Those Who Have Never Heard?* Downers Grove, Illinois: InterVarsity Press, 1995.

Shipps, Jan. *Mormonism: The Story of a New Religious Tradition.* Urbana: University of Illinois Press, 1985.

Shoemaker, Donald P. "Why Your Neighbor Joined the Mormon Church," *Christianity Today* 19, 11 October 1974.

Smith, George Albert. *The Teachings of George Albert Smith.* Edited by Robert and Susan McIntosh. Salt Lake City: Bookcraft, 1996.

Smith, Joseph. *Lectures on Faith.* Salt Lake City: Deseret Book, 1985.

————. *Personal Writings of Joseph Smith.* Rev. ed. Edited by Dean C. Jessee. Salt Lake City: Deseret Book, 2002.

————. *Teachings of the Prophet Joseph Smith.* Selected by Joseph Fielding Smith. Salt Lake City: Deseret Book, 1976.

————. *The Words of Joseph Smith.* Edited by Andrew F. Ehat and Lyndon W. Cook. Provo: BYU Religious Studies Center, 1980.

Smith, Joseph F. *Gospel Doctrine.* Salt Lake City: Deseret Book, 1971.

————. *Doctrines of Salvation.* 3 vols. Compiled by Bruce R. McConkie. Salt Lake City: Bookcraft, 1954-56.

————. *Selections from Doctrines of Salvation.* Salt Lake City: The Church of Jesus Christ of Latter-day Saints, 2001.

Snow, Lorenzo. *The Teachings of Lorenzo Snow.* Edited by Clyde J. Williams. Salt Lake City: Bookcraft, 1984.

Sperry, Sidney B. *Paul's Life and Letters.* Salt Lake City: Bookcraft, 1955.

Stackhouse, John G., Jr. *Evangelical Landscapes: Facing Critical Issues of the Day.* Grand Rapids: Baker, 2002.

————. *Humble Apologetics.* Oxford: Oxford University Press, 2002.

Stanley, Andy. *How Good Is Good Enough?* Sisters, Oregon: Multnomah, 2003.

Statement of the First Presidency of The Church of Jesus Christ of Latter-day Saints, 15 February 1978.

Stein, Robert. *The Method and Message of Jesus' Teachings.* Philadelphia: Westminster, 1978.

Stott, John. *Authentic Christianity from the Writings of John Stott.* Edited by Timothy Dudley-Smith. Downers Grove, Illinois: InterVarsity Press, 1995.

————. *Why I Am a Christian.* Downers Grove: InterVarsity Press, 2003.

Talmage, James E. *The Articles of Faith.* Salt Lake City: Deseret Book, 1975.

————. *The House of the Lord.* Salt Lake City: Deseret Book, 1969.

Taylor, John. *The Gospel Kingdom.* Salt Lake City: Bookcraft, 1964.

Teachings of Presidents of the Church — Brigham Young. Salt Lake City: The Church of Jesus Christ of Latter-day Saints, 1997.

Teachings of Presidents of the Church — Joseph F. Smith. Salt Lake City: The Church of Jesus Christ of Latter-day Saints, 1998.

Trumbow, Jeffrey. *Rescue for the Dead: The Posthumous Salvation of Non-Christians in Early Christianity.* Oxford: Oxford University Press, 2001.

White, Joel R. "'Baptized on Behalf of the Dead': The Meaning of 1 Corinthians 15:29 in Its Context." *Journal of Biblical Literature* 116, no. 3 (1997).

Widtsoe, John A. *Evidences and Reconciliations.* Salt Lake City: Bookcraft, 1960.

Williams, Peter W. *America's Religions: From Their Origins to the Twenty-first Century.* Urbana: University of Illinois Press, 2002.

Woodruff, Wilford. *The Discourses of Wilford Woodruff.* Selected by G. Homer Durham. Salt Lake City: Bookcraft, 1946.

Wordsworth, William. "Ode: Intimations of Immortality from Recollections of Early Childhood." In *English Romantic Poetry and Prose,* edited by Alfred Noyes. New York: Oxford University Press, 1956.

Index of Subjects

LDS = Latter-day Saints

Welch, John W., 149n.17
Wentworth Letter (1842), 57
Wesley, John, 40, 59, 62, 109
White, Joel R., 130n.26
Whiting, Michael F., 153-54
Whitmer, David, 47
Whitney, Orson F., 37n.14, 47
Widtsoe, John A., 108n.43
Wilkinson, Bruce, 108-9
Willard, Dallas, 113

Williams, Peter W., 13
Williams, Roger, 40, 158
Woodruff, Wilford, 1, 14
Woods Museum (Chicago), 156
Wordsworth, William, 18

Young, Brigham, 1-2, 9, 14, 26, 59, 84-85, 88, 92, 102, 105-6

Zwingli, Huldrych, 40, 62

Index of Scripture References